GW00776230

THE BATTLE FOR BETTER DESIGN

THE HISTORY OF THE ROYAL FINE ART COMMISSION

ROBERT BARGERY

Foreword by

LORD FOSTER OF THAMES BANK O.M.
PRESIDENT, ROYAL FINE ART COMMISSION TRUST

UNICORN

Published in 2024 by Unicorn an imprint of
Unicorn Publishing Group

Charleston Studio
Meadow Business Centre
Lewes BN8 5RW
www.unicornpublishing.org

ISBN 978-1-911397-96-0
10 9 8 7 6 5 4 3 2 1

Designed by Blacker Design
Printed by Finetone Ltd

Contents

Photo: Frederic Aranda

Foreword

Lord Foster of Thames Bank OM
PRESIDENT, ROYAL FINE ART COMMISSION TRUST

This is a timely book. Timely because it marks the centenary of the foundation of the second Royal Fine Art Commission in 1924 and timely because it reminds us of the importance of quality in the present era, when public buildings that ought to be a source of lasting civic pride are often designed for the short term. 'When we build, let us think that we build for ever', said Ruskin. In an era of PFI schools and hospitals with lifespans as short as thirty years, that message is too often forgotten, with the result that resources are squandered. Those resources may be material, they may be financial, or they may be the unrealised potential of those left to live and learn in failing buildings.

There were two Royal Fine Art Commissions. One was Prince Albert's, dealing with art and sculpture at the Victorians' new Palace of Westminster. The other was its twentieth century successor, concerned with reviewing building projects and seeking to improve them. They had different remits, but both were essentially concerned with getting the best design outcome. Both brought a message that buildings should be the product of meticulous analysis mixed with imagination and a deep understanding of context. Such buildings will tend to last.

I have a personal interest in both Commissions. As a peer of Parliament I inhabited Albert's complete work of art at the Palace of Westminster, and as an architect I presented to the second Royal Fine Art Commission. I may now be the only person alive who has done both those things. It means I have seen the work of both Commissions at close quarters and I have admired that work.

Prince Albert's legacy at the United Kingdom's Parliament is literally uplifting – amid the daily grind of legislating, the eyes are raised and the mind elevated by the soaring spaces of the building. Partly because of Prince Albert, art and architecture exist there in perfect union, reminding occupants of all the possibilities of life.

Similarly, the twentieth century Commission pushed all those involved in development projects – clients, planning authorities, pressure groups and of course architects – to deliver quality for the public. This is a complex process – often a battle, as the title of this book says – of negotiation, churn, surprise and disappointment, relentless design evolution. The twentieth century Commission was central to that process, one among many competing interests but for me a key one, partly because of its unique stance: at the same time deeply interested but completely impartial. It stood above the fray, intelligent in its criticism, measured in its judgements, always aware of the need to kindle rather than kill the creative spark than can make the difference between great and good architecture.

Romance and Royal Commissions are not natural bedfellows, but for over a century and a half the Albert Commission and its twentieth century successor dedicated themselves – sometimes to the point of exhaustion – to the task of making our buildings the best they could be. They stuck to that task not for financial gain or partisan advantage but because the people of this country deserved no less. For that service both Commissions deserve, in turn, our gratitude and respect.

PART I

Decorating Parliament

PRINCE ALBERT AND THE FIRST
ROYAL FINE ART COMMISSION 1841–1863

Baptism of fire

On the night of 16 October 1834, the old Palace of Westminster, seat of the British Parliament, was almost completely wrecked by fire. Workmen disposing of cart loads of wooden tally-sticks, which after centuries of use had finally been superseded as a means of recording Exchequer debts, burnt them in stoves under the House of Lords and set the whole place alight. Hardly anything survived apart from Westminster Hall. The trail of destruction was shocking. But as with most great fires before and since, this one presented an opportunity. A national pantheon had to be remade, more or less from scratch. That meant quantities of painstaking work under expert direction. 'Now, gentlemen, there's a fine chance for you', said a porter at the Royal Academy to pupils in the library. Before the embers were half-cooled, minds high and low had turned in various ways to renewal.

And so the first Royal Fine Art Commission arose, on the face of it, from a single cataclysm and had a single task: to devise a scheme of decoration for the vast new building, and to oversee its execution. In truth, though, the Commission was more than just a response to a terrible accident. It is easy to fall into a Whiggish fallacy of seeing history as an inevitable succession of events, the fulfilment of a destiny. It is never quite like that, except in retrospect. But even so, the creation of the first Royal Fine Art Commission was governed by factors that by a mixture of chance and design came into perfect alignment in the 1830s. The Commission was a product of forces that had been gathering pace over decades. And with the burning down of Parliament, those forces found their means of expression.

First among them was a climate of intervention in an area that had tradtionally been governed by personal taste and private patronage. The antecedents were already in place, beginning with the setting up of the Royal Academy in 1768. In 1802, a Committee for the Inspection of Models for National Monuments, a very Gallic concept, had been set up in imitation of Napoleonic *dirigisme*. It became known as the 'Committee of Taste', a term applied, with more than a hint of mockery, to any English group of connoisseurs gathered to pontificate on matters of aesthetics. The British Institution was set up in 1805 and campaigned (unsuccessfully) for state prizes for artists – in other words, a form of public subsidy. The National Gallery came next in 1824, its foundation approved by Parliament with vocal support from the Prime Minister, Lord Liverpool.

The interventionist tendency gained momentum after the Great Reform Act of 1832 and the election to Parliament of radical members far more accepting of state activism. In 1835, pivotally, came the establishment of a Parliamentary Select Committee on Arts and Manufactures, chaired by William Ewart, one of Joseph Hume's Philosophical Radicals. The committee's work gave rise almost straight away to Government Schools of Design in London, Manchester and Newcastle. Sir Charles Eastlake, first (and only) Secretary of Albert's Royal Fine Art Commission, was instrumental in promoting the London one, based at Somerset House. Thus a group of highly cultured but also highly influential men, straddling the worlds of art and politics, had already formed by the late 1830s; if the need arose for high-level advice on matters of public amenity and design, there were by now

Opposite: *Queen Victoria opening Parliament in 1859*, John Nash, lithograph 1859. (© *Victoria and Albert Museum*)

The Burning of the Houses of Parliament, J.M.W. Turner, watercolour and gouache on paper, 1834–5.
(© *Tate, London*)

plenty of practically minded, astute experts who were ready and willing to give it.

The advertised purpose of the select committee was to examine the relationship between the arts and manufacture and how training in and popular knowledge of the first could help the second prosper. The surface question, in other words, was a utilitarian one: what could the arts do for the economic betterment of Britain? But there were deeper considerations. State control of arts policy and education, it was supposed, would give the best chance of enhancing British prestige and of directing the greatest artists towards socially useful work; there was little room here for flattering artists' egos or tolerating individual ostentation.

An awareness of the need to boost prestige implies vulnerability, a feeling that national pre-eminence is under threat. And indeed a worriedly envious eye was kept at the time on Franco-German achievements in the arts. If, as Clausewitz said in the 1820s, war was a continuation of politics by other means, then art was in some ways a continuation of war by other means. Disputes on the battlefield had been resolved. But the action, intellectually and artistically, had moved to Germany in particular. Heidelberg University was the leading factory of ideas. The state art studios at Düsseldorf were turning out technically proficient history painters whose works moulded and bolstered national identity. And the woeful temporary accommodation of the British National Gallery contrasted badly with the functional and aesthetic power of Schinkel's Altes Museum in Berlin (completed 1830) and von Klenze's 1836 Alte Pinakothek in Munich. In the face of such self-assurance, there developed a sense of inferiority and a feeling that Britain was falling far behind her main competitors, not only in the creation of powerful symbols such as museums and galleries but in the use of art as a means of public improvement.

Somewhat under duress, then, the British political class

came to an accommodation with two alien creeds, those of state patronage and managerialism; they understood their practical efficacy, understood that the fine arts could deliver better results for the nation if organised, financed and controlled in a professional way. But deeper still – and in a way a curious bedfellow to that strain of utilitarianism – was a conviction that those same fine arts could be morally elevating. The destruction of the Palace of Westminster happened just at a time when the high didactic seriousness of the early Victorians was forcing out the last vestiges of Regency frippery. Its burning and rebirth were almost a morality tale in themselves: an accidental event certainly, but purgative nonetheless. And if the zeitgeist, which Parliament both followed and actively promoted, favoured state intervention, then suddenly – providentially almost – Parliament offered itself as a crucible.

A princely berth

By the early 1840s, then, the circumstances, people and political philosophy, allied to slightly injured national pride, were all in place. The times could hardly have been more propitious for the founding of a standing Royal Fine Art Commission. But all these currents were strengthened by yet another compelling factor, hardly foreseeable even months before: the arrival on the scene of Prince Albert. Not only was a new Parliament building needed; not only was there a new, exceptionally young monarch with (from August 1841) a new Government, led by Peel; from 1840 there was also an energetic, highly intelligent and cultured new consort seeking a *rôle* in his adopted land where, as a German, he was viewed at least initially with suspicion. From this perspective, the emergence of the Royal Fine Art Commission was something of a *deus ex machina*.

There was, certainly, a prosaic reason for establishing a Royal Commission. It had been immediately preceded, in April 1841,

by a second select committee which almost exactly shared its terms of reference: 'to promote the fine arts in connection with the rebuilding of the Houses of Parliament'. Peel, Ewart and the connoisseur Lord Francis Egerton were among its members. This committee, though, was party political, unable to sit in Parliamentary recesses and liable to automatic dissolution whenever Parliament was dissolved (as it was in June 1841). As such it was impractical as a means of supervising a lengthy capital project of national importance.

But even allowing for that procedural rationale, it is not too fanciful to suggest that the Royal Fine Art Commission was created in part as a vehicle for Albert. A substantial job, safely removed from partisan politics and perfectly fitted to Albert's cultural interests, certainly answered a need. Two retrospective assessments offer some insights into that thinking. Lord Salisbury, as Prime Minister, argued in the House of Lords in 1901 that the Commission was in effect a constitutional device to allow Albert a means to express his artistic ideas:

The Prince's position was one of delicacy and peculiarity. He could not, by the courtesies and practice of our Constitution, avowedly exercise executive authority, and it could only be through the action of some Commission that he could bring his great influence to bear and carry out, at least in some degree, the completion of the great artistic designs of which his mind was full ... If it had not been on account of his great influence, of the power he could bring to bear, and of the assistance he could give in all departments of government, I doubt very much whether the Commission would have had the effect it has had ... I believe the work of the Commission was the work of the Prince Consort, and practically of nobody else.

Admittedly, Salisbury was arguing against Lord Stanmore's proposal of a second Royal Fine Art Commission, and it therefore suited his debating purpose to suggest, a shade hyperbolically, that the first Commission amounted to nothing without Albert; but for the suggestion even to be made indicates that Albert's appointment to the Commission's chairmanship was seen, and intended, as more than simply the filling of a vacancy.

Lady Eastlake, widow of Sir Charles, gave a slightly more contemporary view in her *Quarterly Review* obituary of Albert in 1862, describing Peel as looking 'with a puzzled yet practical eye upon this grand and anomalous impersonation of Waste Power' and adding that he 'gladly hailed the opportunity of giving it some definite application in the direction of the decoration of the New Houses of Parliament'. Doubtless Peel's pleasure was mixed with relief: Victoria herself, aware that Albert had landed in what Lady Eastlake later called a 'jealous, insular, mistrustful nation', was anxious that her Prime Minister should find a formal outlet for Albert's talents, and quickly. The Royal Fine Art Commission was the perfect answer, satisfying both Queen and Consort. In a note from the 1860s, Victoria wrote that Albert 'felt he owed to Sir R. Peel his first initiation into public life, for this Commission was the commencement of his connection with the leading public and literary men of this country. It taught him more, he said, than anything else he had done, and he talked of it with pleasure'.

One of the Royal Commission's unofficial functions, then, was the education and acclimatization, even Anglicization, of a twenty-two-year-old who had been a student in Bonn only four years before. The benefits, though, were mutual: there was nothing unwarranted about the Prince's appointment. His schooling in Germany had been comprehensive, with private art history classes at Friedrich Wilhelm University leading to familiarity with the contemporary fresco work of Peter von Cornelius, then (if not now) considered a master of the genre. In 1838, Albert had embarked on the customary *Kunstreise*, a German variant of the Grand Tour following a route south across the Alps. At Munich he had met Julius Schnorr von Carolsfeld, one of the Nazarene school of German Romantic painters whose cornerstone was a rejection of what they saw as the spiritual emptiness of Neoclassicism. For them, frescoes were the perfect repudiation: 'they belong to that spot on earth where they were created', said Cornelius, 'and so are in the most beautiful unison with God, nature, time and surrounding space'. Didactic frescoes had recently been finished at the Glyptothek and Pinakothek in Munich, while von Carolsfeld was painting new ones for Ludwig of Bavaria in the Neue Residenz.

All this gave Albert an introduction both to the practical application of the fresco technique and to the mechanics of royal patronage. On arriving in Britain, then, he was reasonably well versed in the latest fashions in architecture and particularly in architectural decoration. The fact that these fashions harked back to mediaevalism mattered little; rather the opposite, as Britain was developing a parallel fondness, both in literature and in painting, for its chivalrous past.

Her Majesty's Commissioners

Albert's opportunity for co-option to the artistic establishment came in September 1841, when Peel wrote to the Queen formally recommending that the select committee's work be carried on 'through the medium of a Royal Commission'.[1] Assent obtained, he asked whether Victoria would support Albert's being invited 'to place himself at its head'. This request was naturally received with equal enthusiasm. On 30 September, Peel announced the two developments to the Commons, in doing so referring to Albert's new position as the 'presidency', a term thereafter used interchangeably with chairmanship.

Whatever the terminology, Albert was without question the executive head; if there was nothing unwarranted about the Prince's appointment, neither was there anything nominal. His active and detailed direction from the very beginning showed remarkable self-assurance, given that he was a mere twenty-four months beyond his teenage years and found himself presiding over a committee of distinguished experts. Perhaps it was in part his very youth, and unapprenticed newness to England, that saved him from being awed by a group that included five past, present or future Prime Ministers (Melbourne, Peel, Russell, Aberdeen and Palmerston), two Viceroys (Canning, of India, and Carlisle, of Ireland), the Lord Chancellor (Lyndhurst, son of the painter John Singleton Copley) and, even more to the point, men of culture as eminent as Macaulay, the historian Henry Hallam and the art connoisseur Samuel Rogers. To add piquancy, Charles Barry attended meetings of this twenty-nine strong group as an observer, mainly to prevent subversion of his architectural designs for the new Palace of Westminster.

There was, to be sure, more than a touch of avuncularity, even paternalism, in some of the elder statesmen's attitudes to Albert. Peel, after all, had been his vocal champion and Albert reciprocated the affection, making a show of supporting Peel from the Commons gallery during the Corn Laws crisis of 1846 and – according to Victoria – seeing Peel as a 'second father'. Albert was no less fortunate in his Secretary at the Royal Fine Art Commission, Sir Charles Eastlake, an art historical titan who rivalled him in his familiarity and intellectual sympathy with the Nazarene School. Again, the rapport was immediate. 'The light showed his beautiful face to great advantage', Eastlake, then nearly fifty, wrote breathlessly after meeting Albert for the first time. To some extent, he, Albert and Peel formed a sort of triumvirate of Platonic Philosopher-Kings, with some believing that their combination of vitality, statesmanship and expertise made a wider committee redundant. Henry Cole, founder of the Victoria & Albert Museum, wrote in *The Westminster Review* in 1842 that 'if we could not have had Prince Albert, we

would have been ready to accept Sir Robert Peel as dictator'. *Blackwood's Magazine* saw the three of them as a bulwark against the 'stinting, coldly calculating false economists'.

Among the wider group of Commissioners, Albert was clearly able to hold his own as *primus inter pares*. He had been canny enough to take a detailed interest in the Commission's composition, recommending to Peel in his first letter in English on the subject that professional artists be excluded. Their opinion should be sought when needed, he argued, but their permanent presence would inhibit the laymen, in which category he doubtless included himself, and encourage a damaging deference. 'I only give you my crude views and do not wish to press them against the experience of others'. Peel agreed, as he did also with Albert's insistence on non-partisanship. 'I rejoice that party distinction is excluded from my *national* undertaking', wrote Albert on seeing Peel's final list of proposed members.

Having achieved a balanced commission that avoided political and artistic cliques – there was in fact one token artist, George Vivian, but no-one with whom he could make common cause – Albert felt comfortable, and the sentiment seemed to be returned. Lady Eastlake, reflecting on those earliest days of the Commission in her 1862 obituary of Albert, noted that any initial doubts disappeared as 'members of the Commission realised that none of the hereditary possessors of galleries and patrons of art ... could be compared with the youthful President in knowledge of the conditions of art or in sympathy with the artist mind'. Even allowing for a little deferential hagiography and the lionizing of the newly-dead, we can assume there was some substance to that, not least because the same sort of appraisal of Albert in his twenties was made by sober professionals of the calibre of Robert Rawlinson, the engineer and sanitarian: 'To an architect he could talk as an architect; to an engineer as an engineer; to a painter as a painter, to a sculptor as a sculptor; to a chemist as

Sir Charles Eastlake, Sir Francis Grant, pen, ink and wash on paper, 1853. (© *The National Gallery, London*)

The Fine Arts Commissioners, 1846, John Partridge, oil on paper, *c.*1846. (© *National Portrait Gallery, London*)

KEY TO THE PICTURE OF

THE MEETING OF THE FINE ARTS COMMISSION. 1846.

Key to the Picture of the Meeting of the Fine Arts Commission, 1846, Sir George Scharf, pen and ink and wash, 1872. (© *National Portrait Gallery, London*)

a chemist; and so on through all the branches of engineering, architecture, art and science'. Lady Eastlake added that, when discussing art, Albert 'applied Germanic thoroughness to a subject which he took more seriously than most Englishmen were prepared to do, and he talked, if at times a little ponderously, much good sense about it'.

Wider aims

If Albert's words were quietly impressive, so too were his actions. It is true that he was fairly conservative in his interpretation of the Commission's brief. Its formal remit, 'to inquire whether advantage might not be taken of the rebuilding of our Palace of Westminster ... for the purpose of promoting and encouraging the Fine Arts, with direct reference to the moral wants of our nation', implied that the Westminster work was a means to an end; viewed liberally, it could almost have allowed a nationwide campaign of education and training. Albert sensibly chose – although the choice would have been forced upon him by financial constraints – to concentrate on the immediate task; any wider benefits could filter down through example and osmosis. That is not to say, though, that wider considerations were absent from his calculations. Far from it: he was anxious to use the Westminster project first to encourage a British School of history painting and secondly to fortify the position of the Sovereign, and in a wider sense anchor the Albertine monarchy, in the febrile, reform-minded world of the 1840s. This was not, in other words, Art for Art's sake.

On the first point, British performance was widely disparaged and seen as a shadow of the Germans' sophisticated accomplishments. The imaginative, and logical, solution was to consult German experts and import their methods and techniques; and if not Germans then certainly Germanophiles, among whom Eastlake was pre-eminent. His

translations of Goethe's *Zur Farbenlehre* (*Colour Theory*, 1840) and Franz Kugler's *Handbuch der Geschichte der Malerei* (*Handbook of the History of Painting*, 1842) had cemented his reputation as an art theorist fully conversant with German thinking. More critically, his essay *On Fresco Painting* was the foremost English guide to mural techniques and the seminal text for those who, like Eastlake, thought Parliament should be decorated in fresco on account of its capacity 'to develop the highest qualities of art'. The surest route to matching the Germans was to imitate them; and doing that, in the 1840s, meant mastering the art of fresco.

Albert's second wider aim, that of bolstering the monarchy in an age of reform, added a more deeply political dimension to the Westminster project: this was not just the literal remaking of a building but a metaphor for an evolving constitutional settlement. The Hanoverian practice of direct political intervention had effectively ended, leaving hanging a question posed by the Duke of Wellington before Victoria's accession: 'How is the King's government to be carried on in a reformed Parliament?' Barry's architecture answered this in part; strongly encouraged by Albert and Peel, he created a ceremonial axis that allowed the Sovereign to pass in State from the Royal Robing Room through the Royal Gallery direct to the House of Lords. Thus could Victoria and her successors be made manifest as the 'dignified' part of the Constitution, as Bagehot would later put it. Albert's intention was to reinforce this message through decorative choices: far from being a casual or accidental assemblage of images, the selection and placement of paintings was for him a finely-calibrated exercise in semiotics. Parliament was still, lest it be forgotten, a Royal Palace.

The Prince's priorities were not necessarily, in any explicit sense, those of the Royal Fine Art Commission as a whole, but the high degree of sympathy among its members allowed him a good deal of latitude. The Teutonic influence among

Commissioners and their advisers was strong. Sir Benjamin Hawes (M.P. for Lambeth) had gone as far as commissioning ceilings from Cornelius. George Vivian had studied in Munich. Henry Bellenden Ker, a barrister, shared Albert's admiration for von Carolsfeld.

With this preponderance, it was hardly surprising that the Commission leant strongly towards fresco, and it was inevitable that it soon occurred to some to suggest the use of German artists, including Cornelius: after all, they were far more technically proficient in fresco than any British counterpart. *The Athenaeum* magazine, a constant commentator on the fresco debate and never short of a barbed comment, counselled against dependence on native artists: 'No matter how lofty the walls are, if the national taste be low … patronage must entail middle-class productions'. Albert himself was rumoured to agree and to have offered the job to Cornelius before Eastlake objected, supposedly threatening resignation on the matter. All that is uncorroborated anecdote. Certainly any such move by Albert would have been absurdly counterproductive, undermining any prospect of creating a cadre of skilled British fresco artists. It might even have been politically dangerous for him: to use foreign artists for a British Parliament building would have been seen as eccentric at best, and such quick recourse to his countrymen would have smacked too obviously of divided loyalties.

Becoming *frescanti*

The decision to rely on British talent meant, however, that a gaping skills gap had to be filled, and urgently, if the vast interior walls of Barry's Parliament were to be painted to the standard required. Plugging the deficit was not a straightforward matter, fresco being a notoriously unforgiving medium that depends on speed and confidence in execution and offers no scope for last-minute changes. For some,

the high degree of difficulty was part of the attraction: the Scottish artist William Dyce, who as one of only three British artists with any practical experience of fresco work was not wholly disinterested, thought that works in fresco gave 'more of the artist's genius than art in oil … He must leave out a great many secondary beauties and apply himself to the higher qualities in art'. The necessary discipline would, he thought, force an improvement in the standard of English drawing and 'liberate it from its concentration upon mere effect'.

The Commission began the process of trying to recruit potential *frescanti* by announcing, in its first report of April 1842, an open cartoon competition. Its nervousness about using Westminster as a proving-ground, without much evidence of native accomplishment, was plain. 'We have not yet been able to satisfy ourselves that the art of fresco-painting has been sufficiently cultivated in this country to justify us in recommending at once that it should be so employed', the report stated, before concluding optimistically, in a similar vein to Dyce, that 'as the resources of art become circumscribed, so the artist's aim becomes elevated'. Nonetheless, it was leaving nothing to chance. The advertisement was accompanied by detailed technical information, including a treatise on fresco painting by Eastlake, and strict guidance on what was expected. Artists were invited to submit drawings in chalk or charcoal 'not less than ten nor more than fifteen feet in their longest dimension, the figures to be not less than the size of life, illustrating subjects from British history, or from the works of Spenser, Shakespeare or Milton'. But, it warned,

a judicious selection and allocation of subjects is secondary in importance only to their efficient design and execution. How far the designers of the British school will prove themselves adequate to the occasion, or deserving of state patronage, remains to be seen: we are most apprehensive that the ornamental will predominate, and the spirit of the conception be sacrificed to an accumulation of showy accessories. The artists should bear in mind, that although the paintings are intended to decorate the architecture, it is with creations of mind, not with imitations of material objects: the walls should seem instinct with life, character, and action – not merely gay with glittering pageantry.

It was made clear, too, that 'precision of drawing' was sought, together with 'a style of composition less dependent on *chiaroscuro* than on effective arrangement'. This challenging prescription was a clear steer towards sober, didactic Germanic treatments and away from empty dramatics.

Entries were to be submitted by the first week of May 1843, with a total prize fund offered of £2,000, including three top prizes of £300. This financial incentive, coupled with the prospect of a highly prestigious commission, brought forth one hundred and forty entries. After judging by a panel chaired by the Prime Minister, the three top prizes were awarded to G.F. Watts, Edward Armitage and C.W. Cope, all then comparatively unknown – more established artists, it was widely supposed, had been unwilling either to risk their reputations or to set aside their far more lucrative fee-paying work.

All the entries were shown in the summer of 1843 at Westminster Hall, in an exhibition opened by Victoria that attracted huge public interest. 'Screens were erected along the side walls ... with a long central screen', all crowded with rows of anonymous cartoons – although many were speculatively attributed within days. Indeed, the voyeuristic thrill of seeing the work of Richard Dadd was one notable draw: driven insane by sunstroke while painting the pyramids, he had killed his father only days before and had achieved instant notoriety. Controversy also attended the winning Armitage entry; this was thought to be so derivative of Delaroche that Delaroche

himself was maliciously alleged to have worked on it. Armitage was obliged to certify that the work was his and had been wholly completed in Britain.

For the first two weeks, the average daily attendance was one thousand eight hundred, at a shilling a head; thereafter entry was free and Westminster Hall was packed 'with most respectably dressed people', according to *The Times*. Eastlake was more gratified by the strong working class attendance and especially their preference for the sixpenny catalogue over the cheap edition prepared with them in mind. Estimates vary, but at least half a million people came in total. Revenue from ticket and catalogue sales was such that the Commission was able to award a further ten prizes of £100 each.

Capturing the popular imagination in this way was fine as far as it went, but the public view was essentially untutored. More relevant to the project's viability was the artistic quality on offer. Critical reception was mixed but broadly positive, even from a trade press whose default stance was cattiness. Some periodicals even managed a backhanded compliment: Charles Cope's *Trial by Jury* was praised by *The Illustrated London News* as 'the only one of the prizes we should wish to see painted indelibly on the walls of the legislature'. Henry Townsend's *Fight for the Beacon*, one of the lesser-prize winners, was also notably well received.

The Commission had enough confidence in its own expert judgement to consider the potential on show to be more than adequate. Eastlake, a stern but discerning judge, reported to Albert that 'a few may be called truly excellent'. The Edinburgh artist William Bell Scott reported that 'the high excellence astonishes everyone'. And there was indeed sufficient quality among the daunting quantity for Albert to pronounce himself 'delighted at the realisation of my prophesies and wishes': perhaps a slightly premature declaration of 'mission accomplished', but born no doubt of relief that the usual naysayers' pessimism had proved largely unfounded.

Opposite: *First Trial by Jury – a study of the accused*, Charles West Cope, pencil and charcoal on paper, 1841 (© *Parliamentary Art Collection*). Exhibited in 1843 at Westminster Hall and awarded one of the £300 top prizes.

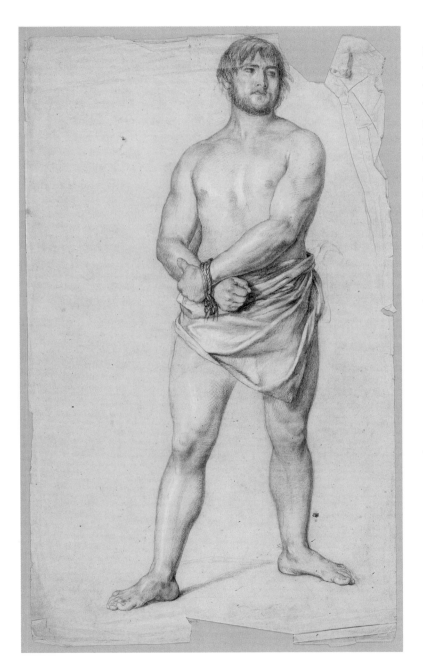

Fortified by the experience, and under pressure from Peel to find out all it could about 'the mysteries of the art', the Commission embarked on a detailed investigation of the technical aspects of fresco. C.H. Wilson, director of the Government School of Design at Somerset House, was despatched to Italy to assess the methodology of Renaissance *frescanti* and the condition of antique frescoes. Eastlake contributed papers on damp protection and invited Cornelius, as the acknowledged master of fresco, to visit London to offer advice. Michael Faraday was asked to comment on the suitability of different types of lime as a plaster base. The generally positive findings from this exhaustive preparatory work encouraged the Commission to invite artists to submit specimen works in fresco, with 'not less than two applications of the superficial mortar'. Two further exhibitions were held, in the summers of 1844 and 1845. The catalogue for the second praised the courage of artists who, 'with the approving voice of the nation, readily plunged into the new course of experiment and labour to try their skill in a process so often declared to be incompatible with their rooted habits' – not least by that habitual polemicist Ruskin, who had been a noted sceptic: 'I have not the remotest hope of the elevation of English art by means of fresco', he wrote to the portraitist Joseph Severn. 'It is not a material that gives us thoughts, passions or powers'.

Such indeed had been the conventional wisdom: the English were expressive colourists in the manner of Turner, quite unlike the hard and linear Germans. But under the influence of Albert, who detected in English art a tendency to 'bribe the senses with rich colouring and voluptuous forms', this was fast becoming a minority view. The latter two exhibitions generated if anything even greater public enthusiasm than the first: *The Athenaeum* detected 'a national mania' for fresco, with the country in a 'fine frenzy'. Treatises such as Mary Merrifield's *Art of Fresco Painting* (1846) found a ready readership. The prevailing view was that Britain was witnessing the birth of a native school of fresco painting. For Albert and his Royal Fine Art Commission, sole begetters of this extraordinary phenomenon, it was something of a public relations triumph.

Translating this tentative start into convincing and commanding finished works remained a challenge, however. Here, Albert's practical activism came to the fore. Using Edward Blore as architect, the Dresden-born engraver Ludwig Gruner as art adviser and the Casa Bartholdy in Rome (decorated by the Nazarenes) as inspiration, he built a pavilion in the gardens of Buckingham Palace 'to offer our artists at once a high motive and fair opportunity to try their powers in this new-old method'. It became a highly-variegated canvas, with a room in the Pompeian style by Augustine Aglio, eight lunettes inspired by Walter Scott's Waverley novels and an octagonal room of frescoes derived from Milton's *Comus*. Victoria and Albert made frequent impromptu visits to inspect progress and made a positive impression on the artists. 'Courting conversation, and desiring rather reason than obedience, they have gained our admiration and love', reported Thomas Uwins. Albert was proud enough of the results to publish an illustrated account by Gruner, thus broadcasting works that would otherwise have been hidden from public view. *The Art Union* thought it confirmed that 'our artists are at least equal to any others in Europe', while allowing itself the minor carp that two of the subjects were identical while another three 'are nearly similar, yet presenting, even in their monotony, an inconsistency; for we have three different ladies on three different chairs'. The result, it said, 'proves the absolute necessity of a presiding mind'.

That was a fair conclusion, and one not lost on Prince Albert. The pavilion had always been intended as an exercise in trial and error and the experiment had helped clarify the artistic pecking order. William Etty, who had failed to impress

with a trial lunette, was dismissed (with what, in a fit of pique, he called a 'German' payment of £40) and was replaced by William Dyce, the insult made worse perhaps by the fact that Dyce had declined to enter the 1843 competition. The reasons for his non-entry are not clear. Ford Madox Brown, not always a reliable witness, speculated that he was 'hopeless of his work attracting the English approbation of the day'. More probably, he calculated that as the only British artist with any real claim to competence in fresco, he had no need to audition. If so, he was absolutely right. Borne on praise from Cornelius – who a little disingenuously professed himself redundant in Britain while Dyce was around – he was privately invited to submit a design once the competition was over. And now, at the summer pavilion, he was again brought in late to add lustre. His status as Albert's *beau idéal* was assured. In short order, Dyce was asked to paint a fresco of *Neptune resigning his Empire of the Seas to Britannia* for a staircase at Osborne House; and it was in conversation with Dyce at Osborne that Albert conceived the idea of decorating the Queen's Robing Room at Westminster with subjects from *Le Morte d'Arthur*, recently popularised by Malory, which he saw as the British equivalent of the German epic *Das Nibelungenlied*.

The politics of painting

Unsurprisingly, then, it was also Dyce who received the Robing Room commission, the first awarded for the Parliament project. He began the fresco cycle in June 1846 with *The Baptism of Ethelbert*. As work progressed along the spine of the Palace, including the Royal Gallery and the Lords and Commons chambers either side of the Central Octagonal Hall, he was joined by Charles Cope, Daniel Maclise, John Herbert, John Horsley, Edward Ward, John Tenniel, Joseph Severn and William Thomas; all of them narrative artists with solid reputations but nonetheless young (Thomas was in his mid-twenties) and inexperienced. Before starting, Cope and Maclise took the precaution of visiting studios in Munich to hone their technique while Dyce, showing remarkable diligence and commitment, went to Italy to analyse frescoes at first hand, absorbing a vast amount of information on pigments, paint adhesion, the practicality of combining fresco and tempera, the problems of using ultramarine and the damaging effects of candle smoke.

The legendary and mediaeval subject matter of this inaugural phase was uncontentious, aside from a comical episode where Dyce, presumably having read *Le Morte d'Arthur* for the first time, realised that its occasional raciness made it a poor choice for a setting as chaste as the Sovereign's Robing Room. He worried aloud to Albert, who had asked him to concentrate on 'the moral qualities venerated in Chivalry', that the text 'turns on incidents which, if they are not undesirable for representation under any circumstances, are at least scarcely appropriate in such an apartment'. Such difficulties were fairly easily fixed by editorial discretion. Largely uncontroversial, too, was the sculpture selection, once the Commission had scotched Barry's suggestion that memorials at Westminster Abbey and St Paul's 'not calculated to excite in the mind of the beholder emotions of piety and devotion' might be shifted across to the Palace as makeweights. A sub-committee including Lord Macaulay settled easily on subjects for what was, in effect, a Temple of British Worthies: Alfred, Elizabeth, Robert the Bruce, Bede, Hooker, Samuel Johnson, Cowper, Walter Scott, Reynolds, Flaxman, Hampden, Clarendon, Burke, Fox, Chatham and Pitt.

Other choices were more problematic. A spat arose, for example, over whether foreign events should be depicted, with Sir Martin Archer Shee, President of the Royal Academy, approving and the historian and antiquarian Lord Mahon (later Earl Stanhope) vigorously objecting. In a letter to Peel (whose position as Prime Minister with the ear of Albert made him an obvious focus for complaints) Mahon protested that 'I would not more consent to admit foreign scenes to decorate a British House of Parliament than I would an alien to sit amongst its members'. Peel and Albert clearly agreed, as Mahon was shortly afterwards appointed to the Commission and put in charge of the sub-committee that selected subjects.

Predictably, though, the real problems came with the depiction and arrangement of domestic events. Chronicling the British pedigree, while easy enough to welcome as a general aspiration, was harder to put into practice: where geographical distance might have lent a degree of objectivity, no such detachment was likely for matters closer to home. Although the Commission was avowedly non-partisan, the Westminster project was a delicate exercise in iconography, and thus deeply political. Skill was needed to skirt the pitfalls. The Cromwellian period was an obvious source of anguish. It could hardly be ignored, particularly in a newly reformed Parliament, but how was it to be treated? Any direct representation of Cromwell himself was resisted, despite agitation in Parliament. But beyond that a compromise was reached, with depictions confined to those showing sacrifice or heroism on both sides. And so the burial of Charles I was included, but not his execution. The King was shown raising his standard at Nottingham, but also failing to arrest the Five Members in the House of Commons in 1642. Bringing the curtailment of monarchical and aristocratic power right up to date, agreement was also reached on an illustration of the passing of the Reform Bill – an event hardly more than ten years old, and thus far more the realm of contemporary politics than of history.

Such matters, though requiring diplomatic footwork, were not too awkward. The tensions became much more acute after July 1846, when one Royal Fine Art Commissioner (Peel) was ousted as Prime Minister by another, the Whig Lord John Russell. Albert, as we have seen, found Peel highly *simpatico*,

The Meeting of Wellington and Blücher after the Battle of Waterloo, Daniel Maclise, waterglass, 1861 (© *Parliamentary Art Collection*). Detail, Royal Gallery.

and he demonstrated his partiality by insisting that he remain a Commissioner. Relations with Lord John were far less easy, and the painting scheme had to be modified mid-stream to take account of newly ascendant Whig sensibilities. It would not be too extreme to call it, as some did, an 'iconographical crisis'. The Commission's next report, written by Eastlake and issued just a month after the change of Government, confined itself to the laconic statement that it was 'not expedient to complete the series of paintings at the present period'. In other words, work was suspended to accommodate a row. What emerged from the ruckus was a marked downplaying of the monarchical emphasis and a parallel upgrading of parliamentarianism. Albert's scheme for the spine corridor had been a model of iconographic clarity, with the glorification of Britain reaching its zenith in the inner sanctum of the Royal Gallery, where military victories were celebrated. To reach that point, the visitor passed walls depicting Britain sunk in a slough of ignorance, then resurgent as it dispensed justice and brought liberty. In a way it was an impeccably Whiggish interpretation of history as a progressive march towards the light. But there was no doubt about where the light ultimately shone: on monarchy, placed firmly at the apex. This was too much for the Whigs, and they came to power just in time to change it. Albert's allusive 'War and Peace' allegories were kept, but moved from the Royal Gallery to the far more mundane St Stephen's Hall. The symbolism was clear: military triumphs were to be treated as straightforward narrative history, not appropriated as a visual apotheosis of Queen Victoria.

In the event, the Royal Gallery was reserved for works that, while still martial, focussed on the tragic rather than the glorious aspects of war. They also conveyed subtler, even personal messages. The principal painting, *The Meeting of Wellington and Blücher after the Battle of Waterloo*, was commissioned in 1858 and entrusted to Daniel Maclise, long a favourite of Queen and Consort. In 1843, Victoria had given Maclise's *Scene from Undine* to Albert as a birthday gift, and Albert had later chosen him to execute a fresco in the Buckingham Palace summer house. The Waterloo painting was a *tour de force*, impressive not just for its sheer size (forty-five feet wide by ten feet high) but for its obsessive detail: almost a hundred men and twenty horses, many of them dead or wounded, litter the battlefield around the mounted generals. Wellington and his Prussian ally von Blücher shake hands in front of an inn sign inscribed '*a la Belle Alliance*' – the Prussians' preferred choice for the name of the battle but also a lightly coded reference to the impending marriage of the Princess Royal, then only seventeen, to Crown Prince Frederick of Prussia. Out of tragedy came catharsis.

Whether Maclise's grand narratives were wholly accurate portrayals of history is another matter. Wellington himself doubted that he had met von Blücher in the circumstances shown, causing such alarm among Commissioners that the Queen, via her daughter (by now the Prussian Crown Princess), rushed to obtain confirmation from von Blücher's decrepit *aide-de-camp* that the scene had indeed happened. And while the details for his depiction of Trafalgar were certainly correct – he borrowed Nelson's coat from Greenwich Hospital and the War Office went to the trouble of running up uniforms to help him – Nelson's death on the quarterdeck is choreographed in a way that departs from historical truth. The nitpicking went on: Edward III never, perhaps, conferred the Order of the Garter on the Black Prince; representations of Saxon dress were pored over by a new breed of antiquarians keen to parade their scholarship. But the Royal Fine Art Commission understood that to convey messages in art usually requires some sort of imaginative interpretation. It might have baulked at some of the more mawkish sanitisations, such as one artist's attempt to hawk a portrayal of 'King Bruce, in a retreat before the English, making way for a sick woman borne in a litter, and checking the pursuers'. But for epic treatments, the essential message was what counted. 'That a work of art should be absolutely faithful to the description from which it is taken', said Eastlake, 'might sometimes be fatal to its success.' Peel was brusquer, telling all concerned to push on and ignore the pedants.

Trials and tribulations

Authentic or not, Maclise's work was received with acclaim. But if he and other artists triumphed it was often in the face of practical difficulties. A hint of these is given by the fact that *The Meeting of Wellington and Blücher* is not a pure fresco at all, in spite of the almost make-or-break importance attached to the fresco method and the physical and mental energy expended in trying to understand it. When Maclise attempted a fresco of his cartoon, he found the difficulties of painting properly onto wet plaster insuperable. The soldiers' uniforms were so detailed that only minute parts could be painted at a time, leading to endless tricky junctions between the work of one day and the next. And the light was poor, or (worse) was turned into a hallucinatory kaleidoscope by being filtered through Pugin's stained glass, with lions dancing on Wellington's face and von Blücher turned green by the shade of hippogryphs.

By August 1859, Maclise had had enough and wrote to Eastlake abandoning the job unless he could complete it in oil. At this point Albert, sensing an unravelling of the whole project, intervened. On the face of it, his initial response was uncompromising, even a touch condescending:

If Mr. Maclise feels disgusted at the dry and rigid materials for his production, and longs for oil, it is because he feels pain in the struggle to have cast away the peculiar means of producing effects in finishing up minute details in which he excels. But a grand historical work requires the sacrifice of these details; and fresco is a protection to Mr. Maclise against himself, and insures his rising by this work to a

height as an artist which he cannot himself comprehend as yet. Try to inspire him with the prospect of this result and to make him endure the penance and artistic fasting, which is to ensure to him the entrance into the artist's paradise – fame!

Luckily for Eastlake, who must have wondered what to do with this instruction, Albert suggested the adoption of a modified painting method called waterglass or stereochrome, a German invention pioneered by Professor J.N. von Fuchs in 1825. Essentially it involved fixing watercolour paint to the wall with syringefuls of sodium or potassium silicate, combining ease of application – it allowed the artist to work on completed ground – with the sought-after matt finish of fresco. Albert despatched Maclise to Munich and Dresden to assess the method; he returned convinced of its merits and with the zeal of a convert produced a technical paper that the Commission appended to its 1861 report. Other artists experiencing difficulties were encouraged by Albert to make the switch: John Herbert, for example, dropped *buon fresco* for his *Moses and the Tables of the Law* in the Peers' Robing Room and took it up again in waterglass, eventually finishing it in 1864 after six years' interrupted labour.

In truth, no medium was entirely suited to the new Palace of Westminster. Even oil, though the instinctive choice of many English artists and sometimes tried despite Albert's strictures, was an imperfect match; Ward and Cope found that 'the gloss of surface, necessarily characteristic of painting in oil, was detrimental to their effect', by which they meant that shiny oils could barely be made out from any likely vantage point. Like Herbert, both artists transferred to waterglass, Ward reluctantly but Cope less so, having studied at first hand the beneficial effects on Maclise. But the problems with fresco, pure or modified, were too deep-seated to be solved by a coating of sodium. Whatever its pedigree, fresco was a bad choice for a polluted, rainy city like London, and especially for a London building sitting on a river and thus subject to damp. It took three or four years for the plaster to be dry enough for paint to be applied, and even then work was often confined to the summer months. But far worse was to follow: the artist Richard Redgrave reported that several murals, including those of poets in the Upper Waiting Hall, were 'hardly completed when decay seized them: the colours underwent destructive changes, flesh tints became painfully livid, greens disappeared, blues and browns changed places – a general mildew seized the whole. The ground itself blistered, became loose and disintegrated'.

In his expert advice to the Commission, Cornelius had discounted the dangers of damp and atmospheric pollution, believing the bigger problem to come from nitrates in masonry, unseasoned timber and imperfectly-burned bricks. But this miscalculation left the frescoes even more vulnerable: the supposed solution, separating the plaster from stone and brick by means of a lath framework, simply created an airtight space in which damp accumulated and was then trapped.

As if being attacked from behind was not bad enough, the murals were also ravaged from the front. In the 1850s, coal consumption released about a million tons of sulphuric acid into London's air every year, and the problem became even worse when limits on the sulphur content of gas were relaxed. Toxic vapour droplets, impossible to repel, ate away the frescoes' carbonate layer and penetrated the plaster, converting both into gypsum that was then lost through slow dissolution. Increasingly desperate attempts were made to arrest the decay. Following advice from Dyce and Cornelius, Albert had the frescoes sponged and rubbed with pellets of stale bread. Cope treated his with a solution of paraffin wax. Others tried flagellating the paintings with slings of leather and linen, 'using all the force a man could give to a side blow'. Nothing really worked. Artists were reduced to

retouching their work again and again, some for the rest of their lives. Cope was one of them. As he put it in his volume of reminiscences, 'How much of life has been wasted in, as it were, writing on the sand'.

Environmental conditions were not the end of it. Producing complex paintings in cramped, ill-lit conditions amid the hammering and sawing of a building site – and one in which Parliamentarians continued to sit and work – was a challenging and sometimes fraught business. When the long-suffering Cope started work in 1846, on his return from Germany, he faced 'considerable difficulties; plasterers and masons were busy and there were many visitors'.

Although he was too diplomatic to mention it, one of them would undoubtedly have been Albert, who, to his credit, was always trying his best to offer practical help. When, for example, Maclise was struggling to work in crepuscular gloom, with what dim light there was refracted through stained glass, Albert had the offending glass removed and took the trouble to devise an elaborate system of reflectors to act as diffusers and ensure a more even light. But his interventionist approach and well-intentioned perfectionism did not always make things easy. When Mr. Punch comically joined in the fresco mania by starting a mural himself, the cartoon showed him sweating under close supervision. 'Prince Albert can hardly be persuaded to quit my *atelier*', read the caption.[2] Dyce would have recognised the scene. 'When you are about to paint a sky seventeen feet long by some four or five broad', he said, 'I don't advise you to have a Prince looking in upon you every ten minutes or so – or, when you are going to trace an outline, to obtain the assistance of the said Prince and an Archduke Constantine to hold up your tracing to the wall, as I have had.'

For some of the sculptors, labouring to produce delicate figurative works, the *Punch* cartoon might also have resonated. John Gibson, down at Osborne for a sitting with Queen Victoria, suddenly found Albert next to him. 'Will you permit

Maclise under difficulties in the House of Lords, Charles West Cope, pencil on paper, c.1847. (© *Parliamentary Art Collection*)

me?', asked Albert. He then took the modelling tool and, according to Gibson, 'worked away changing many parts. He worked for ten minutes at it'. Eastlake, who was present and taking notes for Gibson's edification, recorded that 'His Royal Highness remarked the chin was much too full and large for the Queen and the drapery hanging from the arms, though much admired, produced an oval form that is much too alike under the arms. And in examining the crown, the Prince observed that the usual form of the *fleur-de-lis* is much more graceful and more intelligible than the ornament you have used, and indeed His Royal Highness went on to sketch the form as he felt it should be'.

Barry's architecture, too, was sometimes an impediment. Cornelius observed that 'the available spaces for painting in Gothic buildings are ... unfavourable; the pointed arch and the acute forms produced by the simplest groinings in the ceilings are difficult to fill satisfactorily'. Richard Redgrave complained that the spaces available in the Lords Chamber 'were quite unsuited to the proper display of high art in any medium. The three paintings opposite the throne are so deeply recessed that they are seen as in a dark hole'. Maclise tried to solve the problem by framing his compositions, so that they read independently of the architecture, though at some further sacrifice of dimensions. But many other works were compromised. Horsley's *Spirit of Religion*, for example, seemed notably pinched. And Sir George Bowyer M.P. fretted that some paintings were 'perfectly unintelligible'. Dyce's *Baptism of Ethelbert*, he said in rather literal-minded vein, showed the King 'to all appearance ... prepared for a whipping rather than a baptism. The font was so small he could no more get into it than into a teacup'. *The Athenaeum*, more perceptive in its criticism, praised the art but still lamented its placement: 'it shines forth but out of place, almost out of sight'. Sculpture was also affected. When Sir Benjamin Hall M.P. (who lent his nickname to Big Ben) visited John Thomas in his studio to inspect progress on his statues of the Magna Carta barons, he noticed the 'extreme narrowness' of their shoulders. 'Mr. Barry will not allow us room for them', replied Thomas.

Just as intractable, in a way, were the deeper structural and political issues that swirled around the project. One was a certain mutual suspicion between the Commission and Barry, leading to attritional turf wars. Like Albert, Barry was a perfectionist, and thus keen to control as many aspects of interior design as possible. He had been confined, to his annoyance, to non-figurative ornament and stained glass, while the Commission controlled figurative sculpture and painting, but he fretted about what might be called mission creep: that the Commission would by degrees extend its reach to encompass all aspects of interior design, including furniture, panelling and glass. In fact, Commissioners had no such ambitions; allowing Barry responsibility for any infelicities and budget overruns in those areas had its advantages. But the arrangement did lead to some decorative artists recommended by the Commission complaining of non-employment when Barry chose to place work elsewhere. He had no room, for example, for Samuel Rogers, whom Commissioners had specially recommended for 'those parts of the woodwork of the House of Lords in which great richness of effect and delicacy of execution are required'. And there is no doubt that Barry, ever the canny adversary and an accomplished opportunist to boot, managed his architectural design in such a way as to seize back as much control as he could. When the Commission was agonising over fresco methodology, for example, he took advantage of the prevarication by letting Pugin loose on the House of Lords. The Chamber ended up so covered in gilt and elaborate chasing that no painting could ever have achieved any sort of dominance. The ruse was repeated in several other rooms, where yards of wall space were taken up with lavish furnishings.

Another underlying problem, and even more of a recurrent

Queen Victoria with Justice and Clemency, John Gibson, marble, 1855 (© *Parliamentary Art Collection*). Prince's Chamber.

theme, was funding. Tensions were hardly surprising given that the public works overseen by the Royal Fine Art Commission were aesthetic rather than functional. In such circumstances pennypinchers – especially those with secondary agendas – were watching for signs of extravagance. Creating great art while trying to keep them satisfied would always be an awkward balancing act. The Commission received public funds of £4,000 a year; this had to be authorised annually by Parliament, giving M.P.s plenty of opportunity to complain about value for money. Some of them made a point of doing so, and the delays in fixing on fresco, followed by the steady and seemingly irreversible deterioration of completed works, only encouraged them. Bernal Osborne, Liberal Member for Middlesex, was a particular gadfly, developing something of an *idée fixe* that public money was being 'grossly and wantonly wasted' and warning the Commons with more than a touch of sarcasm that 'whenever a Commission was appointed of gentlemen of great taste, they might depend that the public purse was in great danger'. Warming to his theme, he suggested that 'nothing could be more absurd than to go on spending money on pictures which would not fetch £5 if they were to be hawked all through Europe'.

Such views could not be entirely written off as those of a Philistine obsessive. The Treasury too sought explanations whenever expenditure overran. Cumulatively, over the years, the questioning had a corrosive effect. By 1861, Albert was writing to Lord Palmerston (by then Prime Minister) to protest that the Commissioners' position was 'not that of a Government department, nor of trustees of a public institution, asking for expenditure for their speciality, but of a body appointed by the Crown, on an understanding with Parliament'. He concluded, successfully, with something of an ultimatum: 'if the Encouragement of the Fine Arts is either no longer an object of Parliament, or we possess no longer the public confidence, the Commission should be dissolved ...'

Faced with such forensic scrutiny, any public body might edge towards circumspection, even parsimony. Some artists considered the Royal Fine Art Commission to have done exactly that: their feeling of being short-changed was another running sore. In other words, an opposite (if not wholly equal) pressure had to be borne by the Commission, that of artists agitating for more money. Eastlake found himself renegotiating contracts in an effort to keep them happy – a prime reason for the cost overruns that annoyed the Treasury. Cope managed to increase his remuneration for the Peers' Corridor from £450 to £700 per panel. Maclise, not usually vocal in his own financial interests but backed by *The Athenaeum* magazine in its best polemical tone of mock outrage, managed to raise his payment for the Painted Chamber to £1,000 each for thirteen smaller panels and £3,500 each for two larger ones – although the victory was a fleeting one as the smaller ones were later cancelled. Herbert also had his contract cancelled after receiving only £5,000 of the £9,000 originally agreed. And Edwin Landseer, commissioned in 1850 to paint three hunting oils in the Peers' Dining Room, was forced to accept an 'absurdly inadequate' £1,000 after the Commons refused extra funds to cover a higher payment. He agreed to undertake the work 'only under the influence of his patriotism'.

Success or failure?

With all these tribulations, some of the kind that attend any major capital project, it is remarkable that the Royal Fine Art Commission achieved as much as it did. But was the Westminster project in fact a success? As always, yardsticks were different for different people. Some saw it as an avowedly moral exercise, a method of exciting patriotism in adults and inculcating it in children. The M.P. Thomas Wyse, for example, gave a dewy-eyed account of the impact of Ludwig of Bavaria's patronage of mural painting in Munich: 'I have seen

Opposite:
The Baptism of Ethelbert, William Dyce, watercolour sketch for fresco, 1865. (© *Parliamentary Art Collection*)

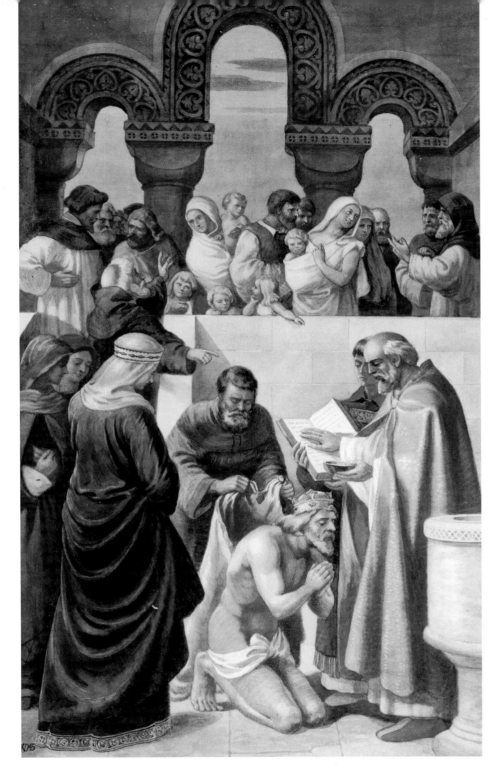

the peasants of the mountains of the Tyrol holding up their children, and explaining to them scenes of Bavarian history almost every Sunday'. Eastlake was slightly of this tendency too: his 1848 tract *On the Philosophy of the Fine Arts* was essentially a statement of faith in the capacity of art to bring moral refinement to the working man.

For those harbouring such high-minded hopes, disappointment was bound to follow: the British polity was too mature and stable for moral inculcation to be necessary and the man in the street too naturally sceptical for it to work. But as a simple exercise in bringing art to the people, the Westminster project paid dividends. The vast and enthusiastic crowds that had queued, and paid, to attend the cartoon exhibitions were ample proof. A breadth of public exposure to art had been achieved that was unprecedented in an era before public galleries and museums.

Did this exercise in state patronage, unique in its scale, raise the general standard of English art? Here again the balance sheet is probably in credit. For sure, no enduring excellence in the art of fresco developed, but the Parliament project did inspire a vogue for ambitious narrative murals, the most obvious progeny being the Pre-Raphaelite interiors at the Oxford Union, painted by the youthful trio of Rossetti, Morris and Burne-Jones in the late 1850s with Arthurian legends as the (by then slightly hackneyed) subject matter. Contemporary with that was a huge allegorical fresco – *Justice, a Hemicycle of Lawgivers* – at Lincoln's Inn by G.F. Watts, who though nominally on the Commission's roster was given few opportunities, to the chagrin of some who recognised a great talent. Even more interesting, in that they adapt the form to contemporary concerns, were William Bell Scott's 'Iron and Coal' murals at Wallington Hall in Northumberland, also from the late 1850s, and Ford Madox Brown's 1880s series at Manchester Town Hall depicting commerce and the textile industry.

It is also true that there was robust, even savage, criticism of individual works at Westminster, some of it from people competent to judge. This had been so from the beginning of the project, when a vitriolic commentary on the cartoon exhibitions had dismissed the Commissioners as 'gay idlers in taste'. Later, in 1858, *The Quarterly Review* considered the murals to reveal 'little else than coarse unfinished daubing, hasty inaccurate drawing and academical *tours de force* scarcely superior to what may be seen on the papered walls of a French café'. More lightheartedly, *Punch* reworked an aria from Balfe's 1843 opera *The Bohemian Girl*:

> I dreamt that I slept in the House of Lords
> and I also dreamt – which puzzled me most –
> That the figures were all the same.

And when the wearisome Bernal Osborne affected to apologise for having confused the face of Cordelia with the nose of Regan, his fellow member William Cowper suggested that he had confused both with the dragon in Watts' *St George*.

Such barbs, then as now, are an occupational hazard in England. But they were counterbalanced by solid praise that became on the whole more generous with time, in spite of the continuing decay that by the last quarter of the nineteenth century made some paintings mere shadows of the original. Eastlake told Albert that he thought Dyce's Arthurian frescoes in the Robing Room 'superior to the best German work of this kind'. Perhaps deference coloured his perspective, but he had the comparative knowledge and the critical faculties to judge. Cope's frescoes drew praise from Holman Hunt, another discerning critic. But Maclise's paintings, wrought at such emotional cost and physical effort, were admired most: even when faded almost to a monochrome, they were widely thought to have retained their 'sombre realism and expressive power'.

The twentieth century was kinder still: critical distance lent enchantment and the opportunity for measured assessment away from the babble that attends the birth and infancy of any big production. A century on, when Victoriana was distinctly unfashionable and the reputation of mid-Victorian narrative painting in particular was at its nadir, some were still inclined to ridicule works that seemed saccharine and overwrought to modern eyes. As Edward Reynolds pointed out in *The Spectator* in 1949, a mental adjustment was needed to understand them: 'one must re-create a world of illustrative art, scarcely troubled by the rivalry of the camera and insulated against all those brilliant inventions in the treatment of light which were leading France towards the triumphs of Impressionism'. But at the same time, there was growing appreciation of the skill displayed by the (often young) artists chosen by the Royal Fine Art Commission. And Maclise continued to win admirers. For Clare Willsdon, his Royal Gallery work succeeded in its skilful synthesis of French and Germanic trends, recalling the Pavillon du Roi of Louis Philippe at Versailles. The *Death of Nelson* mural, she thought, was a secular *pietà*. The art historian Thomas Boase, writing in 1954, was also complimentary. By any standard, he argued, Maclise's paintings 'remain major works … In his sprawling, twisted corpses he has painted some of his grandest figures, using to the full his remarkable power of foreshortening and his wide range of anatomical knowledge. English art in the high romantic vein has seldom reached such narrative power and found such force and range to set it out'.

To what did all this virtuosity add up? Was the whole greater than the sum of its parts? Again, judgements differ, not least across time, but there have always been voices ready to acknowledge the depth of the Commission's achievement in difficult circumstances. Even some M.P.s joined in: John Stanford, the Member for Reading, told the Commons in 1850 that the cartoons were 'splendid works of genius that

The House of Lords in Session 1851, Joseph Nash, bodycolour on paper, 1851 (© *Parliamentary Art Collection*). Above the Bar of the House are Daniel Maclise's *Spirit of Justice* (left) and *Spirit of Chivalry* (right), either side of John Horsley's *Spirit of Religion*.

The Judgement of Daniel, John Herbert, oil on canvas, 1880 (© *Parliamentary Art Collection*). Detail, Peers' Robing Room.

gave triumphant contradiction to the charge that Britain was deficient in great painters'. *The Spectator*, generally a candid friend and perceptively critical when necessary, offered a favourable assessment when reflecting on twenty years of the Commission's labours in 1861: Albert and his Commissioners had 'undoubtedly fulfilled their office in promoting the fine arts; we may date a revival in art from the time of the Cartoon Exhibition in Westminster Hall, and several painters have risen to eminence and academic honours who were then unknown, and would have been till now'. C.L. Eastlake, the architect nephew of Sir Charles, took a similar view in the 1880s. Before the Royal Fine Art Commission, he noted,

> no public encouragement worth mentioning had for some time past been given either to painters or sculptors. They were now associated in the completion of a grand national work. The display of prize cartoons in Westminster Hall had the effect of bringing under public notice the talents of many an artist who might otherwise have long remained in obscurity. The technical details of fresco painting, which for centuries had been forgotten in this country, received scientific attention; and if the issue has not been altogether satisfactory, it is from no want of pains or extent of research.

Similar judgements were made in the twentieth century, the more authentically as deference and filial piety had by then no purchase. Lord Stanmore, addressing the Lords in 1901, argued that the general standard of English art had been 'wonderfully improved. No-one who looks at the average run of English pictures at an exhibition of the Royal Academy, and who remembers what they were sixty years ago, as unfortunately I can, would hesitate for a moment in saying so. This I believe to be due in a great measure to the Prince Consort's efforts, and not a little to the work of the Commission'. And Boase,

never short of an acerbic judgement when he thought one warranted, took the view in 1954 that the Westminster project 'resulted in a series of frescoes which remain, though neglected and little admired, the most remarkable English attempt in that medium since the close of the Middle Ages.'

An end and an afterlife

As events came together to provide the perfect conditions for creating the Royal Fine Art Commission, so they conspired to end it. The premature death in 1861 of Prince Albert, personification of the whole enterprise, removed at a stroke its driving force. But even before that, there had been a gradual loss of vitality.

The artistic fashions of the 1840s began to look anachronistic. Constant arguments over funding were gruelling. The endless battle against physical decay, a kind of Sisyphean labour, was draining and even harrowing. More fundamentally, the ideological imperative was less pressing, with Britain firmly at peace and the constitutional settlement that had seemed so fluid in the 1840s now embedded and secure. And while he never lost interest in the Westminster project, Albert himself had sought more varied outlets for his prodigious talents and energies. Buoyed by the huge success of the 1851 Great Exhibition, he increasingly diverted them to other endeavours, not least the improvement of public education, the promotion of commerce and the advancement of science. Eastlake, too, spread himself more thinly, becoming President of the Royal Academy in 1850 and adding to that the Directorship of the National Gallery in 1855. And ordinary mortality had culled by more than half the ranks of those who had stood with Albert at the outset. Peel had died in 1850, Rogers in 1855, Macaulay in 1859. 'All my Commissioners are dead almost', he said to the Queen in the spring of 1861.

With Albert's own death, the Government grant, long

a source of contention, came to a sudden halt with only about half the planned paintings completed. The Queen, sentimentally attached to Albert's *début* project, intervened with Gladstone, then Chancellor of the Exchequer, to secure an extension, allowing the Royal Fine Art Commission to limp on until 1863, when it announced its own dissolution in its thirteenth and final report. 'The term of our prescribed duties has now arrived', it said. 'The whole scheme of decoration ... has been decided, and, trusting that the series of works now in progress can be carried on to their completion, it does not appear to us that the commission need be continued to superintend the execution'. Work did indeed continue, or rather sputter on piecemeal, under the aegis of a committee that included Sir Charles Eastlake until his death in 1865; but the focus had shifted decisively from art to money, with the greater part of mental effort dissipated in negotiating artists' fees and other banausic tasks. Dyce died in 1864, his work unfinished; but Cope carried on until 1869, Ward until 1874

and Herbert as late as 1880, when his *Judgement of Daniel* was finally hung in the Peers' Robing Room. Blank spaces were covered in Pugin wallpaper, while experts debated for decades, on and off, the best methods of preserving the fragile works amid worsening pollution. This shadowy afterlife continued through the twentieth century and beyond, sustained by private donations. Further murals, in oil, were added in 1910 and 1927 and it was not until 2010, when the Armada series conceived by Albert to replace the sixteenth century tapestries destroyed in the 1834 fire was finished, that the chapter begun in 1841 was finally closed. The Commission itself, though, had effectively died with Albert. Without his unique animating spirit, its focus and forward propulsion were lost. As Lord Salisbury put it forty years afterwards, 'there was no power that could carry on the work to which he devoted himself, nobody fit to take up the work that death compelled him to drop'.

Opposite: Nicholas Grimshaw and Partners' Waterloo International Terminal (1993), built to accommodate Eurostar trains running between London and Paris. Evident from the picture is its quality as an airy, light-filled space, but that was almost sacrificed when the developers proposed adding office blocks above the terminal. The Royal Fine Art Commission played a major role in preventing that – a success that, a quarter of a century on, is little known or acknowledged. One view that was thus preserved through the glass is of the Shell Centre, the first true London skyscraper, which the Commission supported in the mid 1950s. *(Reid & Peck / RIBA Collections)*

PART II

Design Champion

THE TWENTIETH CENTURY
ROYAL FINE ART COMMISSION
1924–1999

I | Fresh impetus

Prince Albert's death in 1861 left his Fine Art Commission rudderless. A penny-pinching Exchequer sank it soon after. His unfinished work of decorating the new Palace of Westminster with art and sculpture drifted, as we have seen, to a posthumous conclusion.

It did so slowly and unsurely. Ill-paid artists tinkered in grim conditions, their work sometimes disintegrating before their eyes. The Palace of Westminster, filled with air filthy with coal dust and hard by a river polluted with raw sewage, became almost uninhabitable; a shroud had to be hung in its riverside windows in an effort to keep out the foul atmosphere. Faced with decaying murals, the Board of Works covered them, as Lord Stanmore put it, 'with a vulgar wall-paper, and there they are, behind it, obliterated'. High art, he complained, had given way to the most commonplace upholstery.[1] The miserable hiatus persisted for forty years, sustained by an assumption (never tested) that to breathe new life into the Fine Art Commission, and thus get things moving again, would be an act of lèse-majesté that Queen Victoria would resent and resist. The charnel house aura of the Palace of Westminster somehow seemed a fit echo of the mournful Court. Albert's death had left the place a memorial stuck in suspended animation.

These bonds of propriety were cut in 1901 with the death of Victoria. As soon after as decency allowed – five months, as it happened – Lord Stanmore proposed a motion in the House of Lords to bring back a Royal Fine Art Commission, which he saw purely in the context of the Palace of Westminster: an apolitical body set up to finish, then embellish and expand, the work of Prince Albert. The halting progress of the past forty years meant that some opportunities had been lost forever: John Everett Millais and Lord Leighton could never now be commissioned and Edwin Landseer's Monarch of the Glen, painted for the Peers' refreshment room, was now in private hands. But Westminster could still be a living illustration of the island story, still be used as a canvas for the encouragement of Art across the nation.

In other circumstances, Stanmore's timing might have been ideal: most fundamental institutional reform is done early in the life of a regime, before inertia sets in and events intrude. But this was merely the start of a new reign; the Prime Minister, Lord Salisbury, was by contrast limping towards the end of his third ministry, and in truth he was never one for government intervention where inaction was an option – his tendency was to wait until civil servants had presented a proposal and sum up with a brisk 'far better not'. It was hardly surprising, then, that he resisted Stanmore's motion, relying on rhetoric to shore up some thin arguments. A special machine without Albert steering it would founder, he thought; worse (as if standing Royal Commissions were an untried novelty), vesting powers in a permanent body would undermine the normal processes of executive government. Predictably, the coup de grâce was financial: Stanmore's plan, 'however admirable in an artistic dream', was, he feared, 'calculated to cause a cold shudder in the back of a Chancellor of the Exchequer'. Lord Rosebery, his predecessor as Prime Minister, thought Lord Salisbury's reasons 'as usual, somewhat unexpected'. But they were enough to kill off the idea of a new Commission in the Albert mould.

Nonetheless, there was a sense of a gap needing to be filled, a gap that went far wider than decorative detail at the Palace of Westminster. Even in the mid-nineteenth century, there were stirrings. Albert's Westminster project was demanding enough, but his remit, referencing as it did a resurgence of the artistic prowess of the nation, had always carried the potential for something bigger, almost a culture-led moral rearmament in the face of growing German supremacy. That sense was reinforced by Albert's status as a polymath who could hardly be constrained by a single building project. In the event, his determination to focus on the job he was given meant that he interpreted his mission narrowly, and so his Fine Art Commission never troubled itself with the broader question of improving the public realm across the country. But behind the scenes he took an interest, complaining towards the end of his life to William Cowper, First Commissioner of Works, that 'anything more abominable than most of the drinking fountains that have been erected in Hyde Park I never saw'. Even Victoria was sometimes moved to aesthetic outrage when personally affected, as for example by Queen Anne's Mansions, built in 1873 in her line of sight from Buckingham Palace to the Houses of Parliament. The 1894 London Building Act introduced an 80ft height limit in direct consequence.

In the 1901 debate on the Stanmore motion, the Earl of Wemyss broached, for the first time, a wider Fine Art Commission, one that went beyond the Palace of Westminster to monitoring architecture generally. 'What is wanted in this country is a permanent body which should have control over official architectural eccentricities and put a check on engineering monstrosities such as we see in some of the bridges over the Thames.'[2] He argued for models of proposed buildings to be displayed for comment, anticipating the design review method ultimately adopted by the twentieth century Royal Fine Art Commission. Warming to his theme, he launched an assault on specific public buildings, beginning with the new Admiralty Building at Horse Guards, and particularly on the secrecy that attended their planning. Greater transparency, and appraisal by an expert advisory body, would, he reckoned, filter out the worst offenders.

Lord Wemyss's idea was left hovering until the Great War, the horror of which had a profound effect on perceptions and attitudes. Something better had to emerge from the destruction and loss. It could not be business as usual, and certainly there was pressure to make art less rarefied, to bring it 'down from the mountain tops to permeate each detail of a man's everyday life', as The Times put it in March 1921. 'Too little care is taken officially to save us from unnecessary ugliness', it said. Its proposed remedy, a committee of taste composed of sculptors, painters and architects to choose sites for statues and a standing committee of designers to oversee street decorations for occasions of national importance, was 'being discussed in many quarters with an eagerness that shows that the beauty of London, and anything making for its increase, is an intimate concern of thousands not given to theorizing on aesthetics'.

The agitation was largely focussed on small, ordinary and common things: not power stations but pillar boxes, not government buildings but sand-boxes and street lamps. Indeed, the President of The Royal Institute of British Architects at the time gave a spirited defence of the pillar box, pronouncing it beautiful because it was so exactly fitted to its purpose. 'It is round for the safety of passers-by. It has a curved top to drain off the rain. It has a firm base, a flap over the aperture to keep letters dry. There is nothing superfluous at all.' The chief

agonies, then, were over things that insistently intruded on the daily existence of Everyman – and what we now call street furniture was more likely to do so, on the whole, than a single, avoidable building.

At the same time, there was a greater willingness after the War to countenance state direction. In 1919, Sir Charles Villiers Stanford had suggested that music should be fostered by the state. 'Why not the Arts too?', asked the Society of Architects. This pro-intervention sentiment was not as strong as after the Second War, nor was it by any means the default stance in Britain. Critically, too, 'state' did not mean 'government'. Advocates of a committee of taste wanted, if anything, to take control away from government and vest it in independent experts; most were at pains to say that 'officials' (by which they meant government employees) should be excluded. But still there was a feeling that intervention of some kind might be tried in response to the cataclysm of war, even if the authors of that cataclysm were nation states. And we have, too, the genesis of the idea that the tastemakers might be a challenge to government, not its handmaiden.

Opposite: Cannon Street Railway Bridge, built in 1866, widened in 1893 and photographed here by John Gay in 1968. Comprising five spans supported on massive cast-iron columns, it was one of the huge utilitarian engineering structures in central London that prompted The Earl of Wemyss in 1901 to call for a new Royal Fine Art Commission for the twentieth century, empowered to control the design of major public works. (*Historic England Archive*)

II | American precedent

If something needed to be done, it was already being done elsewhere. The French had a well-established Ministry of Fine Arts, but the more compelling precedents were in America. What Britain was groping to conceive was already fully-fledged across the Atlantic. America was increasingly viewed as the pathfinder and innovator, the model to be followed and even copied. And it had a prototype, in the form of the United States Commission of Fine Arts, set up by Congress in 1910 to appraise development proposals in Washington and advise the federal government.

Hard work was needed to grind out a proposal suitable for Britain. The graft was done by an informal, self-appointed coterie that managed to hold together through the early 1920s despite internal tensions, personality clashes and a certain amount of mutual suspicion. Even more impressively, it achieved its goal despite political flux and pressing matters of state (such as negotiating German war reparations) of the kind that would have made it hard for any government to pay much attention to arrangements for deciding the appearance of pillar boxes.

The main actors in this drama were a mix of politicians, civil servants and architects, between them a potent blend of emollience, practical acumen and bloody-mindedness. The prime movers were Sir Lionel Earle, Permanent Secretary at the Ministry of Works; his political master, the 27th Earl of Crawford[3], First Commissioner of Works; two senior architects, Sir Reginald Blomfield and Sir Aston Webb, the latter President of the Royal Academy; and finally an *éminence grise* in the shape of Viscount Lee of Fareham, who had served as Lloyd George's Minister of Agriculture and now, with a peerage, had a berth that gave him continuing political influence.

To a man, they favoured emulating American practice, Lee perhaps influenced by his close and direct experience of the United States; as military attaché in Washington after the Spanish-American War of 1898, he had become an intimate of Theodore Roosevelt. Earle admired the American Fine Art Commission's work in designing and beautifying American military cemeteries after the Great War. For all of them, though, adoption of the U.S. template meant one thing above all: avoidance of a government ministry to regulate artistic endeavour. Earle had seen enough politicians in action in his long career to know that their performance was variable and unpredictable; he described Sir Alfred Mond, Crawford's predecessor as First Commissioner, as 'knowing nothing about art', and he worried that transient ministers were the wrong people in whom to vest executive authority on artistic matters. *The Times* agreed: a ministry, it thought, risked being 'expensive, cumbrous, autocratic and partial, and certainly subject to the common dangers of political appointment, with which the arts have less concern than any other human activity'.

To bolster the case, Earle sent the social reformer Sir Hubert Llewellyn Smith to Washington in late 1921 to assess how the American Commission worked and how well the model would translate to Britain. Llewellyn Smith was encouraged by what he found. The U.S. Commission had been so well received that Executive Orders of the President had quickly extended its scope beyond statues and fountains to cover public buildings in the District of Columbia; then any new structures that significantly affected Washington's appearance, for which purpose the Commission sometimes selected architects and organised competitions; then 'any questions involving matters of art with which the Federal Government was concerned'; and from that came a general tendency for Acts of Congress to stipulate that the Commission's advice be sought before any 'matter of art' was finally determined. In addition, it informally advised State governments and public authorities. All in all, it was an impressive *curriculum vitae* for a body still not much more than ten years old. The Commission's chairman, the librarian Charles Moore, reported that its advice was almost always adopted, the only noteworthy exception being an intervention on the design of medals where it had 'given an amount of time entirely disproportionate to the results achieved'. Llewellyn Smith asked if he ever found the limitation of the title to 'Fine Arts' embarrassing. 'We would if we ever paid the least attention to it', Moore replied. 'But we do not.' The circumstances were not, of course, exactly parallel to those in Britain: Llewellyn Smith noted that the American Commission was helped by the unitary government structure in Washington, with no municipality alongside the federal government, giving it an obvious gap to fill and a clearer field; and he cautioned that London, being so vast and complex, was a tougher challenge. But he felt able to send a broadly positive report back to Earle.

If independence from government was seen as important, so too was independence from professional bodies seeking to advance a sectional interest. Crawford and Earle at the Ministry of Works were constantly fretting that the Royal Academy was trying to hijack the mechanism of an independent body for purposes of self-aggrandisement. At worst they saw its President, Aston Webb, as a pestering infiltrator, all his offers of help written off as having an ulterior motive. It is true that the offers were frequent, were pressed hard and went well

beyond the call of duty. The new body could have offices at Burlington House, Webb said. Royal Academy staff would provide clerical support. Webb himself would raise funds privately to cover the first year's operating costs, to avoid a call on the public purse in straitened times – on the face of it a generous gesture, but probably more a canny device to allow the new body to be set up quickly without Treasury funds and therefore without Treasury approval. In short order Webb indeed raised £100 'from a sympathiser', about half the sum needed, and was confident of doubling it.

But all this activity, from someone who technically had no locus in the matter, served only to inflame Earle's cynicism. He told Crawford that the Royal Academy 'wanted to get the kudos for this initiative'; and while it is probably a good sign to have people fighting to claim credit, Earle found it galling as the Academy had, in his view, been 'supine' when it came to defending the cause of good design in the public realm. 'The new body will be doomed to failure', he thought, 'if it becomes a child of the Academy'. In February 1922, Crawford (never much given to diplomacy) was sufficiently nervous to ask Webb outright whether the whole scheme was an 'Academy stunt'. Of course not, Webb protested. And in truth he was an old man in a hurry. He knew that the wheels of bureaucracy turned slowly and that opportunities had to be seized before peacetime inertia set in. Blomfield agreed: 'If we don't do something now', he told *The Times*, 'we probably never shall'.

The turf wars became more acute when discussion turned to who might sit on the new body. Here again, Webb caused alarm by suggesting that the Royal Academy should nominate most of the members, and that the President of the Royal Academy (at the time Webb himself) should be a member *ex officio*. Again, Earle was dismissive, complaining to Crawford that 'the thing is bound to be a failure if it is to be composed largely of the stereotypes such as we find among Royal Academicians. I should like to rope in the Whistlers, the

Augustus Johns and the Burne-Joneses of the day, and types of men who, as a rule, have a very poor opinion of the Royal Academy as a body'.

A second point of contention was the balance between professional and lay members. Webb and Blomfield, predictably as architects, wanted professionals to dominate, with Blomfield lamenting 'the English habit of handing these things over to amateurs'. But where he merely sought a majority of 'trained and competent artists', Webb went further and argued that only the Chairman should be a layman. Crawford was unimpressed, telling Earle that 'laymen may often be fools but artists invariably quarrel; and I myself think that a larger measure of lay membership is necessary'.

And then there was the question of how members would be chosen. Here again Crawford, who remained involved despite having been replaced as First Commissioner by Sir John Baird when the Lloyd George coalition collapsed in October 1922, worried about undue influence by professional bodies. He swatted away one proposal circulated within the Ministry of Works in 1922 that had two-thirds of a twelve-strong body nominated by external organisations: two each by the Royal Academy and R.I.B.A. and one each by the London County Council, Society of Sculptors, London Society and the Tate Trustees. Discarding that idea, Baird came back with the suggestion that the King should be the ultimate appointer, acting on the advice of his Prime Minister. This was better: Earle saw it not just as a happy borrowing from America, where Fine Art Commission members were appointed by the President, but as 'a check in the event of any really undesirable member being pressed on the Commission'. It did though raise the question of how the Prime Minister himself would come by names. Some thought he should pick from candidates suggested by expert panels, but that idea was dropped as an absurdity as soon as it was realised that any panel worth having would comprise all the best people. Crawford told Earle that 'we should all shrink from

the laughter caused by its transpiring that the committee of selection had unanimously selected itself!'

In the event, Baird simply decided that he would put a list of names to the Prime Minister 'based on the best advice I can obtain'. It was not, of course, a simple matter at all, as the question of who was and was not a suitable candidate introduced a whole new area of disagreement. The official papers record a series of unsavoury judgements as unsuspecting artists and architects had their professional and (more often) personal defects examined. Crawford was the most caustic appraiser, sometimes attributing negative comments to others: of the architect William Lethaby, he said to Baird that 'Lionel Earle will tell you that he is a perfectly hopeless and impossible person on a committee when called upon to record a judgement – his vacillation on such occasions is little short of maddening'. Lutyens he thought 'very little good at committee meetings – he is always fantastic and frivolous. I would much prefer [Herbert] Baker'. The artist William Rothenstein was marked down for having 'a very ugly name, though I do not think it less euphonious than Ruthersten, by which his brother has just re-baptized himself'. Avray Tipping and Lawrence Weaver he wrote off as 'pure journalists and amateurs of the first water'. And Albert Richardson he described as 'on the cranky side – moreover we do not want another cockney or another professor'.

In the end it was the Foreign Secretary, Lord Curzon, who broke these various deadlocks. In some ways he was an improbable saviour. He was exceptionally busy trying to deal with the large geopolitical questions that were swirling about unanswered. And of all the main players, he was the most sceptical of the need for a Commission, worrying that it would interfere with local authorities and become a source of local contention. Earle reassured him that it would 'always be on the side of the Angels', and he was finally won over by Earle's clever claim that, had it existed, a Commission would have prevented the installation in 1914 of a fresco cycle by Sigismund Goetze at the Foreign Office. This, for Curzon, was something of a litmus test: he regarded the murals (depicting the triumph of the British Empire) as an act of vandalism.[4]

Once convinced, Curzon was a formidable ally. Baird knew this and offered him the chairmanship of the new Commission. Curzon declined, but Baird still made sure that he was shown the evolving plans, on the basis that the Cabinet would approve anything on the subject of art and architecture of which Curzon approved. Where he came into his own, though, was not in finessing details but in negotiating a way past political hazards, of which there were several. The early 1920s were years of such domestic flux that coaxing through non-urgent reforms required all Curzon's skills; without him, the whole enterprise of creating the Commission might easily have foundered. The Treasury almost sank it in September 1922 by asking for it to be postponed on grounds of cost – 'we do not wish to initiate any new service which is not immediately and essentially necessary' – but Curzon stepped in at Baird's request and forced the Treasury to back down. And when Lloyd George resigned as Prime Minister a month later, throwing the plans into yet more doubt, his successor Bonar Law was persuaded to leave the matter open until Curzon returned from a Reparations Conference. By 1923, a cancer-ridden Bonar Law had himself been replaced by Baldwin, who agreed to put the question to the Cabinet, but again delayed until Curzon was back from an Imperial Conference. Baldwin then, quite unnecessarily, held another General Election, hoping for a personal mandate. He miscalculated badly and lost his majority. And so he too went, albeit staggering on for a few weeks while a new Government was formed. Improbably, it was during that period of limbo, a week before Christmas in 1923, that the outgoing Cabinet finally approved the establishment of a 'Commission of Fine Arts'.

Pushing the proposal through in these circumstances could easily have backfired. Ramsay MacDonald was in the process of forming the first ever Labour Government, and now a new body was being foisted on him as almost the last act of a defeated Conservative administration. Crawford was nervous: 'I am beginning to get a little shy of making this large and novel departure in policy two or three days before the change of Government', he wrote to the Ministry of Works, 'but I suppose if the matter were deferred until the new Government comes into office, the delay might again be serious.' The King, too, was dubious, Downing Street telling Baird that 'the King approves of the Cabinet's proposal but is rather doubtful whether, in the present circumstances, it is wise to attempt to run the measure through'. Here again Curzon weighed in to good effect, suggesting that 'it might be politic, and anyhow courteous, to submit the panel and the reasons for the creation of this body to the Leader of the Labour Party'. Baldwin took his advice. Brought into the outgoing Prime Minister's confidence in this way, MacDonald put up no obstacles. Rather the opposite in fact: Baird told Lord Stamfordham, the King's Private Secretary, that MacDonald 'cordially welcomes the idea and raises no objection at all to the immediate appointment of the gentlemen who have been suggested should His Majesty see fit to nominate them'.

That final list of gentlemen, after all the toing and froing, again showed Webb's enduring influence. Apart from Webb himself, it included four of his nominees – Sir Reginald Blomfield, the painter David Cameron, the sculptor Sir George Frampton and the architect Alfred Gotch. Crawford was offered the chairmanship, which he accepted 'with great reluctance' – shades of *nolo episcopari* – with Curzon serving as a lay member and Sir Edwin Lutyens, in spite of Crawford's reservations, joining as the second architect member. The landscape architect Thomas Mawson[5] made up the nine, three of whom were serving presidents of professional institutes.

The Fine Arts Commission – a working title by which it

W.R.
1922

Opposite: Sir Edwin Lutyens by William Rothenstein. The two sat together on the Royal Fine Art Commission for most of the 1930s. Lutyens, a founder Commissioner, effectively had life tenure owing to his eminence and served twenty years until he died in 1944 – the fourth longest term of office after Sir Philip Dowson, Lord Holford and Lord Lee of Fareham. Such lengthy terms gave the Commission a powerful collective memory: the sequential service of just three Commissioners – Lutyens, William Holford and Elizabeth Chesterton – spanned the seventy years from 1924 to 1994. (*Sanguine and black & white chalk, 1922. National Portrait Gallery, London*)

was still known even at this late stage – was at last appointed by the King on 24 January 1924. Baldwin had finally resigned eight days before, after losing a vote of confidence, with MacDonald replacing him as Prime Minister. Thus by an accident of timing (and ironically, given the circumstances of its dissolution in 1999), the creation of the Royal Fine Art Commission was almost literally the first act of Britain's first Labour Government. An accompanying press notice stated that the Commission had been 'set up on the lines of the American Fine Arts Commission … It is hoped that the efforts of the Commission, as in America, will result not only in a marked improvement in the artistic character of monuments and public buildings, but also in the saving of many thousands of pounds'. The imitation of American practice, and the use of good design to avoid waste and extravagance, were presented to the public as clinching arguments.

In the rush and political turmoil, and notwithstanding the fact that the Commission had already been set up, a few matters of detail remained unresolved. These were settled, on the whole pretty casually, in the first half of 1924. One question was the name. The working title of Fine Arts Commission was a borrowing from the United States, rather than a conscious harking back to Prince Albert's Commission, but even so it was seen as not quite right for a body focussing on architecture. Crawford had told Earle in May 1923 that 'I do not very much like the name, which suggests enterprise outside the range of the Commission's sphere; but I am at a loss to suggest any alternative'. So too was everyone else. Even the exact constitutional status of the new body remained uncertain for a couple of months after its creation. Eventually the two matters were settled together in March 1924, when the Treasury and Home Office agreed that the new body should be a Royal Commission and the founding Commissioners decided that, on balance, they preferred 'Art' in the singular.[6] And so it became the Royal Fine Art Commission.

Also still unclear in the opening months were the Commission's terms of reference. Crawford himself came up with the formula that the Commission would 'inquire into such questions of public amenity or artistic importance as may be referred to them by any Department of State, and give advice on similar questions when so requested by public or quasi-public bodies, or where it appears to the Royal Commission that their intervention would be advantageous'. 'I don't quite like the word 'intervention'', Earle told the Treasury. 'It smacks too much of Poincaré and the Ruhr.' 'Assistance' was ultimately chosen. Nor was he keen on 'public amenity', which he thought would 'include the placing of lavatories, which could hardly come under the purview of this important body'. But those words stayed.

Even less clear was the geographical scope of the Commission. There were plenty of informal views on the matter: Blomfield thought that for practical purposes it should confine itself to London. But formally, did its writ run in Wales and Scotland? No-one quite knew. Crawford told Earle in March 1924 that 'as far as the original Treasury minute is concerned, there is no territorial limit – that is to say that not only are Scotland or Wales not excluded, but as drawn the minute would authorise the Australian Government to invite our opinions'. The Treasury reassured him that only buildings put up by the Australian government in London would be covered.[7] The Commission should proceed on the basis that it covered England and Wales. Northern Ireland, created only three years before after Irish partition, was never mentioned.[8]

These points resolved, the King was able, on 30 May 1924, to sign a Warrant of Appointment, with all members greeted by their Sovereign as Well-beloveds except Curzon, who (as a marquess) was designated as 'Entirely-beloved'. This cemented the name and terms of reference. The Royal Fine Art Commission, already up and running for four months, was officially born.

III | In action

The Commission was delivered into a receptive world. As always, there was a smattering of low-level carping about the cost of the enterprise, and some resentment about busybody interference, but these were isolated episodes. *The Times*'s positive judgement was far more typical, and also revealing in its recognition that the task was huge, the problems deep and the results unlikely to be quick. It hoped for

> *'the gradual inducement of a standard in public art, which will make itself felt all over the country, to the discouragement of eccentricity, vulgarity, and waste. The knowledge that such a body exists cannot fail to bring upon it very rapidly an increasing rush of demands for its advice, in years when there is much building and rebuilding, when towns are expanding and garden cities and other means of relieving congestion are needed on all sides, and big schemes are on foot for the housing of the artisan classes and not all the war memorials are finished and in place. There is no hurry – or rather, though there is here and there grave need for prompt action, haste can be of no service in what is ultimately a matter of education.'*

At first the Commission was purely reactive, able under the terms of its warrant to become involved only when asked by public bodies. As an 'on-call' adviser its repertoire was strictly limited, but within those limits it did useful work. From the beginning there was an atavistic interest in the Palace of

Westminster, already by the 1920s suffering from structural problems. The Anston stone used by Sir Charles Barry to build the Palace had been hit hard by pollution, but to make matters worse it had been defective, with plentiful fractures that caused spalling. And in some places it had been wrongly bedded during construction; weaker points such as pinnacles had had to be reinforced with cast-iron rods. In 1927, the Office of Works asked the Commission to approve the use of Stancliffe stone for repairs, as recommended by a technical report commissioned by the Government. No, said the Commission; although Stancliffe was hardier in the face of atmospheric pollution – and in the 1920s there were still plenty of airborne toxins – that would lead to differential weathering. More importantly, its colour was wrong, and insuperably so. 'It is a sandstone which quickly assumes a complexion of uniform blackness, and contrasts most unbecomingly with a yellowish limestone such as Anston'. It would start piebald and then get gloomier and more oppressive with every passing year, ending up a 'dead dirty colour', according to Sir Reginald Blomfield. Alternatives were suggested by various sources – artificial stone, terracotta, even refacing the Palace in Portland stone – but the Commission instead advised quarrying defect-free Anston, now a possibility owing to technological advances since the 1850s. Privately, Blomfield blamed Barry: 'he should never have agreed to all that confectionery. Had he followed the manner of the Horse Guards, the cost would have been reduced by at least a quarter, and he would have left us a far more convenient building which would have complied with one of the first essentials of Architecture – that it should stand up.'

Whatever its reservations about Barry's architecture, the Commission positioned itself as something of a defender of the decorative works inspired by Prince Albert. In 1926 a House of Lords Select Committee resolved that all relevant projects be submitted to the Commission, giving it a powerful locus. And it was not shy of making a decisive impact. Within a year it had derailed the Earl of Iveagh's cherished plans for a Peers' war memorial in the Royal Gallery that would have comprised two marble statues by John Tweed and mural panels by Frank Brangwyn on the theme of the 'Pageant of Empire'. The Commission pounced: the Victorian gilded statues that would have to be sacrificed to make way for this ensemble were 'integral to the original decorative design', while the sixteen Brangwyn canvases, 3,000 square feet in area, would overpower Daniel Maclise's epic narratives of Waterloo and Trafalgar and, worse, would be 'so emphatic as to require that all their surroundings shall be brought into subordination'. This was awkward; the project sponsor was a peer acting from noble impulses in a noble cause. But in a vote, the House of Lords backed the Commission. Brangwyn was appalled, understandably given that his sample canvases had taken seven years to paint. By 1933 they were reduced to doing the rounds of the *Daily Mail* Ideal Home Exhibition at Earl's Court, before going into storage at Kenwood.[9]

Not that the Commission was in principle opposed to adding to Albert's legacy: Lord Crawford personally supervised the production of a cycle of murals in St. Stephen's Hall, on the theme of 'the Building of Britain from Alfred to the Union with Scotland'. Sir Henry Newbolt chose the subjects. David Cameron, by now knighted, acted as project director and (in spite of his name) Sir William Rothenstein was engaged to paint the tortuously titled *Sir Thomas Roe, Envoy from King James the First of England to the Moghul Emperor, succeeding by his courtesy and firmness at the Court of Ajmir, in laying the foundation of British influence in India, 1614*. The murals were unveiled by Baldwin (now back as Prime Minister) in June 1927 after three years' labour; a speedier exercise than the Victorians had managed, but working conditions were easier and no time was wasted wrestling with the fresco method that had driven Maclise and others to distraction in the 1850s.[10]

In these tentative inter-war years, the Commission's focus was less architectural and its workload lighter than *The Times* had expected, in the main because there was still some confusion about what it was for. Its name was largely to blame, creating a sense that its job was to pronounce on things ornamental and decorative. This is reflected in the miscellany of design problems on which its advice was sought by public bodies: anything from mess waiters' uniforms at the Royal Naval Hospital at Greenwich to decorations for the 1935 Silver Jubilee and the 1937 Coronation. For the Jubilee, the Commission deputed Lutyens and his fellow architect William Curtis Green to act as advisers, but they came in too late to have much effect. Dispirited by the experience, they recommended that in future competent designers should be brought in early to supervise commemorative decorations. The opportunity to put that into practice came quickly, with a Coronation following the Jubilee in short order. Giles Gilbert Scott and Grey Wornum were appointed as design advisers: but perhaps that was more heft than was necessary, as the results were a touch po-faced: a series of long vertical pennants, hung either side of poles along The Mall, seem in hindsight uncomfortably reminiscent of Nuremberg, while a temporary annexe built outside Westminster Abbey to serve as a robing room turned out rather Lutyens-like in its monumental gravity.

Equally quirky was the Commission's input into the design of firemen's helmets, on which it was invited to comment in 1936 by the London County Council. The traditional brass helmets were unsafe because of their low resistance to electrical currents; as a result it was decided to replace brass with cork and rubber, but it was far harder to fashion these lighter and bulkier materials into elegant designs. The Commission was nothing if not diligent, analysing the designs in minute detail and receiving presentations from the Chief Fire Officer, who brought along a specimen helmet in maroon. Lord Crawford suggested blue, with a red crest and cartouche, together with a redesign of 'the ugly square upon the throat of the man's tunic to make a more becoming strip of colour'. Other Commissioners made suggestions too, which Sir William Rothenstein painstakingly painted onto plaster models made by Sir William Reid Dick. In the end the Commission recommended black helmets for the ranks and white for officers, both with gilt flashes. The version approved for manufacture in November 1936 used the same colour for officers and men, but the Commission was satisfied with its input, stating in its 1937 report that 'the top-heaviness which we feared would be inevitable has been avoided'.

Mesmerising attention to detail was also given to the design of the George VI postage stamps, especially the definitive issue that visually defined his reign. The Commission had not been consulted on the Edward VIII definitives, and these were poorly received when issued in August 1936 – as it turned out, nearer the end of his fleeting reign than the beginning. *The Manchester Guardian* was especially critical, in particular disliking the use of a photograph as the basis for the effigy, and successfully agitated for the Commission's involvement when, after the Abdication, the whole design process had to be repeated. On this occasion, though, there was a far greater rush, as the date set for Edward's Coronation was kept, with George VI being crowned instead. The design was an inspired collaboration between Edmund Dulac, who sculpted the effigy, and Eric Gill, who did the lettering. The Commission pored over it, ironically suggesting that the King's head might

be better photographed than sculpted, and the effort paid dividends: this time *The Manchester Guardian* praised the stamp as 'the best since the Penny Black'.

Statues and monuments were more common fare. The Commission had taken over the functions of the Ministry of Works' Sites Committee, and so more by default than design it found itself with powers under the Public Statues Act of 1864 to veto the erection of statues in London. And it acquired this power at precisely the time when monuments were proliferating – not empty, perfunctory monuments either, but emotionally-charged ones raised to the dead of the recent war. Creating them was sometimes more an exercise in catharsis than an artistic endeavour, and as such the art sometimes suffered. Harold Nicolson called the result a 'futile jumble'[11] and the Commission fairly rapidly concluded that saturation had been reached; once the best sites had been taken, compromised sites did no favours either to the work itself or to those seeking the peace to contemplate it. Memorials should be refused, it said, unless they had artistic value. That did not mean that they had to be conventionally beautiful. War, after all, was nothing if not ugly. When Lord Gerald Wellesley described Charles Jagger's proposed Royal Artillery Memorial at Hyde Park Corner as 'one of the most terrifyingly ugly things in central London' (to be fair, it was in full view of Apsley House, his family seat), the Commission by contrast saw something with real emotional power – massive, eloquent, literally awful, refusing to sanitise the dreadful truth of war.

Even more controversial was Alfred Hardiman's equestrian statue of Field Marshal Earl Haig, proposed for Whitehall in 1928. The design was not universally admired – a firm of military tailors complained that a cavalryman would never have allowed himself to mount 'a circus horse of such ostentatious vigour' – but the real controversy centred on siting. The Commission wanted it in the middle of the carriageway, bringing the glorious dead and their Cenotaph into direct dialogue with

Opposite: The choice of a site for Alfred Hardiman's 1928 statue of Field Marshal Earl Haig was so controversial that the matter went as far as the British Cabinet, with Ministers backing the Royal Fine Art Commission over Westminster City Council, which had objected to a mid-carriageway position on grounds of public safety. This photograph, showing the grand sweep of Whitehall from Scotland Yard to Parliament, makes clear the soundness of the Commission's judgement in preferring a site in the middle of Whitehall: Haig, seen here mid-scene forward of a mounted Duke of Cambridge, is movingly juxtaposed with the Cenotaph. (*Historic England Archive*)

their Commander-in-Chief,[12] with the two monuments visible together along the great sweep of Whitehall. Westminster City Council thought this would be dangerous – 'many people had practically to risk their lives to place a wreath at the Cenotaph' – and would limit the space available to traffic. Nonsense, said the Commission: growing traffic would soon make the middle of roads places where pedestrians sought refuge rather than encountered danger. The Marquess of Londonderry, First Commissioner of Works, backed the Commission. Westminster persisted. Why not Horse Guards' Parade, or the Mall under the Duke of York's Column, or Pall Mall, or on top of the newish Admiralty Arch, or on the vacant plinth in Trafalgar Square? Barely a site went unexplored. The National Union of Boot & Shoe Operatives weighed in with a suggestion of a site outside Richmond Terrace. The Commission demolished them all, aided by the King who worried that the Mall would become an avenue of monumental statuary.

Eventually, in October 1928, the Cabinet was brought in to break the deadlock – with the tenth anniversary of the Armistice looming, a continuing wrangle would have looked unseemly. It too backed the Commission, at which point Westminster relented.[13] And across the distance of nearly a century the Commission's insistence on Whitehall can be seen to be right: the relationship between Haig and the Cenotaph, although marred by the clumsy interposition in 2005 of the Women of World War II memorial, is still a poignant one.

The Commission's interest in the streetscape went beyond ornamental statuary; it was also closely involved in the design development of functional apparatus, notably the telephone kiosk. Its role in the emergence of Sir Giles Gilbert Scott's red telephone box is justly celebrated, but the project really emerged by accident. It was initiated in 1924 by Birmingham Civic Society, which sent the General Post Office an unsolicited design for a concrete kiosk, believing it to be better than the pedestrian model then in common use. The G.P.O.

asked the Municipal Borough Standing Joint Committee to pull together other designs – a random process that attracted submissions from a motley crew including Westminster Metal Morris Works, D.G. Somerville & Co. and the British Institute of Industrial Art. A Ministry of Works civil servant and an inspector in the Post Office Engineering Department also had a go. The critical reception was damning. 'No-one with any knowledge of design could feel anything but indignation with the pattern that seems to satisfy the official mind', said *The Architects' Journal.*

The G.P.O. appealed to the Commission. Did it share that view? It did, most definitely, adding that 'so many of these kiosks will be erected during the course of the next few years that we look upon the matter as one of national importance'. Chastened, the G.P.O. agreed to the Commission's suggestion of a small competition, limited to three architects, with a prize of £50 for the winner. At the Commission's request, the R.I.B.A. nominated the architects: Sir Giles Gilbert Scott, Sir Robert Lorimer and Sir John Burnet, with Guy Dawber and Walter Tapper in reserve if any of them declined. The G.P.O.'s brief required the kiosk to be made of portable sections not less than 6'8" high internally, rectangular (to allow sufficient wall space for equipment), uniform in colour and reasonably soundproof. Windows were stipulated on three sides starting no more than two feet from the ground, which Lord Crawford thought 'sounds rather ugly, but the G.P.O. insist upon the point in order to obviate offences against propriety'. On the whole he thought these restrictions severe enough to be off-putting; but all three architects took up the challenge. Burnet proposed a cast iron kiosk with a fish-scale domed roof topped by a ventilating funnel, all coloured to match oiled teak. Lorimer's was also cast iron with a teak door, the design kept on 'severely practical lines', though with corner pilasters. Scott's was the majestic K2, its dome derived from Sir John Soane's tomb in Old St. Pancras Churchyard. Full-scale models were inspected by the Commission in May 1924, behind the National Gallery. 'The place is absolutely private', said Earle, 'and the Commissioners can examine them without being annoyed by the curiosity of the general public'. The Commission chose Scott by a whisker, although suggesting that he and Lorimer be given the chance 'to correct any mistakes in detail and to secure that quality of execution which is essential to get the feeling aimed at by the designer'. That cannot have been an appealing prospect for Lorimer, who knew he had come second and that tinkering was unlikely to reverse the result. Tenders were soon being awarded for the supply of the Scott kiosk.[14]

By the mid-1930s, growth in demand for kiosks in rural areas prompted the G.P.O. to seek a more practical model, by which they meant a smaller and cheaper one. Scott had in fact already obliged with his K3, made of concrete and coloured to resemble stippled Clipsham stone, with red glazing bars. Several thousand were made, but trying to produce delicate detail in concrete was difficult and the stone colour was impractical. Production was abandoned and the G.P.O. again reacted to failure by consulting the Commission, saying it wanted 'a worthy substitute for the admirable K2' and was 'prepared to shoulder the not inconsiderable cost, as part of our contribution to the preservation of the country's amenities'. And again it wanted the Commission's blessing. In spite of the abortive work on the K3, Scott was retained, this time emerging with his familiar K6 Jubilee kiosk. At first the Commission tried to persuade him to copy the square windows of the K2 and K3, but Scott resisted — happily so in retrospect, as his rectangular windows with narrow sidelights give the kiosk a distinctively 1930s look.

But the real point of contention was not design but colour. Aware that quantities of the kiosk would be installed in villages, Scott set himself against copying the pillar box red of the K2, fearing it would strike a discordant note amid quiet greys and browns. To begin with he preferred toned white or stone,

then shifted to a 'warm dove grey, light enough to avoid any suggestion of heaviness or gloom but not so light as to allow mud splashes and dirt to show up easily'. The Commission and the G.P.O. both strongly favoured red, regardless of location. For the G.P.O. it had become a kind of corporate livery, but the preference was mainly for practical reasons. If needed in an emergency a kiosk had to be visible, not camouflaged, and it also had to be reasonably resistant to dirt; light colours, the G.P.O. explained to Scott, 'show to a hideous extent all fortuitous stains, such as those caused by dogs and by splashes from passing traffic, and invite and receive scrawls in pencil, some of them indecent, from passing idlers. In contrast even in the least reputable neighbourhoods in London the red kiosks remain without any such disfigurement'. But Scott persisted, nervous of being the author of a kiosk that was resented in villages up and down the country. It was only after three full-size mock-ups, in white, grey and red, were presented for inspection at Burlington Gardens that the Commission's push for red finally prevailed. Even then, there were endless requests for local variations from councils disturbed by the loudness of the new kiosks. At first the G.P.O. relented and permitted local discretion[15] but gradually its attitude hardened. Backed by the Commission, the Postmaster-General issued a circular in February 1939 (ironically just before wartime blackouts) stating that no further departures from the standard red would be allowed.

In amongst all this, there were signs of bigger things to come; a sense that, given the opportunity, the Commission might grapple effectively with wider questions of planning and architecture. With that, of course, came the likelihood of being pulled into controversy, always awkward for a non-partisan body. And indeed in the inter-war years the Commission was embroiled in some fairly impressive rows.

The most embarrassing — mainly because it hinged on whether the Commission had been duped by one of its own members – concerned 4 Carlton Gardens, former home of Palmerston and Balfour and the building that terminated Nash's Carlton House Terrace to the west. The Commissioners of Crown Lands, as owners, wanted to knock it down on the grounds that the house had been empty since Balfour's death and would be costly to bring up to the standards required of a private residence. A replacement building, to serve as offices for a paint manufacturer, was designed by Sir Reginald Blomfield. This was about forty feet higher than both the existing building and Nash's terrace. But in presenting it to the Commission, Blomfield gave the impression that his building was merely the first instalment of a settled scheme to demolish and rebuild the whole of the terrace, which would be built up to the higher level. He even – without the knowledge or authority of the Crown Lands Commissioners and without making it clear that it was speculative – produced a drawing showing No4 as part of a brand-new terrace, faced in Portland stone to harmonise with Buckingham Palace to the west and Admiralty Arch to the east. The Commission took all this on trust and gave Blomfield's design for 4 Carlton Gardens a positive critique. But it fairly soon transpired that the Crown Lands Commissioners had no definite plans to redevelop the whole terrace at all, leaving the Commission in a compromised position: not only had it given its public blessing to a building that would now tower over Nash's terrace, but it had done so on the basis of misinformation; and it had failed, so it seemed, to do anything to defend Carlton House Terrace when it believed it to be in peril.

To make matters worse, the Crown Lands Commissioners tried to rescue matters not by withdrawing its scheme for No4 but by extending it to take in the whole terrace, writing to Crawford in November 1932 to say that 'it would check mischievous criticism of Blomfield's position if he were now appointed to prepare a design for the Terrace for the consideration of the Commission.' Even more egregiously,

they added that they were 'reluctant to bring the names of the King and Queen into any controversy, even in a private letter, but cannot ignore the fact that Their Majesties, after seeing Sir Reginald Blomfield's drawing of 4 Carlton Gardens, *spontaneously* suggested that he should also design the new Carlton House Terrace'. In this the Crown Lands Commissioners miscalculated. A huge outcry arose against the prospect of losing Nash's Terrace. Parliament debated the matter at length. M.P.s and peers queued to denounce the idea and seventy M.P.s lobbied the Prime Minister, Ramsay MacDonald. *Country Life* ran a special supplement in which various luminaries were asked 'Do you think Carlton House Terrace should be demolished? If not, why not?' To which Robert Byron replied 'Do you consider one mentally deficient? If not, why not?' 'Demolish *nothing*', said Hilaire Belloc. Maxwell Fry said that 'viewed as a national asset, Carlton House Terrace stands with such works as the Rue de Rivoli and the Piazza San Marco as a mark of national intelligence'. And Kenneth Clark objected on the grounds that the terrace was 'one of the finest blocks of architecture in London'. It is arguable, then, that the Commission's moment of embarrassment had a salutary effect in that it flushed out, and probably forestalled, plans to demolish a terrace which, in theatrical effect if not in architectural detail, certainly merits Clark's description.

The Commission nonetheless felt bruised. Crawford did his best to defend it in the House of Lords but was sufficiently annoyed to write to the Prime Minister two days before Christmas in 1932, saying that the Commission had been shown 4 Carlton Gardens under false pretences. Generally, though, it was given the benefit of the doubt by an outraged public. The Carlton House Terrace Defence Committee even passed a resolution, moved by the Bishop of Southwark and seconded by Frank Pick, condemning the 'lack of regard' for the Commission. As for Blomfield, he was unabashed, and the correspondence between him and Crawford descends into barely-restrained mutual recrimination. Blomfield had always been difficult, but this was the final breach and he resigned soon after. His 4 Carlton Gardens was in the end built and still stands,[16] but the affair was a complicated mess that redounded to no-one's credit. As *The Manchester Guardian* put it in January 1933, 'The Carlton House Terrace Mystery will rank with the puzzle of why the Pyramids were built'.

Although it backfired badly, bringing the Commission in early on 4 Carlton Gardens had in fact been intended by the Crown Lands Commissioners as a peace offering following a spat over South Africa House in Trafalgar Square, the first major new building in the square since its completion in 1830. This project had been referred to the Commission in 1930 by Christopher Addison, Minister of Agriculture in Ramsay MacDonald's National Government,[17] who had invited comments on height. The Commission obliged, saying it should be limited to eighty-two feet, but went far further and offered unsolicited opinions on elevational treatment. In its view, the new building should be seen as a wing in an architectural composition and should therefore conform in scale and general appearance to Smirke's Canada House, which faced it across the square: low-slung, flat roof, no portico and use of the Ionic order. Instead, the architect, Sir Herbert Baker, had taken his cue from the National Gallery: pitched roof, portico, Corinthian order. And more particularly, he had chosen to carry round the gallery's cornice line. Because the square sloped away from the gallery towards Whitehall, this meant that Baker ended up with a hefty wedge of a building. This satisfied the client, as it maximised internal space, but in the Commission's view it upended the square's architectural hierarchy.

All this was far more advice than the Crown Lands Commissioners, or indeed the South African Government, had either asked for or wanted. They protested that to follow it beyond a few details – the pitched roof was reluctantly dropped – would send Baker back to the drawing board and cause huge delays. Their main counter-argument was that Canada House would probably be demolished in due course[18] – its lease expired in 1963 – and would be replaced by a building that followed Baker's massing. It should not therefore be seen as a model. The Commission, however, was insistent. So too was Addison, who fearing diplomatic embarrassment went to the Prime Minister for backing and got it. At that point the Commission bowed out, no doubt fearing that if it commented further on architectural detail it would be implicated in a design that it saw as fundamentally wrong-headed. A shade haughtily, it told the High Commissioner that 'effective agreement on the question of principle is improbable, and it would accordingly be superfluous to trouble you with further observations'.[19]

The Commission was drawn into several other inter-war controversies by its early tendency to favour the cause of building preservation. A sympathetic hearing was more or less guaranteed in a body containing Lord Curzon and Sir Aston Webb, who in 1923 had said that 'the great strength of our nation lies in our historic possessions, and if we scrap them ruthlessly for temporary considerations of convenience we shall lose one of the things of most value to us'. The painter Sir David Cameron was no less committed, reacting fiercely when, in 1926, the Corporation of London floated the idea of demolishing Custom House to allow for the expansion of Billingsgate Fish Market. 'It is our primary duty', Cameron told the Commission's Secretary Chalton Bradshaw, 'to emphasise the preservation at all costs of the few remaining monuments of old London. The occasional clashing of utilitarian and aesthetic [considerations] is inevitable but our special duty is clear'. The Commission's official view on the Custom House question, communicated to Sir Lionel Earle at the Ministry of Works, made no attempt to pretend that it was first-rate architecture, but noted that it was the most important riverside building between Somerset House and the Tower and expressed 'growing apprehension at the repeated attacks upon the slender number of surviving building of historic interest'. This was firm enough to scotch the demolition plans.[20]

The Commission's second report, published in 1926, trumpeted other successes, such as seeing off a colonnade that would have intruded on the portico of Wilkins's University College London in Bloomsbury, before adding that 'wherever possible, we have advised in the interests of conservation'. This inclination became stronger as threats to historic buildings became more acute. Its seeming indifference to the fate of Carlton House Terrace, though easy for mischief-makers to exploit, was more perceived than actual. In reality, the Commission shared the widespread disquiet about the pace of destruction. And it had a far more significant role to play in these *laissez-faire* days when the conservation lobby was still in its infancy. Before effective planning controls, before the listing system, before conservation areas, largely before national amenity and civic societies, there was something of a vacuum; the Commission, willingly or not, was cast in the role of bulwark against developers, and those who detected an existential threat to their civilised inheritance came to it for a voice.

To call the threat existential is hardly to exaggerate. At times almost no building seemed safe. Soane's Bank of England, Nash's Regent Street and the Adam Brothers' Adelphi were pulled down; so too were Devonshire House, Chesterfield House and other great eighteenth century mansions. Nineteen City churches were earmarked for demolition in the 1926 Phillimore Report. Its recommendations were largely implemented by the Luftwaffe, but even in peacetime it took strong opposition from the Commission and others to deflect the wrecking ball. Anxiety amongst preservationists was deep-seated, even apocalyptic. Sir Reginald Blomfield, admittedly never one to be optimistic when there was scope for pessimism, told the Architecture Club in 1926 that there was 'no reason why St. Paul's Cathedral should not go the way

of the other City churches. The longer I consider this question of building preservation, the more depressed I get'. Clive Bell showed a similar sense of exhausted defeatism when, in reply to the *Country Life* questionnaire on Carlton House Terrace, he wrote: 'Of course I agree with you but it's useless to protest. You haven't a chance. They have pulled down Regent Street and the Foundling Hospital and they will pull down Waterloo Bridge. No building is respected in this country unless it has sentimental associations or happens to be a bit of rubbishy late Gothic'. Eric Gill was equally depressed, if less resigned: 'I don't know if it's any use kicking against the pricks of the commercial world', he wrote. 'But let us kick as long as our toe-nails last.'

The Commission did kick, sometimes hard. Indeed its very first case, in March 1924, saw it kill off, for reasons of building preservation, a bridge across the Thames at St. Paul's that had been proposed as way of relieving cross-river congestion. The Commission objected in principle because of the risk to St. Paul's itself – the rise in motor traffic and thus vibration through London clay so close to its foundations would, it concluded, threaten the stability of the Dome. A catastrophe might ensue. 'St. Paul's Bridge cannot be built and used without grave and imminent peril to St. Paul's Cathedral', it said. 'If the scheme augments an already substantial danger to London's proudest monument, all other objections become superfluous.' The degree of peril was questioned by some engineers, who noted the absence of engineers on the Commission; but deep anxieties had been sown in the minds of the Cathedral's Dean and Chapter, and that was enough.

Almost immediately afterwards, the Commission was caught up in another bridge-related *cause célèbre*, the battle for Rennie's Waterloo Bridge. Demolition was favoured by the London County Council as a radical solution to the problem of subsidence caused by traffic growth; wooden supports and a relief bridge had been erected as emergency measures. The Commission's views were channelled through Curzon:

We have many admirable (and a few appalling) architectural features in our Capital City; but we have not so many of the former as to be content, except for the most overwhelming reasons, to sacrifice one of the grandest among them...We have on the Thames a nineteenth-century bridge finer than any contemporary or later fabric, and as fine as any that were constructed in the great bridge-building epochs of Continental or Eastern countries. Do not let us be in a hurry to deprive ourselves of this legitimate source of national gratification.

Curzon's rhetoric was allied to practical proposals: he suggested keeping the Rennie bridge alongside a new one, if a new one was definitely needed, and argued for a less piecemeal approach to dealing with growth in cross-river traffic. This gave the L.C.C. (which was understandably nervous about destroying a bridge built by statute to commemorate Wellington's victory) a way out, and Curzon's idea was taken up in the form of a Royal Commission on Cross-River Traffic, chaired by Lord Lee of Fareham. Lee's close affiliation with the Royal Fine Art Commission was promising, and indeed his commission recommended against demolition, preferring instead a reconditioning exercise of underpinning and rebuilding. It deferred to the Royal Fine Art Commission on the detail of how to achieve this without damaging the bridge visually; the Commission opted for corbelling out, using a system of coved friezes that left the lines of the Rennie bridge untouched. But this turned out to be no more than a stay of execution. Herbert Morrison and others at the L.C.C. were becoming frustrated at all this romantic fussing over a bridge which, in their eyes, was just a means to cross a river. In March 1934 they finally decided on demolition. In spite of other preservation proposals, and in spite of *The Times* thundering that 'there are other values in life than physical convenience, ease of transit and commercial efficiency', Rennie's bridge went. As a kind of consolation, the L.C.C.'s Improvements Committee asked the Commission to advise on a competition for the replacement. The Commission hesitated, feeling itself complicit in an act of demolition it deplored. But pragmatism won. It insisted on the competition conditions being 'limited to the very minimum to allow the fullest scope to taste, invention and resource'. Sir Giles Gilbert Scott won, and although the Commission had initial reservations about his design, Morrison was in no mood to interfere in the creative process.

Westminster was another focus of the Commission's early conservation efforts. When, in 1937, a memorial to George V was proposed for a site opposite the Palace of Westminster, and Sir Giles Gilbert Scott devised a layout that would have meant clearing several Georgian houses, it worked hard to broker a less destructive plan. The houses were seen by the Office of Works (which owned them) as expendable, indeed obstacles to a view of greater glories: the Chapter House, Jewel House and the Abbey precincts. The Commission, by contrast, saw their value and pressured Scott to produce an alternative scheme that spared two of them, 6 and 7 Old Palace Yard. This he did, but the King George V Memorial Fund rejected it and opted for the original, grander plan. The Prime Minister, Neville Chamberlain, fearing a Commons row, conferred with other party leaders and came out in support of the Commission, at which the Memorial Fund grudgingly accepted the less destructive proposal. *The Times*, unusually, disagreed with the Commission's stance, seeing it as elevating the old too far above the new. 'In the conflict of view between Sir Giles Gilbert Scott and the Commission, the decisive voice has been negative; the resolution to cling to minor monuments is tainted with the characteristic timidity of committees.' That was unfair: a greater timidity would have been to fall in behind Scott, the Office of Works and the Memorial Fund. But as it happened, the Commission's victory was short-lived. The houses it saved were flattened by Germans bombs only two years later.

Conservation skirmishes were happening, of course, across England and Wales. And the Commission did sometimes manage to score successes outside London. In 1930, its opposition persuaded Buckinghamshire County Council to drop a plan to demolish Marlow suspension bridge, dating from 1831 (so about to reach its centenary) and the only surviving bridge in England by William Tierney Clark, a pupil of Telford's and assistant of Rennie's. The council considered it unsuitable for modern traffic and proposed a ferro-concrete replacement, but agreed under pressure to strengthen it. But such examples were too few, and the Commission knew it.

If *The Times*'s expectation that the Commission would be flooded with requests for assistance had not been realised – and they had not, by some distance – the fault lay at least as much in a lack of awareness as in a lack of willing. Frustrated, Crawford went direct to Ramsay MacDonald, asking him to help ensure that public bodies consulted the Commission more readily. The request fell on fertile ground – over the life of the Commission, there was no Prime Minister more willing than MacDonald to offer it genuine, practical support. In July 1931 he wrote to Ministers instructing them to consider what greater use could be made of the Commission. 'Bearing in mind that an unsightly building remains an eyesore for generations, I am anxious to cover the whole field', he said.

Some Ministers replied to the Prime Minister individually, in dutiful and often defensive terms. The Admiralty said 'very advantageous results' had been obtained by the Trustees of Greenwich Hospital from securing the Commission's advice on the design of the Royal Hospital School at Holbrook – no mention was made of mess uniforms. A joint response from Arthur Greenwood (Health), Hastings Lees-Smith (Education) and Herbert Morrison (Transport) had a notably self-justificatory tone, with Morrison attaching a lengthy memorandum, defending the Ministry of Transport's performance, which had its own appendices in the form of Ministry circulars on the design of petrol pumps (1923) and road bridges (1925).

The Prime Minister showed the replies to Crawford, who was unimpressed. In his view they showed the scale of the problem rather than any real understanding of how to solve it. The Board of Education's comments suggested to him

'how little it appreciates the universal importance of proper design and planning. Its statement that 'schools are usually built in one storey, and the opportunities for architectural treatment are therefore limited' is based upon a very curious but very complete misapprehension of architecture; and when they go on to say that 'the schools are normally well set back on large sites, and consequently are unlikely to disharmonise with the general features of the neighbourhood', again I feel that the building branch of the Board of Education must be thoroughly behind the times: this kind of outlook is long since obsolescent. The vast buildings which I see being erected all over the country do justice neither to their very great scale nor to their neighbourhoods, to which they should be not only an ornament but an inspiration'.

Morrison, he thought, 'shows every desire to do the right thing' – he had not yet sullied his reputation in Crawford's eyes by forcing the demolition of Waterloo Bridge – 'but I sometimes wonder if the Department itself is sufficiently well-informed to be able to select and process the technical advice available to it'.

So far so inconclusive. Downing Street asked first the Treasury and then Sir Lionel Earle at the Ministry of Works to push the matter forward. Earle was reluctant to interfere in the affairs of other departments but relented when the Prime Minister asked him personally. Downing Street then asked Ministers to discuss with Earle what changes might be made to improve the design quality of public buildings. Some progress ensued, especially with the Ministry of Transport; Parliament had recently been given a say in the distribution of the Road Fund, essentially a mechanism to alleviate unemployment through road construction, and could therefore put aesthetics on the agenda. 'The bulk of the engineers at present in the Ministry of Transport have no idea, or no concern, about the amenities of the countryside', Earle told Crawford; but this would, he said, change 'very considerably'.

All this was fine as far as it went, but it was becoming increasingly clear to the Commission that the real problem lay in its narrowly-drawn Royal Warrant, which allowed it to go only where asked. It was all too tentative, too timid and indeed too wasteful: by 1931 Crawford was complaining to Sir Russell Scott at the Treasury that 'occasionally the Commissioners find themselves with little or nothing to do'. New powers were needed to extend its reach and equip it for new challenges. What was needed above all was the power to get involved unilaterally. The Carlton House Terrace fiasco had brought this home. Yes, it had been misled; but more fundamentally it was limited to doing what the Crown Lands Commissioners had asked it to do, namely consider the design of 4 Carlton Gardens. The future of Carlton House Terrace as a whole was, in crude terms, none of its business. Not everyone in the outside world appreciated such a nice distinction, or understood why the Commission observed it so rigidly; as a result, it was sometimes criticised for staying silent when some thought it should have been shouting. Crawford, though, was a stickler for proprieties, not one to go beyond his remit. But he felt the restriction acutely and began to lobby for a freer arrangement.

His tactics in doing so were astute, writing to the Prime Minister in April 1933 to suggest that the Commission should be able to veto projects, and only then mentioning that it should also be authorised to volunteer opinions. Naturally, Downing Street was appalled at the prospect of a veto. And

there were plenty of good reasons to deny one, not least the Commission's lack of democratic accountability and the impossibility of giving an independent body executive control over capital spending decisions. But once it had exhausted itself coming up with those grounds for refusal, the Government found itself amenable to the less radical idea of letting the Commission comment on schemes without being asked. Downing Street probably knew full well it was being played – a memorandum to the Prime Minister of June 1933 said that 'it is hard to believe that Crawford will seriously press for powers of control or veto' – but at any rate the strategy worked, partly because of Ramsay MacDonald's indulgent attitude to the Commission. He replied to Crawford in soothing terms, saying that the Commission had done 'yeoman service in the cause of national amenities' and took 'far too modest a view of its achievements'. And he wrote to George V on 31 July recommending an enlargement of the Commission's terms of reference. The King, who was sailing on the Royal Yacht Victoria & Albert, signed a new warrant the next day.

That was not quite the last of it. In 1943, Lord Crawford – by this time the 28th Earl, who had succeeded his father not just in the earldom but, after an interval, in the Chairmanship of the Royal Fine Art Commission – agitated for the Commission to be given the additional power to call for people and papers. No-one was quite clear why, perhaps not even Crawford. The proximate reason was a perceived slight by the Corporation of London, which had shared its plans for the post-war reconstruction of the City five minutes before meeting the Commission and had taken them away again without leaving a copy. But this was an isolated case. The Office of Works and the Treasury, in the person of its Permanent Secretary Sir Alan Barlow, were mobilised to dissuade Crawford. He should ignore the City's rebuff: 'the individual mainly concerned does not reach the normal standard of reasonableness', they said; and besides, hard cases made bad law.

The Office of Works worried that the extra power would 'land the Commission in real difficulty in the long run'. Its prestige had largely come from the fact that it was free from the taint of bureaucracy; by giving the impression that it wanted to assume the role of a dictator in aesthetics, it would risk arousing resentment from local authorities, and perhaps legal challenges that would dent its reputation. Even more importantly, added the Parliamentary Counsel Sir Granville Ram, the supposed power to call for people and papers was unenforceable unless backed by statute, of which there was no prospect at all. It would in any event be trumped by Crown privilege, which entitled departments to withhold documents. As Barlow put it in an internal Treasury minute in November 1943, 'It seems rather a tall order to advise the King specifically to amend the Warrants by adding to it words which are in reality idle words; and I should dislike the task of drafting the answer to any Parliamentary Question asking what the purpose was and what difference it made'. All this was put to Crawford in diplomatic language, but to no avail. He countered that other Royal Commissions, such as the Ancient Monuments Commission, already had the power; that it would have moral force even as a bluff; and that he had been invited on becoming chairman to suggest reforms, only to find himself at once rebuffed. Remarkably, he threatened to resign on the matter, though not before having 'squared Mr. Morrison personally', as the Treasury wryly noted.[21] Faced with this, Barlow and the Office of Works relented, on the basis that as futile gestures went it was less harmful than some, and that the Commission would not be 'silly enough to expect Service Departments to produce details about aerodromes and dockyards'. For what it was worth, the power to call for people and papers was thus enshrined in a further Royal Warrant, in 1946.[22]

IV | Twentieth century challenges

And so the Commission, having been forged in one post-war world, had to reinvent itself in another, not much more than twenty years later. It was, at least, fortified by its new powers – a necessary shot of energy as it emerged from the semi-hibernation of wartime, when it was left without either a permanent chairman or a permanent secretary. Lord Crawford had died in 1940 and Chalton Bradshaw in 1943, of a heart attack at his desk in the Commission's offices in Queen Anne's Gate, depriving the Commission of two key people who had been present since its creation. Bradshaw's secondment to the Ministry of Shipping in the most difficult days of the war had in any event left the Commission unmanned and directionless: his attempts in 1939 to persuade the Treasury to use the Commission as a recruiting sergeant for architects (to superintend public works and defence installations) had been a casualty both of his enforced absence and the Treasury's unwillingness to sanction, still less fund, non-essential work. There was, then, an urgent need to regroup and refocus, not least because the challenges that had surfaced between the wars were becoming more acute.

Comprehensive redevelopment

One of these was the sheer pace of redevelopment and its impact on the urban fabric. Concern about this grew during the 1920s and 1930s to the point where it reached a pitch of genuine alarm. Britain, it was felt, was being asset-stripped. The Carlton House Terrace controversy in 1932 offered a focus for these complaints, uniting as it did all the problems that were seen to be blighting London: shady dealings, lack of transparency, exploitative overdevelopment and a willingness to sacrifice cherished buildings for profit. *The Times* made the point with its usual trenchancy at the end of 1932: 'It will be said that in these days money must come before everything; and one more gem in London's heritage of beauty and history will be 'realized' for whatever it will fetch…The Commissioners of Crown Lands treated Carlton House Terrace as though it was a trifle that did not much matter one way or the other. What did matter, apparently, was getting a little money on the nail'. Just before his death in January 1933, the novelist George Moore wrote that 'the moment they see a fine building they form a plot to pull it down. Yesterday it was Park Lane, to-day it is Carlton House Terrace, and tomorrow it will be the churches in the Strand. All will be destroyed and nothing of beauty will be left in London to indicate that once a civilized people who did not make a god of football and motor-cars lived in it'. It was a familiar refrain for the time, indicative of a mood. In hindsight, of course, the lamentations are not just poignant but ironic. As at Old Palace Yard in Westminster, much energy was spent trying to save buildings that were then destroyed from the air.

War changed the landscape, literally. A blitzed capital needed major surgery, on a scale not seen since the seventeenth century. So too did many provincial cities. And as in the seventeenth century, there were differences of opinion on how far the damaged areas should be not just rebuilt but reshaped. There was in a way no better time to have a Royal Fine Art Commission, the more so because the Commission had put itself ahead of the game. Even before the war, in its annual report for 1937, it had drawn attention to the need for a more comprehensive approach to London planning, to address housing and transport needs. By 1943, this was looking prescient. And the mood had shifted; depression at the destruction of old England, so evident on the eve of war, had by a paradox been lifted by the destructive trauma of war itself. Suddenly *The Times,* on New Year's Day 1943, was saying that 'like Pip in *Great Expectations,* some of us have nursed doubts whether London was not rather ugly, crooked, narrow, and dirty'.

It was then that the Commission, largely dormant during the early years of the war, was prodded awake by a new Ministry of Town and Country Planning that saw its potential in supporting the national reconstruction effort. Others saw it too: in a House of Lords debate in June 1943, several peers pressed for a more forthright and powerful Commission, with Lord Mottistone resurrecting the idea of giving it a veto. 'All buildings in our towns and cities should be under the wise and benevolent aesthetic control of the Royal Fine Art Commission', he said, 'so that monstrosities and horrors shall never occur again'. The new Lord Crawford, making his maiden speech, almost had to dampen expectations, and Lord Lee broke a twenty-year silence in the chamber to caution yet again against well-meaning reforms that might end with a Ministry of Fine Arts. 'There is no guarantee at all', he told peers, 'that a Minister of Fine Arts might not be as ignorant of aesthetic considerations as a Hindu is of skates'. Lord Portal, Minister of Works, brushed aside notions of a veto but made clear that the Government saw the Commission as 'the ultimate authority on matters of taste and aesthetics' and a body with a significant role to play in rebuilding Britain. It was readied for the task by an influx of planning expertise. Patrick

Abercrombie, already a member, was quickly reappointed and was joined by William Holford, his successor as Professor of Civic Design at Liverpool University and a wartime planner in the Ministry of Works. The architect-planner Hubert Worthington was also brought in.

By July 1943, the London County Council and the City of London had both produced draft reconstruction plans for London; the latter's, at the instigation of the Minister of Town and Country Planning (and without much initial enthusiasm on the part of the City) was referred to the Commission for comment. The City's hesitancy was more than a little strategic; at such a critical juncture, it was unlikely to welcome forensic examination of its plans by an outside body of experts. And if it was nervous, it was right to be so. The Commission ripped the proposals apart in a published critique that was followed, a month later in September 1945, by formal rejection of the City's Plan by the Ministry of Town and Country Planning. The Commission had refused point-blank to endorse any plan that failed to provide for the eventual removal below-ground of railway lines and stations, such as Fenchurch Street and Cannon Street – a radical ambition that even now is far from being realised.[23] Secondly, it cautioned against major infrastructural intervention, especially that designed to meet the growing appetite for motor cars; in broad terms the Commission saw the Plan as not much more than a glorified exercise in road-widening. A proposed huge roundabout at the junction of Moorgate and Bishopsgate and a radial hub planned for Tower Hill were deprecated, partly because they would 'destroy the very amenities which the City seeks to preserve' and partly because they and their kind were inimical to good new architecture; 'in many instances', the Commission said, 'proposed street improvements and roundabouts result in plan shapes on which no architect could hope to design a successful and convenient building'. It argued for zoning diagrams to show what massing and heights would be acceptable in what location, as well as enhanced provision of open space[24] and the placing of car parks under new buildings rather than in freestanding multi-storey blocks. And it objected to the City's plan for straightening the approach to St. Paul's Cathedral up Ludgate Hill, preferring to keep the asymmetry that allowed the west front to be revealed gradually on the approach from Fleet Street.

In setting its face against this kind of formalism, the Commission was to some degree re-enacting battles fought after the Great Fire; and it helped ensure that in the twentieth century, as in the seventeenth, London did no more than flirt with grandiosity before plumping for the usual quiet pragmatism.[25] Courtesy of the Commission, then, the City's plans for post-war reconstruction, so long in gestation, were effectively stillborn. In casting around for candidates to make the plan acceptable, the City sensibly if ironically alighted on two people – Abercrombie and Holford – who had been party to its savaging by the Royal Fine Art Commission. Abercrombie got the job, while Holford ended up designing the new Paternoster Square next to St. Paul's, producing a rectilinear scheme that nonetheless respected the kink in Ludgate Hill that the Commission had sought to preserve.[26]

The Commission was by no means always opposed to comprehensive redevelopment. As much as any organisation it was a creature of its time, and just as likely to share a few prevailing orthodoxies. And certainly it was willing to see the positives in radical urban interventions, especially where it meant treating a problem holistically and addressing connected problems such as traffic congestion. In 1960, when Brighton Council asked the Commission to pronounce on three shortlisted designs for an eleven-acre site on the seafront, it found itself steered towards abandoning them all in favour of a planned policy for whole area between the two piers. As a result, revised proposals for comprehensive redevelopment were drawn up and submitted to the Minister of Housing

and Local Government. Similarly, a year later in Bristol, it pushed the City Council to develop comprehensive plans for an area around Wine Street that had lain disused since an air raid in 1940, rather than squandering an opportunity through piecemeal development. There are plenty of similar examples.

But if the Commission was not immune to orthodoxies, it was by no means prey to them either, sometimes to the frustration, anger even, of those on one side or the other who thought they could count on its support. This determination to approach schemes without prejudice meant that it was always likely to speak up for the odd scheme that was damned by local opinion as carrying on the work of the Luftwaffe. The central area rebuilding of Plymouth in 1957 was a case in point, as was a 1952 scheme for St. George's Street in Canterbury, which The Times described as 'bearing a strong resemblance to shops in Poplar' and thus 'not necessarily the last word in suitability for Canterbury'. In Gloucester, though, it assessed a scheme similar to that in Canterbury (and also from 1952) but came to the opposite conclusion, believing that it would do serious damage to a large area west of the cathedral; the Commission fought hard, and successfully, for design improvements.

In formulating its approach to these questions, the Commission was in some ways ahead of its time. Its advocacy, as far back as the 1950s, of something that sounds remarkably like the urban village phenomenon of the 1990s and beyond is notable: 'Most cities have fair-sized inner rings of property, often more or less obsolete, which could be more intensively developed both for business purposes and for living', it said in its 1959 annual report. 'Positive planning for the reconstruction of these areas would make it possible to loosen up the stranglehold on the present central areas and might, at the same time, provide a new pattern for urban living.' Those were intriguing words for a time when the segregation of land uses and the split between commercial centres and residential

Opposite: The sheer scale of destruction and reconstruction in Britain's cities after the Second World War is laid bare in this aerial photograph of Plymouth in 1948, when implementation of the Abercrombie-Paton Watson grand plan for the devastated city centre was underway. Sir Patrick Abercrombie had been reappointed to the Royal Fine Art Commission in 1943 in readiness for exactly this task of dealing, as effectively and sensitively as possible, with the multiple and often conflicting post-war challenges of urban renewal, traffic management and the preservation of historic buildings. *(Architectural Press Archive/RIBA Collections)*

suburbs were more or less axiomatic. In the same report, it also anticipated the flexibility that would flow from technological advances: 'the prestige concentration of office staffs is based on a reluctance to make use of modern improvements in communications which make it both possible and economic to have routine processes done outside the central area and to keep in that area only a small nucleus of executive staff'.

As a rule, then, the Commission supported schemes which it believed to be underpinned by rational planning and a genuine attempt to improve the public realm – as at Paternoster Square, where it defended Holford's scheme against heavy criticism. Conversely, it usually opposed schemes where, in its view, the main motivating factor was to maximise lettable area, and thus the developer's profit. Rapaciousness of this kind was a frequent source of concern in the late 1950s; all those anxieties common in the 1930s about the behaviour of private developers bent on squeezing every last penny from a site began to resurface. Over a period of perhaps fifteen years, the word 'rape' was commonly used to describe the reshaping of Britain's cities; there was a sense that anything was fair game, that developers were chancing their arm, that the noble objective of replanning for the public good was being supplanted by interventions that were neither comprehensive nor really planned but based on how much money could be made and how fast. 'All too often', the Commission said in 1959, 'the dominant motive is to attain the largest amount of lettable floor space that planning legislation will allow in the most sought-after areas...It is not enough to invite private developers to submit their own schemes with little guidance from the planning authority and then to accept the highest bid, whatever architecture may happen to have been included'.

As an antidote, it recommended the preparation of masterplans either by an architect-planner or by local authorities; but where, as often happened, developers were left to produce schemes in something close to a

planning vacuum, controversies arose that rumbled on for years. One such was a scheme for the western side of Charing Cross Road below Cambridge Circus: this originated in 1959 with a brashly speculative proposal from Greencoat Properties, then went through various revisions in the 1960s, all involving huge towers, before re-emerging in 1972 as an even vaster project linked by aerial pedways to a redeveloped Covent Garden. The Commission fought with others to defeat all these. That is not to say that it liked the scheme that was finally built, in 1981 to designs by the ubiquitous Richard Seifert; it criticised this as 'inappropriate both architecturally and socially', but in truth the Seifert scheme was far more sensitive, notably keeping the Welsh Presbyterian Church in Cambridge Circus that would have been demolished by Greencoat.

An even starker illustration of the problem arose (again in 1959) at what was called the Monico site in Piccadilly Circus, an ill-tempered saga and perhaps the archetype of what objectors saw as land grabs by greedy developers. The London County Council had already published a scheme (including *de rigueur* high-level walkways) for the whole circus when developers came forward independently with a scheme for just the Monico site, centring on a slab and podium block emblazoned with a 172ft advertising hoarding.

At first the Commission had been willing to suggest design adjustments, and had achieved tweaks such as a cut in the podium height by five feet. But its resolve was tested by the weight of opposition to the scheme, which was savaged in Parliament as the 'vulgar prostitution of the most famous site in the Commonwealth'; Bernard Levin denounced it in *The Spectator* as 'the Monster of Piccadilly' and *The Times*, in full thundering mode, concluded that 'Piccadilly Circus is too important a focal point to be turned into a hunting ground for speculators'. Wilting under the pressure, the Commission decided to drop its equivocal line and did so in dramatic fashion, waiting until the opening day of the public inquiry,

16 December 1959, to send a public letter to the Planning Minister, Henry Brooke, demanding that the scheme be abandoned. 'It is a mistake in principle', said the Commission, 'to provide what is in effect little more than a gigantic hoarding on a site of this importance'. The developers of course were furious, but the scheme was fatally undermined. Brooke rejected it on the recommendation of the inquiry inspector, Colin Buchanan. And though Sir William Holford was later engaged as a consultant, tasked as usual with rescuing a project through an injection of sober rationalism, it was all too late; the critical moment of opportunity had passed.

Transport revolution

Not entirely coincidentally, the Commission also arrived at just the right time to become immersed in questions of how to accommodate the still newish phenomenon of motorised road traffic. This was a pressing concern from the earliest days: the first problem the Commission confronted, more or less, was the lack of cross-Thames road capacity. At the time, there was a working assumption that road traffic would continue to increase, and that making space for it was a priority. Much administrative activity in the 1920s was devoted to the matter: the Home Counties Traffic Advisory Council was set up in 1924 and Lord Lee of Fareham's Cross-River Traffic Commission in 1926; traffic management plans were drawn up hastily by local authorities in an effort to deal with the arrival of traffic in towns and cities that were not designed for it.

In particular, bridges were put under huge stress. The cables and girders of Lambeth Bridge decayed so badly that it was closed to vehicles in 1910, less than fifty years after opening. Outside London, weight and capacity limits forced heavy traffic to take circuitous routes, adding to congestion and visual blight. Should these weak bridges be replaced, widened, strengthened, underpinned, corbelled out? What design

principles should be followed at a time when stone and brick were being supplanted as materials by steel and concrete? Across its lifetime, the Commission probably invested more time and energy on those questions than on the design of any other building type.

By May 1937, Leslie Hore-Belisha, Minister of Transport, was able to tell the annual meeting of the Council for the Protection of Rural England (which happened to be presided over by Lord Crawford) that 'today, no bridge of importance is constructed or improved without reference to the Royal Fine Art Commission'. In the 1950s and early 1960s – ironically when Lord Bridges was the Commission's chairman, as if the whole thing was nominatively determined – the number of new bridges arising from the nationwide roadbuilding campaign was such that the Commission had to set up a bridge sub-committee. This was chaired by the engineer Arthur Floyd with a rotating membership that at various times included John Betjeman, Basil Spence, Hugh Casson, Frederick Gibberd, Geoffrey Jellicoe and Lionel Brett, who was moved by the sheer weight of labour to protest that 'we are doing the Ministry of Transport's work for it and involving ourselves in an amount of detail on bridge design that tends to weaken our status as the final court of aesthetic appeal'.

The level of detail was indeed astonishing. At one typical meeting in September 1962, the sub-committee reviewed twenty schemes, all presented by their engineers and architects and thus a feat of administration and logistics as well as mental energy. One of those schemes, to give a flavour, was Barnstaple Bridge in Devon, where the Commission's earlier advice on lighting had been rejected by the Ministry of Transport; three Ministry officials attended to discuss the matter, along with three project architects, leading to adoption of the Commission's preferred solution of lighting columns placed on the inside of the parapet and half set into it, with a diameter not exceeding six inches and spaced every third pier, with a mounting height of twenty feet. A couple of months before, in July 1962, the sub-committee was agonising over the exact shade and texture of vitreous enamel tiles proposed for a bridge over the A1 at Barnsdale in Yorkshire, as well as arguing, successfully, that the historic bridge over the A498 at Pont Bethania in Carnarvonshire should be kept as a footbridge, with a new road bridge built at least twenty feet away to prevent excessive scour. And in 1961, commenting on a planned new bridge at Clifton in York, it had advised that 'the facing to the cut-water edges be omitted, the batter reduced, the horizontal joints in the pre-cast concrete carried round the cut-water edge and the nibs masking the joints between the spans eliminated'.

This must have been gruelling work – Floyd's unpaid labours were little short of Stakhanovite – and it serves as a corrective to any perception of the Commission as a body more comfortable dealing in fey generalities. Neither did it stop the Commission acting as ultimate arbiter, as Brett had feared. In 1962, at the same time as all those exhausting sub-committee meetings, the Transport Minister Ernest Marples was writing to Lord Bridges asking if he might include, in the rules for a design competition for a bridge over the River Calder on the M1 near Wakefield, a condition that the chosen design would need the Commission's approval.

When the bridge sub-committee came to be disbanded, in 1963, it was only partly because the number of new bridges had fallen; the other key reason was the Commission's success in agreeing a common design approach with the Ministry of Transport's technical staff, as a result of which it needed to comment only when especially difficult problems or fresh points of policy arose. In the meantime, others could be left to work to its design templates, such as that used for the thirty-nine concrete bridges on the London to Leeds motorway. Its advice was collected in *The Appearance of Bridges*, published by the Ministry of Transport in 1964. The eventual need for a

sequel – *The Design and Appearance of Bridges*, published by the Department of Transport in 1994 – showed, though, that the problem of poor visual design was a persistent one.

The physical impact of new roads on town and country was, of course, enormous, as great as that of the railways a century before. The Commission devoted minute attention to the question of how best to relate trunk roads and motorways to landscape, successfully pressing the Ministry of Transport to retain consultant landscape architects to work alongside engineers on sensitive projects. 'Road building should not be left entirely to the well-meaning but tender mercies of the technicians and the accountants', it argued, or 'ugly and widespread scars will be inflicted on the beauty of Britain'. Reviewing routes for the M40 and M4 motorways connecting London to Oxford and Cardiff, it intervened in an effort to reduce damage to the Chilterns and the Wiltshire and Berkshire Downs, while in 1970 Richard Marsh, the Transport Minister, was lobbied hard to abandon a huge cutting in the Chilterns escarpment in favour of a tunnelled route devised by Geoffrey Jellicoe and Ove Arup. And three years earlier the Commission was embroiled in a row with the Ministry of Transport's Landscape Advisory Committee,[27] chaired by Sir Eric Savill, which tended to the esoteric view that roads through beautiful countryside added value by making that beauty more accessible and visible.[28] Where Savill preferred a northern route across the Downs for the Berkshire stretch of the M4, the Commission, after detailed analysis, favoured a less direct and less environmentally damaging southern route that roughly followed the line of the old Bath Road. The Commission tried to reach agreement with the Advisory Committee, suggesting a joint site inspection, but found Savill unwilling to contradict his political masters; at last even Bridges lost patience and went public, in *The Times* of 19 September 1963, with a denunciation of the northern route. Savill was furious, accusing the Commission of a breach of faith and abuse of privilege, and warning of 'suspicion and mistrust in the future', but in fact the public pressure worked: in 1965 the Ministry of Transport proposed a compromise route that largely avoided the Downs. Bridges told Lord Strang, Chairman of the National Parks Commission, that 'it was a more satisfactory outcome than seemed possible', although (presciently) he worried about the creation of an 'M4 corridor', with access to the motorway acting as a magnet for development. It was, he thought, naïve to suppose that the narrow line of the road represented the full extent of the threat to amenity, and with impressive foresight he pressed Strang to take immediate action to designate the Downs as an Area of Outstanding Natural Beauty. 'Any delay', he warned, 'could be dangerous'.

But in general the Commission was interested in more than simply damage limitation. If motorways had to be built, then virtue should be made of necessity. 'Good landscape design', it said in a public statement in 1959, 'consists in more than the judicious planting of trees and shrubs after the motorway has been built. Motorways should not only be laid out and designed in such a way as to preserve amenities but should in themselves be first-class examples of design, creating opportunities for landscape improvement and urban renewal.'

Those last words are telling, because increasingly major roads were affecting not just the rural but the urban environment. Urban motorways came on the scene in the late 1950s, the most brutal peacetime intervention in major towns and cities in the twentieth century. The Commission was anxious to avoid London and major provincial cities being cut to ribbons, and here too it counselled against letting engineers run the show. 'American experience', it argued, 'has shown that if these roads are conceived solely in engineering terms, they will be destructive, on an enormous scale, of urban values, both financial and aesthetic.' Early collaboration with architect-planners might, on the other hand, redeem them to the point of their being exciting contributors to urban vitality.

Partly as a result of this agitation, the Committee on London Roads, set up in 1957, included both architects and planners, and in 1969 Sir David Serpell, Permanent Secretary at the Ministry of Transport, bowed to pressure from the Commission and created an architect-planner post in his department as a counterweight of sorts to the engineers. But the Commission was not so naïve as to believe that these steps would be a panacea: some proposals were, it thought, so damaging that they were unacceptable in principle, whatever mitigation was planned. In 1971, it shared the general outrage at a plan for an urban motorway linking Covent Garden to the Strand, which would have crashed through the Nash buildings opposite Charing Cross Station.

The Commission also assessed an array of proposals for inner relief roads. These were often touted as a friend of conservation, by virtue of taking traffic away from clogged historic centres, but the advertised benefits were by no means guaranteed. 'We have seen instances of ring roads proposed with little idea of what is to happen inside the ring', noted the Commission in 1960, 'and loop or bypass roads planned which seemed likely to damage those very qualities they were designed to conserve.' This was especially true in top-ranking historic towns and cities. In August 1955, the Commission sent a high-powered delegation comprising Methuen, Brett, Betjeman, Geoffrey Webb and Jellicoe to Oxford to discuss with the City Council ways of relieving congestion on Magdalen Bridge and The High; the latter, as Thomas Sharp put it in *Oxford Replanned*, had become 'the scene of a titanic traffic battle, the collegiate calm obliterated by a kind of free-for-all in which five-ton trucks, sixty-foot lorries, vans, motor coaches and private cars thunder between vibrating college buildings that are almost invisible'. From this nightmarish chaos emerged a notorious plan, pushed hard by the Ministry of Housing and Local Government, to drive a relief road across Christ Church Meadow, as well as turning Georgian streets like Beaumont Street, running from Worcester College past the Ashmolean to St. Giles's, into traffic funnels. The Commission objected strongly – Howard Colvin thought the relief road would 'ruin the meadow and blight its surroundings'. Ultimately, with others, it prevailed, and today Christ Church Meadow remains a scene of bucolic calm, Beaumont Street retains its quiet Georgian dignity and The High is largely free of traffic. In the end, as the Commission foresaw, huge physical interventions were simply unnecessary.

As intrusive schemes kept coming, so the Commission kept objecting: in 1968 to a relief road in Canterbury that would have bisected the city centre, then three years later to a dual carriageway skirting the city walls in York; four Commissioners visited to assess the likely impact and issued a statement abhorring the plan, saying that it would degrade the setting of some of York's finest Georgian buildings. A less intrusive alternative was later devised. Even as late as 1987, the Commission was having to fend off ill-considered proposals: an inner relief road planned for Rye, following the line of the railway, was denounced as a 'serious threat' to the town. Its supplementary barb, expressing 'astonishment that such an outstanding town should not have a proper bypass', revealed its preferred solution, here and elsewhere: a relief road, yes, but far enough out to avoid bringing noise, visual blight and physical damage to the very place it was meant to relieve.

Cars brought other things besides roads, pollution and congestion. They needed to be left somewhere, so where they went car parks followed. Like railway stations in the mid-nineteenth century, these were designed to deliver people to convenient points near city centres, so they rapidly became a major presence – but without the railway station's redeeming feature as a social nexus. Objections mounted from the late 1960s onwards, and not only to visible car parks. The Commission also deplored the policy of putting car parks below London's squares; aside from acting as a magnet for

traffic, these brought with them ramps and caverns which often killed trees and made it impossible for new trees to be planted. Generally, the Commission agreed with *The Times'* judgement that car parks should be sited on the edges of cities, both to repel traffic and to avoid the degradation of city centres by 'cumbersome buildings surrounded by expanses of asphalt'. At the same time, though, it had to deal with practical realities. Manipulating the massing of multi-storey car parks so that they responded sensitively to an historic context was a challenge, but not an impossible one; when it saw the potential for a high-quality bespoke solution, as with Birds Portchmouth Russum's 1989 car park in central Chichester that took its design cue from the city walls, it was more than willing both to work with the designers and to trumpet the results.

Preservation

As the twentieth century progressed, the popular appetite for preservation increased. The apocalyptic atmosphere of the inter-war years had given way to the devastation of war, then to a sense that keeping old buildings was an impediment to reconstruction, even to progress itself. From the heritage perspective the nadir was the decade from the mid-1950s, when one in six country houses in England was demolished and Government ministers had no hesitation in dismissing conservation as a regressive brake on development. Sympathy was scarcer still as Harold Wilson fired up his White Heat of Technology; even his Arts Minister, Jennie Lee, told him in October 1964 that 'we cannot be busy looking after old buildings while living architects are destroyed by discouragement'. As late as 1972, an *Observer* review of Lord Kennet's *Preservation* was able to refer to 'a preservationist cult out of keeping with the modern world'. Saving things was still, just, a niche interest. But a shift in priorities and perceptions came very soon after, fuelled in part by the 1973 oil crisis and growing discontent with levels of consumption and waste. By then, too, private owners had long since had their freedoms curtailed by planning restrictions, historic buildings were valued not just for themselves but for their contribution to their context and local planning authorities could control the detailed appearance of buildings and demand urgent repairs. But these things go in cycles and by the late 1980s there were hints of a backlash, as critics blamed an over-powerful conservation movement for stifling creativity; in protecting one architectural heritage, they were accused of strangling another at birth.

Where did the Commission stand in all this? In a way it was under less pressure to intervene in the second half of the century. As the formal protection apparatus grew and the heritage lobby expanded and strengthened, the Commission no longer had to fight the battles it would have fought in the 1920s. Others were there to do that job. And in a way it was less able to intervene; as its workload increased without a commensurate increase in staff and financial resources, it needed to pick its battles.

Even so, the Commission's approach to road-building and the motor car showed clearly enough that it still had a residual sympathy for old buildings. In its report for 1962–1965, before the Council for British Archaeology drew up its seminal list of towns and cities especially worth preserving,[29] the Commission referred to itself as having 'a special responsibility to historic towns'. And just as the inter-war Commission had among its number several committed conservationists, so too did the post-war Commission, most strikingly in the person of John Betjeman but also in the less obvious form of modernist architects for whom a rigid distinction between old and new was a false dichotomy. Sir Leslie Martin was one of those who revealed himself to be unexpectedly *simpatico*: when an undergraduate at Newcastle University wrote to Lord Bridges in February 1959 asking for help in saving the late Georgian

set-piece of Eldon Square, it was Martin who took the time and trouble to visit the site twice, once in the company of the undergraduate. His recommendation, that the shopping centre scheme threatening Eldon Square be suspended until a new masterplan had been prepared, was rejected by the university on the grounds that the scheme was too far advanced for a major rethink; but one side of the square was kept, and stands today as something of a monument to the folly of demolishing the other three.

If the Commission spoke up for historic buildings, though, it tended not to do so on principle. And indeed there were sometimes disagreements internally. Betjeman thought the Commission should be more devoted to the cause: 'I wish we gave as much time to the subject of old buildings as we do to tinkering with the designs of new and often uninteresting blocks of offices and flats', he wrote to Lord Bridges in 1958, by way of remonstrating against the Commission's relaxed approach to the impending loss of the Coal Exchange in Lower Thames Street. Had the Coal Exchange been built in 1646 or 1746 instead of 1846 it would unquestionably have been preserved, he argued with some justice; 'but because it is by an architect with the comic name of J.B. Bunning and not by Wren or Chambers we submit to its destruction. Yet no-one with an eye for architecture could ignore it. It is not just a funny Victorian phenomenon and compared with the very tame Smirke rebuilding of Custom House opposite and the contemptible Billingsgate Fish Market, it is very fine'. Betjeman's approach, then, was dogmatic but also idiosyncratic: a catalogue of personal prejudices, some inspired and some less so, that could hardly be a basis for the settled policy of a Royal Commission, as Bridges was quick to remind him: 'we shall cease to exercise proper influence', he replied, 'if it becomes our habit to back all appeals for preservation'.

The Commission had, then, to discriminate. And because of this it was sometimes seen as insufficiently committed, insufficiently consistent too perhaps. Lord Esher, writing a blunt piece in *The Times* in 1970, just after he had stepped down as a Commissioner, put it like this: 'While maddeningly obstructive to some, the Commission's policies have seemed complaisant and even Philistine to others, and particularly to the rabid preservationist lobby. Nowadays it is understandable that one should fall into the defeatist attitude that anything new is worse. But the Commission is not a preservation society and has to steer a subtle course'.[30] Deyan Sudjic made a similar point in 1979, when if anything conservation interests were even more vocal. Commenting in *The Observer* on a proposal by the Courtauld Institute to demolish a dozen Georgian buildings in Woburn Square to make way for a Denys Lasdun building, he said that 'whatever line the Royal Fine Art Commission takes, it is bound to make some people very angry. The choice facing the Commissioners, perhaps Britain's last remaining arbiters of taste, is between an elegant modern building and the remains of two Georgian terraces. The Commission stands between conservationists and the champions of modern architecture, now on the defensive'. Professor Frank Fielden, then reaching the end of a ten-year tenure as the Commission's Secretary, told Sudjic that it was 'very difficult to keep a balance when a movement has become as strong as the conservationists'. He and Lord James of Rusholme, the then Chairman, had tried to steer the Commission on a consensus course, neither neglectful of conservation nor an obstacle to progress, but as a result it was often caught in crossfire. 'We are criticised whichever way we decide', said Fielden. That was not necessarily a bad thing: its ability to annoy people from both sides of the argument suggests it often got the balance about right, and indeed the desire to have the Commission as an ally was a compliment in itself, implying that its influence ran deep.

In general, though, the Commission managed to rise above the fray, speaking up for some buildings and accepting the loss of others based simply on its assessment of their value, and sometimes the value of what was proposed as a replacement. Those it defended form an eclectic group, and it sometimes defended them before their cause was fashionable. Straight after the war it had opposed demolition of George Gilbert Scott's St. Agnes Kennington, a Gothic Revival church of 1877. In 1956, and indeed for years afterwards in what turned out to be a decade-long saga, it objected to the demolition of Thomas Colcutt's Imperial Institute in Kensington, erected for Victoria's Golden Jubilee in 1887 and woefully out of fashion by the mid-twentieth century. Its chances of survival were even slimmer given that the site was wanted for a new Imperial College of Science and Technology, with the physicist Lord Cherwell and others arguing that only a clean slate would give the architects the freedom to create the facilities needed if Britain were to keep pace in the fields of pure and applied science. Again, the choice was caricatured as one between nostalgia and thrusting progress, and no decade was more likely to plump for progress than the 1960s. Unsurprisingly given the temper of the times, the Government decided that 'the urgent need to increase this country's output of scientists and technologists must be the decisive factor'. But it agreed to meet the Commission to explain its decision, and out of that came a compromise: Colcutt's striking campanile, the centrepiece of the Imperial Institute, would be kept. And so it was, a victory of sorts for the Commission.[31]

Even Georgian architecture was still out of fashion in the early 1950s, when Holy Trinity in Leeds was earmarked for demolition by a Ripon Diocesan Pastoral Committee which thought it had 'no future as a cure of souls'. The Commission helped save it. And in its annual report for 1954 it reminded the Church of England that its responsibilities went beyond pastoral care and did not cease when a church happened to be post-mediaeval: 'there are Georgian and Gothic Revival churches which are masterpieces of their kind and are entitled to at least as much consideration as a Norman or Gothic building which sometimes has little more than its age to recommend it'.

Often too the Commission fought for war-damaged buildings that were placed in further peril in peacetime, when their futures were considered against a background of austerity. It was a vocal proponent of keeping the Nash terraces in The Regent's Park, which remained at risk for more than a decade after the Gorrell Committee first considered their future in 1946. It took until 1957 for the Crown Estate Commissioners to decide to preserve them, and then only if it could be done without undue expense; practical restoration plans had to wait another five years, until 1962.[32] St. John Smith Square, the baroque masterpiece of Thomas Archer, was also left languishing as a bombed-out shell; with the support of the Commission, it finally found a new use as a concert venue in the 1960s.

The City of London churches, forty-eight of them within a square mile, posed another difficult problem. Not one came out of the war unscathed. Two were destroyed; seventeen were left burnt-out shells; eleven were severely damaged; the remaining eighteen had lesser structural injury. Five of them — St. Katharine Cree, All Hallows London Wall, St. Anne and St. Agnes, St. Mary Aldermanbury and St. Dunstan in the East — were left at grave risk of demolition. Should they be sacrificed for the site value, in order to generate funds for other repairs? The Commission, as much as anyone, wrestled with this dilemma, examining the architectural merits of each threatened church and in 1958 making recommendations (jointly with the Central Council for the Care of Churches) to the Bishop of London. St. Katharine Cree (a unique example of a Laudian church), All Hallows (by Dance the Younger) and St. Anne and St. Agnes (by Wren) were, it said, of outstanding importance: 'nothing should be allowed to stand in the way of their complete restoration'. St. Mary Aldermanbury, also

by Wren, had been seriously damaged but should be fully restored. It argued for the retention though not restoration of St. Dunstan's, but that too showed nice aesthetic judgement as the Gothick design lent itself to an afterlife as a picturesque ruin. All in all, the Commission's robust intervention had a decisive impact in staving off extensive demolition. The Church of England's final plan, published in November 1958, provided for the restoration of St. Katharine Cree as premises of the Industrial Christian Fellowship; All Hallows for the Central Council for the Care of Churches; and St. Anne and St. Agnes as a church for refugees. The tower of St. Dunstan's was kept and still stands alongside the preserved shell of the church. St. Mary Aldermanbury was fully rebuilt, albeit not in London; in 1962 its remains were shipped to America and the church was reconstructed at Westminster College in Fulton, Missouri, where Churchill had delivered his Iron Curtain speech in 1946.

Other historic fabric, notably iron railings, was threatened by the British government rather than the Germans; in 1941, Lord Reith's Ministry of Supply used its emergency powers under the 1939 Defence Regulations to requisition 'all unnecessary iron or steel railings in the country for scrap use in iron and steel works and foundries'. An exemption was granted for railings of special artistic merit or historic interest, by which was meant 'specimens of the finest craftsmanship and design': but none post-1820 as those were assumed to be reproducible after the war. There followed a rush to identify railings that might qualify; rejected claims were appealable to a panel that included Sir Albert Richardson, giving the Commission a voice of sorts in what in many ways was a desperate process. The Commission was lobbied, and lobbied in turn. Richardson went beyond his brief to recommend the retention of the (post-1820) railings lining Park Crescent in The Regent's Park, while Charles Holden dashed round to Bloomsbury to report that 'there is a length of elaborate Victorian Gothic railing enclosing a garden at the corner of Montague Place and Malet Street', although he was not hopeful of saving it as the Home Office had 'just carried away about thirty feet of R.I.B.A. railing' from Portland Place.

Acting collectively, the Commission had some success, extracting from the Office of Works an assurance that the railings at Maids of Honour Row in Richmond-upon-Thames would be preserved.

And after the war, it had to repeat the process in reverse, lobbying for the reinstatement of iron railings in London squares that were disfigured for years afterwards by various types of cheap and supposedly temporary substitute: anything from chainlink fencing to wooden palings, hedging weldmesh, close-boarded oak and steel railings. Meetings followed with the London County Council and the aristocratic estates that largely owned the squares, but the greatest success came in 1959 when Lord Bridges, a Whitehall insider *par excellence*, managed to persuade the Treasury to allow tax relief on the cost of reinstating railings removed under the Defence Regulations.

Elsewhere, the Commission argued the conservation case in several other *causes célèbres*, although many of them, like the attritional war over the Imperial Institute, were probably unwinnable battles. It pressed hard in 1966 for Sir Gilbert Scott's choir screen to be kept *in situ* at Hereford Cathedral, countering the Dean's judgement that it was an incongruous Victorian excrescence that looked unpleasant in its dilapidated state but would look even worse if restored to its full garish polychromy. The Commission thought, by contrast, that although the screen was suffering an 'aesthetic eclipse', it was likely in time to be valued, if not as a masterpiece then certainly as a competent piece of craftsmanship and 'a worthy monument of the piety and skill of a great age of churchmanship' – a view that required a sophisticated willingness to look beyond fashion and admit the claims of posterity. It was not in fact a view held unanimously within the Commission, Geoffrey Jellicoe being a notable dissenting voice who sided with the Dean, but the pro-screen majority, led by John Piper, forced the issue to the point of a public statement that firmly backed retention.'[33] Similarly, in 1961 Lord Bridges made a last-minute plea to the Transport Minister, Ernest Marples, in an effort to save the Euston Arch, suggesting that if necessary it should be rebuilt on an adjoining site. The pleas were refused by the Prime Minister, Harold Macmillan, although efforts to rebuild the Arch continue even today. Bridges' successor, Lord James of Rusholme, was no more successful in 1978 when he tried hard to persuade Peter Shore, the Environment Secretary, to spare the eighteenth-century Cutler Street warehouses in Aldgate, partly on the grounds that the proposed replacement, an office building by Richard Seifert, was inadequate.

Conversely, where a replacement had the potential to take its place as the valued heritage of the future, the Commission was more than willing to sacrifice an historic building to make way for it. In 1979, it sided with Richard Rogers in his efforts to replace Sir Edwin Cooper's Edwardian Lloyd's Building with his own Hi-Tech version, praising the Rogers design as 'brilliant' and likely to be 'one of the most remarkable buildings of the decade'. Twenty years earlier, in 1957, it had supported the demolition of Someries House, an altered Nash building in The Regent's Park, to make way for Denys Lasdun's Royal College of Physicians.[34] And there are plenty of other instances where the Commission demonstrated that its support for conservation causes was anything but automatic. It raised no objection to the demolition of the Old Deanery in Salisbury Cathedral Close in 1948 to make way for a diocesan training college, or the demolition of a Georgian terrace in Abercromby Square in Liverpool in 1965 to make way for university buildings, or (ironically given its earlier interest) to the proposed 1951 redevelopment of Carlton House Terrace, behind the retained Nash facades, to create new premises for the Foreign Office.

Tall buildings

'I wish I could reduce the height of all buildings to the width of the streets in which they stand and in no case higher than eighty feet, with these heights again ruled by the aesthetic needs of historic buildings.' So said Sir Edwin Lutyens in a letter to the Commission's Secretary, Chalton Bradshaw, in March 1936, as part of a highly prescriptive wish-list that extended to wanting all buildings higher than their neighbours to have side walls designed in sympathy with their facades.

It was a militant statement of disaffection with rising heights and the apparent disorder to which they led, and it found a sympathetic audience within the Commission, not least in Lord Crawford, who in an internal minute in 1935 argued that unless restrictions were firmly enforced, 'historic landmarks will disappear from view and the ragged and untidy outline of present-day building will prejudice the future beauty of the metropolis'.

The tall buildings that aroused such anxieties were tall only in relative terms; by any absolute standards they were modest. Queen Anne's Mansions, which as we have seen annoyed Queen Victoria so much that it led to height restrictions in London, was only 180 feet. And when in 1934 the Commission first addressed the question, indeed devoted almost a whole annual report to it, it singled out for criticism two tall buildings that today would hardly register as such: Faraday House, an international telephone exchange in Queen Victoria Street, and Unilever House at the northern end of Blackfriars Bridge, both of them significantly higher than their immediate surroundings but by no stretch of the imagination towers. The problem was their effect on St. Paul's when seen from Southwark. 'Two beautiful views have been disastrously blocked', the Commission said. By this time, the height limit in London of 80 feet, given statutory force as recently as 1930 under the London Building Act,[35] was having less and less effect in keeping buildings low; developers started to treat the limit as

a target to aim for, so it tended to encourage higher buildings rather than otherwise.

This appetite for tall buildings grew even stronger, and harder to suppress, as technical capabilities improved. Using its powers of discretion – granted under both the 1930 Act and the 1932 Town and Country Planning Act – the London County Council began to allow exceptions, in particular sanctioning taller blocks on the riverfront: Adelaide House by London Bridge rose to 120 feet and the Shell-Mex Building on the Victoria Embankment to 130 feet. In March 1934, *The Times* wrote that 'the need for high buildings is held to be indisputable; and good architects believe that, with good design and good planning, they can be built so as to make the new London airier, lighter, and easier to move about in than the old. All the better, therefore, is it to have a body like the Royal Fine Art Commission, alert to see what damage has already been done by bad design or by bad planning, and quick to advise how more such damage can be prevented.' The Commission suggested an early form of planning gain: 'in return for the increase of money value gained by increase in height, those who receive concessions should give something in exchange, such as a set-back from the pavement or provision of wide angles of light in the building itself.' And by mid-1936 the Commission was beginning to set out some principles. Its efforts, it said, had 'always been directed towards moderation in altitude', consistent with 'the London tradition of low structures', and it argued for height zoning in order 'to preserve an equable skyline, maintain selected silhouettes, check violent irregularities and protect historic buildings from being overwhelmed by their neighbours'. Context, in other words, was central to any sensible assessment of tall buildings. As they were not isolated objects, their location was critical. In itself, Faraday House was a well-designed and well-made building; in many contexts it would not even be considered tall. But where it was it was both tall and damaging.[36]

Despite these anxieties, and to some degree because of them, London until the mid-1950s was still a low-rise city, with St. Paul's Cathedral at 370 feet physically and visually dominant; in fact its dominance had been increased by war damage. In 1956, Queen Anne's Mansions, then eighty years old, was still the tallest residential building in London. Among non-residential buildings, St. Pancras Chambers (270 feet to the tip of its tower), Senate House at the University of London (210 feet) and Battersea Power Station, with its 337 feet chimneys, were the highest. Tall buildings were still few and far between.

However, 1956 was a pivotal year. By then the pressure to build skyward was mounting and the statutory limits that had applied since 1890 were becoming unsustainable. *The Manchester Guardian* surveyed the scene and declared that the 'battle of skyscrapers now appears to be won'. The Shell Centre on the South Bank was proposed at 331 feet, the Barbican at 300 feet. Many others were queueing up for permission. 'It may be taken for granted that architects will begin to take heart, feeling that they need no longer behave like an audience at the Players' Theatre which offers mock obeisance to Queen Victoria'. The consent of the London County Council was still required for any building above 100 feet, but its Town Planning Committee had no appetite for capping heights as a matter of principle. Quite the opposite: its message was that towers up to 300 feet would be allowable in many parts of London.

The result was a maelstrom: developers pushing the boundaries, central and local government becoming increasingly unwilling and unable to resist. The Commission, dedicated to assessing each proposal on its merits, was as usual caught somewhere in the middle. Broadly it held to its advertised line that well-designed towers in the right location were acceptable. And as a rule it favoured clustering towers, a policy that was both logical (in that a location that worked for one tower was likely to work for others) and effective

(in that it allowed towers to meld into a coherent and even pleasing group).

Where did this leave the Commission in practice? Its wish to avoid a Manhattan-style cliff of towers around the edge of the Royal Parks, and thus preserve their sense of *rus in urbe*, led it to oppose the Hilton Hotel in Park Lane, partly because it knew that as soon as one tower was allowed, there would be a clamour for more; and precedent would be a powerful weapon in the developer's armoury. When first consulted on the Hilton in 1957, it argued, a little quixotically, that the normal 100ft limit should apply. Over the next two years, as the project evolved, the height did indeed fall from 380 to 320 feet; so the Commission had some effect, but by no means enough to make a material difference. On the Knightsbridge side of Hyde Park, it managed to cut the height of Bowater House[37] from 260 to 144 feet, largely by shifting accommodation from the tower to the podium, and it scored a significant success in killing off a 1967 plan for thirty-storey cruciform hotel near Lowndes Square which would have been prominent from Hyde Park. But by this point as soon as one scheme was defeated another was proposed.[38] And any hint of planning constraints to come did little more than encourage a rush of applications from developers hoping to get their schemes through while they could. When the London County Council agreed in principle in 1960 to a limited number of tall buildings overlooking the Royal Parks, as long as they did not appear as an 'enclosing wall', the Commission knew full well that this would serve only to prod developers into action; the earliest applicants, after all, would not be the ones filling the wall.

As in its approach to comprehensive redevelopment and new roads, the Commission was never dogmatic and never entirely predictable in its response to tall buildings. Although it objected to the Hilton, it raised no fundamental objection when consulted in 1970 on Basil Spence's Knightsbridge Barracks for the Household Cavalry; given the choice between a long, low block and a slim tower, it preferred the latter. And sometimes its view changed over time. In 1959 it successfully objected to a plan for a 240 foot tower on the site of the disparaged Queen Anne's Mansions. It initially welcomed the replacement scheme, a 186 foot building by Fitzroy Robinson and Basil Spence for the Home Office, then criticised it on account of its impact on both Queen Anne's Gate and St. James's Park, before finally accepting it as a well-realised architectural statement. The first *volte face* was by no means sudden; it took place over about four years, from 1964 to 1968, as the Commission's attitude towards this kind of gargantuan building hardened. Spence, never an emollient character, was furious. 'It is absolute nonsense to suggest that the building is not in tone now', he said, or more probably shouted. 'Four or five years are a mere tick of the clock for a building...This absolutely explodes the whole validity of the Commission'. *The Architects' Journal* raised the tempo even further by alleging that Spence's drawings misrepresented the building to make it look less obtrusive in views from St. James's Park. Like Blomfield before him, Spence reacted badly to having his integrity impugned and denied the allegations with vigour. 'The criticism of this building is a fundamental affront to my reputation as an architect', he said, before roughing up anyone else who had dared to be negative. 'Why should Osbert Lancaster command respect as an architectural critic?' he asked. 'He should stick to Maudie Littlehampton.'[39] And Lord Molson, who had told The House of Lords that Spence would go down in history as the perpetrator of two monstrous buildings on the edge of Royal Parks,[40] was repaid by Spence in kind: 'he will go down in history as the worst Minister of Works we have ever had; during his period of office they produced some of the worst buildings in London'.

Besides the Royal Parks, the Commission continued to be protective of St. Paul's Cathedral, in some ways a tougher assignment as the City of London, generating constant demand for more office space, was next door. Faraday House

and Unilever House were mild-mannered compared with the assertive buildings that came later. The first of these was Bucklersbury House, occupying an entire block between Cannon Street, Walbrook and Queen Victoria Street. Its bulk was one thing, at 450,000 square feet, but another concern was its height, 140 feet over fourteen storeys, level with the base of the dome of St. Paul's. At a quarter of a mile to the east of St. Paul's, Bucklersbury House was outside the area of formal height control and the City Corporation was inclined to approve the scheme, taking the optimistic view that people would 'live to admire such a building, in which there would be fresh air and sunshine, while the fog would be down below'. For the Commission, though, it was too big and too high, and faced with the prospect of planning approval it decided to make its objections public – an unusual step at a time when it was still deeply formal, coy even, in its methods. John Betjeman, then a Commissioner, supplemented this with his own vivid criticisms: 'It will ruin the view of the Wren spires in relation to St. Paul's. It is the beginning of something we hoped we had seen the last of in Faraday House, starting to turn London into a kind of New York, with a few museum pieces built by Wren preserved in great chasms'. The spat that followed dragged in Harold Macmillan, then Minister of Housing and Local Government, who promised the Commons in June 1953 that he would consider the Commission's criticisms. In the end, he decided to wave the building through, leaving the Commission to advise on elevational details and again risk association with a building it disliked. In this more limited task of lightening the building to make it less oppressive the Commission claimed some success, edging the architect, Owen Campbell-Jones, away from a 'between-wars Bank of England style' to something 'completely contemporary'. In its annual report for 1953 it concluded that 'if, when Bucklersbury House is completed, the public shares the Commission's feeling that its bulk is excessive, there may be consolation in the thought that its architectural treatment, but for the efforts of the Commission, might have been very much worse'.[41]

Even in the context of St. Paul's, though, the Commission was sometimes hard to read. There was a hint of wistful regret in its judgement that the 290ft Mies van der Rohe tower proposed for a site opposite Mansion House in 1968, and only finally rejected after a public inquiry in 1984, was too tall for a site less than five hundred yards from St. Paul's. Two Commissioners clearly favoured the scheme: Lord Holford thought it would appear as a kind of plain, bronze curtain, almost complementary as a backdrop to the cathedral dome, and Sir John Summerson later lamented the lost opportunity to bring drama into the City. The Commission as a whole sometimes gave in to this underlying sense that a tower, as architecture, could be an adornment that would gain by extra height. At a late stage in the design process it encouraged Gollins Melvin and Ward to go with their instincts and add height to their 1969 Commercial Union Tower in Leadenhall Street, an immaculately detailed glass box and the closest equivalent in London to Mies's Seagram building. And in 1970, when the City Corporation asked Richard Seifert to design an alternative, and lower, version of his 600ft NatWest Tower following protests in the House of Commons that it would interfere with St. Paul's, the Commission surprised many by saying that it preferred the taller version.

That was probably wise. Generally, the Commission got into greatest difficulty with tall buildings when it tried to lop off storeys in an effort to make them less intrusive. Impractically, it suggested knocking 90 feet off the Mies tower, which would have been fatal to its delicate proportions. A decade before that, in 1957, it did in fact succeed in cutting four storeys off New Zealand House in Pall Mall, thereby reducing the height from 237ft to 200ft. Still not satisfied, it asked the New Zealand Government to shave off another four storeys. This time the High Commissioner took it upon himself to refuse

without referring the matter back to Wellington, explaining that 'we hope to avoid a mediocre compromise which has all too often resulted from a desire to placate every shade of opinion'. Mediocrity was what he got, though, in the view of many; not only was the tower stunted, so too was the podium, which the architects, RMJM, had designed to extend across the adjoining site then occupied, and today still occupied, by Her Majesty's Theatre. Despite the mangled result, *The Times* showed its usual generosity in its assessment of the Commission's role. 'The battle does not redound to the discredit of the Royal Fine Art Commission', it said in March 1957. 'The Commission's role is that of watchdog on behalf of the public, and if it does not point out the ways in which a project like this may be contrary to the general interest who else will do so?'

Conversely, the Commission was most successful either when it worked closely with architects to refine a tower's detailed design or when it managed to prevent a tall building altogether. Those invisible successes are far easier to forget than the still-prominent scars of failure: who now remembers that in 1964 a tower was proposed by Macmillan Publishers directly behind the National Gallery, intruding on views of the Haymarket Theatre from St. James's Square along Charles II Street, or that a 435ft tower was drawn up by Dennis Lennon for the Criterion site in Piccadilly Circus in 1968? That scheme, as *The Times* reported, was 'unveiled with fanfare by the Greater London Council only five weeks ago but now looks like following its many predecessors into limbo. The G.L.C. have now shuffled back on to the fence after its unanimous rejection by the Royal Fine Art Commission'. And understandably, few would appreciate the subtle interventions made by the Commission to improve the design of the Euston Tower, London's tallest office building when completed in 1969. As at the Commercial Union Tower, the Commission nudged the architects towards a lighter solution using glass curtain

walling, and then encouraged them to accent the vertical members by using natural anodised aluminium; the contrast with window frames in dark grey aluminium gave a much slimmer overall effect.

As with comprehensive development and road-building, the mood shifted decisively against tall buildings in the early 1970s. The collapse of the Ronan Point tower block in East London in 1968 effectively destroyed it as a model for council housing, symbolising the death of the utopian dream of streets in the sky. And in the wake of the oil crisis, towering office blocks were much more likely to be dismissed as irresponsible advertisements of conspicuous consumption. But the commercial market for tall buildings was still resilient, partly because planning permissions had been banked in easier times and partly because there was still significant demand for office space, at least in London. Although *The Times* remarked in March 1975 that 'giant property development schemes are being shelved; the blockbuster approach to planning has abated', it went on to note that

'in the City, projects designed during the go-ahead Sixties, for a prospect quite different from the one now facing us, are still being forcefully carried out. The architectural damage done since the Second World War is extensive and disheartening: the skyline around St. Paul's, for example, has been one of the proverbial tragedies of the past twenty years. But what we shall see in the next few years, unless the City Corporation shows a change of heart, will be destruction on a scale unprecedented since the days of the Luftwaffe, or perhaps of the Great Fire, and the construction of some of the most extraordinary and unnecessary architecture to be found anywhere'.

There was life left, too, in plans for tall buildings along the Thames, a natural habitat for towers as the views were

expansive and the problems of overshadowing far less. Initially, the Commission even recommended the river bank as a suitable location for tall buildings; it was perfectly happy with the Vickers Tower in Millbank, which it reviewed in 1957, and three years earlier it had taken an indulgent view of the Shell Centre, a twenty-two storey tower by Sir Howard Robertson on the Festival of Britain site and the first commercial building in London really to warrant the term 'skyscraper'. Commissioners took a detailed interest in the design, visiting the site to assess its likely impact, and here too they advised an increase in height – by one storey, in order to make the tower more dominant over the subsidiary buildings at its base; these, it thought, should be lowered by a storey to accentuate the effect still further. The developers insisted that it was economically infeasible to reduce the height at any point, so to bring the proportions closer to those wanted by the Commission they raised the height of the tower by two storeys – a deliciously canny exploitation of an aesthetic argument to achieve an increase in lettable area.[42]

It was reasonably easy to be indulgent towards single, isolated towers like the Shell Centre, conceived almost as a piece of urban sculpture on a festival site and set well back from the waterfront. Indulgence was harder to sustain later on, especially at the beginning of the 1980s when, as Deyan Sudjic put it in *The Guardian*, a 'tidal wave of development' threatened to overwhelm the South Bank of the Thames from Vauxhall to Tower Bridge and beyond. In 1980 there were live applications for 6½ million square feet of riverside offices, some of them architecturally distinguished, such as Richard Rogers' Coin Street plans for Greycoat Estates, but others very far from that. The worst offender, proposed for a site on the Albert Embankment across the river from the Tate Gallery, was a 500ft tower designed by Abbott Howard for European Ferries and nicknamed the Green Giant on account of its tinted glass. Sudjic noted that its 'crude projections, unresolved angles and extraneous lumps look more like accountancy than architecture, the vertical projection of a profit-and-loss equation'. The Commission agreed. Its Secretary, Sherban Cantacuzino, complained that 'we asked for an elegant tower and instead we've been given a monumental slab'. The architects fought back: 'We don't design to suit the Royal Fine Art Commission', they said. 'They have become just another bureaucratic hurdle'. But in this instance an insurmountable one: the scheme was defeated by sheer weight of opposition.

Apart from the uninspired architecture and overdevelopment of the site, a further concern about the Green Giant was that it would set a precedent. Lord Duncan-Sandys, President of the Civic Trust, foresaw a 'forest of towers' along the Thames. Similar worries surfaced a decade later at Canary Wharf, where the Commission fretted that in another ten years 'the entire area opposite Greenwich could be devastated by vast buildings'. But unlike the Green Giant, Canary Wharf was impossible to stop: the *laissez-faire* planning regime, designed to aid regeneration of the old London Docklands by means of enterprise zones, meant that three towers taller than any in Europe could be approved by the London Docklands Development Corporation in the record time of two weeks without reference to the Commission. No consultation took place on the effect on views from Greenwich Park across the river, and the Secretary of State for the Environment, Kenneth Baker, refused a public inquiry. Discussions between the Commission and the developers finally took place in November 1980, but the Commission was entertained very much on sufferance; it was made clear by the developers that they would resite or abandon their 850ft towers only if forced to do so by retrospective legislation that withdrew their development rights – in which case they would expect substantial compensation. The Commission was in a ludicrously weak position. It did nonetheless manage to extract one concession,

with Skidmore Owings Merrill agreeing to shift the western skyscraper from the centreline of Wren's Royal Hospital, but it was a minor change that did little to soften the overall impact.

Where normal planning controls applied, the Commission usually encouraged the adoption of policies for tall buildings that took account of their wider effect, including on historic views and settings. Some English cities had such policies; in the 1960s Douglas Murray had done one for Oxford and Geoffrey Jellicoe for Gloucester, and Liverpool's was widely considered an exemplar for its recognition of the contribution that well-designed and sited towers could make to visual planning. But most cities did not, with the result that proposals for tall buildings were judged in isolation as and when they arose, without any real guiding sense of what heights might be acceptable where. Even London relied on a curious mix of formal prohibitions, in the shape of St. Paul's Heights, and informal ones based on the known or supposed preferences of the London County Council and the Royal Fine Art Commission. The result was confusion, guesswork – and exasperation. In a 1961 leader, *The Times* said that 'it should at least be possible to reach some agreed policy as to where tall buildings are best sited. Yet there is no sign that any such policy is even in view.' And while the Commission did in fact try to persuade the Government of the wisdom of such a policy, telling the Housing Minister, Henry Brooke, in 1961 that 'the fringes of the Royal Parks at least should be inviolate from overlooking and intrusion', nothing came of it. Nor did it in 1980 when, as part of its response to the Green Giant proposal, the Commission recommended to the Greater London Council a more restrictive policy on development along the south side of the Thames; its ideal was something analogous to St. Paul's Heights, with protection for historic views allied to guidance for architects on designing for sensitive contexts.

The Commission's long experience across the country

indicated a widespread need for exactly that kind of coherent approach. Without city-wide policies, the Commission still achieved significant successes; but it was forced into the thankless and exhausting task of pursuing one flawed and arbitrary scheme after another in an effort to make them better, in the process gaining an unfair reputation for having an animus against tall buildings when its sole interest was to improve them in the public interest.[43]

Street clutter

If there was a note of ambivalence in the Commission's approach to many of the rising challenges of the twentieth century, there was one about which it could be unequivocal. It always hated street clutter.

That aversion was very apparent between the wars, when it would hardly be an exaggeration to say that there was a fear of visual apocalypse. The detritus of modern pursuits was seen to be spreading everywhere, well beyond the street in fact. A memorandum by the Royal Academy submitted to the Prime Minister in 1931 painted a depressing picture:

'The destruction now proceeding at such an alarming pace of much of the charm and beauty of our country compels us to make an urgent protest...The country has been subjected to a wave of ruthless materialism and destructive commercialism. In many parts the face of England has been ignobly and irrevocably transformed. Ugly, mechanical uniformity is rapidly displacing the varied and natural beauties of our land ... Advertisements deface the frontages of unworthy buildings, often built of material foreign to the soil and climate. Country lanes and ancient streets are disfigured with asphalt paths, concrete kerbs, and petrol-filling stations. Craftsmanship has been superseded by mass production'.

Much of this found a ready audience in the Royal Fine Art Commission. Lutyens told the Incorporated Society of Architects and Surveyors, at their tenth anniversary dinner in November 1935, that 'sky-signs, illuminated signs, floodlighting – an uncultured form of decoration, the very antithesis of Nature's ruling – all join in one loud clamour of advertisement. As things are moving it has been calculated that in less than a century we will be left without trees and little land to build upon. The land will be as desolate as though a plague of locusts has passed by'.

At the time, advertising controls were in their infancy: serious attention was given to stemming the blight (a particular problem along new roads) only in 1937, when Hore-Belisha pushed advertisers into reining in their habit of filling as much space as possible with garish signs. But even with these small advances, and the steady growth in local by-laws aimed at curbing the worst excesses, there was still much to complain about. In January 1938, Lord Crawford sent a lamentation on clutter to Sir Patrick Duff at 10 Downing Street: 'London as a whole is being congested by a variety of pavement signs and protuberances', he said. 'I can count at least forty of them. There seems no control, still less any effort to harmonise them, or to curtail these forests of vulgarity. As for the blue monsters erected by the Police, they are frankly scandalous'. The note to Duff covers a letter from Crawford to Sir Samuel Hoare, the Home Secretary, asking him to review the design of these new police call boxes, which 'reflect no credit on our powers of invention or our sense of fitness. The general scheme is ill-proportioned, and the detailed treatment is so unsuitable that one assumes it was designed by a journeyman-carpenter. Anyhow the mouldings are commonplace and meagre, and in fact there is no trace of understanding of architectural design'.[44] Duff was not about to get the Government involved: 'When so many of the population seem to be intent upon destroying beauty in towns and country something in the nature of a crusade to change the mentality of the ordinary person as well as of those in authority is called for', he wrote in an internal Downing Street minute in February 1938. 'And this, of course, is no concern of the Ministry of Works.' But he agreed with the diagnosis: 'the great increase of mechanical contrivance is giving more free play than ever to what we must regretfully admit is the innate vulgarity and lack of taste of the English'.

There was, then, plenty of outrage before Ian Nairn's *Outrage*, the title given to the celebrated *Architectural Review* issue of June 1955 that traced a route across England plotting the visual effects of all the paraphernalia, from road signs to bus shelters, that had, he thought, reduced tracts of England to 'subtopia'. Nairn was not short of allies: apoplexy has a way of increasing in inverse proportion to size of offence, so small things are especially liable to inflame passions, the more so when multiplied. One ally was John Betjeman, in whom the topic brought out his best demagogic tone; a favourite *bête noire* was street lighting, on which he was never far from a furious attack. In *The Times* in August 1950, he launched an onslaught on 'the craze for erecting lamp posts like concrete gibbets with corpse lights dangling off them in old country towns'.[45] And another ally was the Commission, which had been vocal on the matter longer than most, and certainly long before Betjeman joined it and lent his own unique inflection to its protests.

The Commission was keen to make practical points where possible, recommending that redundant equipment be swiftly removed and that the various statutory bodies take every opportunity to combine equipment, instead of each littering the streets with its own impedimenta. But as it happened, it too was exercised by street lamps, reserving a special dislike for concrete columns, which were commonly used after the war because of the shortage of steel. Not only was there more and more street furniture, but much of it was made

from cheaper and thus inferior materials; and to add to the difficulties hardly any of it was subject to ordinary planning controls, the 1947 Town and Country Planning Act having exempted everything from directional signs and traffic control equipment to street lighting. Some residual controls were still exercised by The Ministry of Transport under its emergency wartime powers, which bizarrely remained in force (along with rationing) into the 1950s, but meetings between the Commission and most of Attlee's Transport Ministers (Alfred Barnes excepted) were largely stilted affairs, held only when some transcendent purpose came into view, such as the need to 'tidy up' in preparation for the Festival of Britain in 1951.[46]

Advances were therefore bitty and incoherent. Frederick Gibberd, in an address to the Town Planning Institute shortly after he joined the Commission in 1950, gave a bleak assessment of the overall visual effect. 'Our towns have become mean and squalid places', he said, 'and every day we make them more mean and more squalid'. He might have been speaking for the Commission, which in its annual report for 1953 complained that the results of a lack of effective control were 'profoundly disturbing', at the same time issuing a call for vigilance. Practising what it preached, it devoted enormous time and energy to questions of lamp-post siting and design in the 1950s, generating such a flood of work that it almost swamped itself. Some of this work was in the cause of improving standard designs, which often meant making them smaller and thus less intrusive; regulations in the early 1950s required posts to be 25 feet high and the Commission promoted research to improve technical performance, so that a shorter post would give as wide a spread of light. And some of it was aimed at making the light itself less unpleasant, in particular through the encouragement of alternatives to sodium and fluorescent light. Here again its input was detailed and practical; it even had some success, in 1956 persuading the City of Westminster to suspend the installation of fluorescent lights in St. James's and Pall Mall while it looked into colour-corrected mercury vapour. But on the whole the growth in motor traffic made local authorities wary of deferring to an aesthetic body on what they saw as a matter of public safety.

Much of this work was an unglamorous trudge through lesser-known highways and byways, attempting to save sensitive environments from a nasty orange glow emitted from the top of crude concrete posts. The routine was leavened by occasional well-publicised spats, almost always in affluent neighbourhoods with articulate residents.[47] The so-called Battle of the Street Lamps in St. John's Wood in the summer of 1956 was one such. Others were in Chelsea, where the Commission recommended grey-green lamps with narrower-shafted columns; in Eton, where it suggested lanterns fixed to buildings; and in Kensington, where the Commission managed to lengthen the council's list of streets and squares where old-style lanterns would be kept. There was, then, some success, but on the whole it was a thankless and ill-rewarded task.

Fortunately, it was not one the Commission had to bear alone. Not only were local preservation societies increasingly organised and vocal, but other bodies, some of them Government-sponsored, were emerging to take a detailed interest in the burgeoning field of industrial and product design, including what came at this time to be known as street furniture. The Council of Industrial Design, set up at the end of the war, began to claim more territory, releasing the Commission from the obligation to deal not only with lamp-posts but with finicky matters such as street nameplates, parking meters and garage signs.[48] At the same time, the Civic Trust arrived to take over a good deal of the exhausting work of campaigning and proselytizing.

Increasingly, then, the Commission, having done much to draw attention to the problem of clutter, was largely freed from the daily grind of dealing with it[49] – for which it was grateful not least because it was then better able to concentrate on the business of architectural design. It kept up a sporadic involvement in most of the areas in which it had developed expertise, to the occasional exasperation of its architect members: in 1958, Lionel Brett complained to Lord Bridges that 'all of us have spent long periods in country towns of middling importance marking down the precise siting of every one of hundreds of new lamp-posts – the sort of work any good planning officer, local architect or civic society could do'. Eminent men, he implied, were being used as drudges, laying waste their powers.

He must have felt similarly when the Commission, having happily ceded to the Council of Industrial Design the task of producing a guidance booklet on the design of street furniture, asked him and his colleagues to review the draft. Through gritted teeth, Brett damned it with faint praise ('it can do no harm'). Others were harsher: the art historian Geoffrey Webb deplored its 'scout-master' tone and John Summerson said that 'if it is for secondary schoolchildren it is satisfactory...but there is too much play with the past. A Georgian bollard may be all right but any fool can see that it is not elegant'.

And so the disengagement from banausic tasks was gradual. But by 1966 the Commission was politely declining to comment on Anthony Wedgwood Benn's proposals for a rectangular, pole-mounted post-box, and such turf wars as there were with the Council of Industrial Design were gentlemanly sideshows. The last of these, in 1965 over the interior design of the new transatlantic Cunard liner to replace the *Queen Mary* and *Queen Elizabeth*, arose only because Sir Colin Anderson, the Commission's then Chairman and a shipping man, had decided views on what he saw as the 'deplorable provincialism' of Cunard's internal decoration and furniture.[50] In the 1970s, the Commission assessed designs for the Silver Jubilee street decorations, but there were few other digressions. Given the luxury of cherry-picking, the Commission had finally mastered the art of discrimination.

It did however choose to retain an interest in lighting, though more and more in the context of light pollution. In 1994, in response to a growing tendency to light motorways and other roads – the Institute of Lighting Engineers estimated that 100,000 new lights were being installed annually – the Commission tried to amend the Government's Environment Bill to make public lighting subject to ordinary planning controls. And it issued a counterblast in the form of a polemic called *Lighten our Darkness,* one target of which was floodlighting, which though intended to celebrate notable buildings quite often had the effect of flattening the architecture and bleaching out any subtleties. The Commission accused architects, owners, developers and planners of 'attempting to outdazzle one another for commercial, prestigious or civic gain'. If architectural lighting is now hugely improved – and the Crown Estate's work in Regent Street serves as an exemplar of what can be achieved – then some credit for that might reasonably be given to the Commission.

Throughout the post-war period, again up to the 1990s, the Commission also kept up a sentimental attachment – a proprietorial interest, even – in telephone boxes. Here it was never quite willing to cede responsibility to the Council of Industrial Design or its successor, the Design Council. In 1957, when the Postmaster-General Ernest Marples sought a new kiosk better able to house equipment for trunk dialling, he invited the Commission's involvement. The news of the redesign was broadly welcomed: *The Manchester Guardian* was typical in saying that 'at last – and none too soon – we may see a Post Office telephone kiosk designed in a twentieth-century manner. That sad semi-Georgian hybrid designed by Sir Giles Gilbert Scott is the only kiosk that many of us remember'. *The Times* added that 'a change is long overdue. The present kiosk, with its vestigial classical cornice and pediment and its Georgian-style window-panes, has for years been noted with amusement by visitors from abroad who have expressed a

feigned surprise that the instrument inside is not in Georgian style too'. Neville Conder, Frank Howe and Misha Black were invited to produce designs for a modern replacement but the project fell into abeyance and when it resurfaced in 1962 only Conder was retained. His design had a superficial family resemblance to Scott's work, with two scarlet strips on glass walls, but it was never manufactured for public use.

In the 1980s, when British Telecom threatened to abandon the Scott kiosk altogether, it had lost its negative connotations and come to be revered as what is commonly called an 'icon'.[51] Many did disappear, or were mutilated by having their glazing bars removed, but by the mid-1990s the kiosk's value as a tourist attraction not only won it a late reprieve but led British Telecom to install large numbers in central London. Deregulation of the payphone market meant, however, that other providers were clamouring for lucrative sites on which to put their own (exceptionally ill-designed) kiosks. IPM wanted to install ten thousand, New World Payphones five thousand. It was, in many ways, an atrocious mess, with little prospect of resolution given that kiosks were still exempt from normal planning controls. In an effort at mitigation, the Commission in 1996 backed New World in its fight for the right to use the Scott kiosk – a controversy that generated the last (and very supportive) *Times* leader on a Royal Fine Art Commission matter. And in a parallel effort to make some sense of the visual anarchy unleashed by deregulation, the Commission issued a circular on the design and siting of kiosks and even toyed with the idea of a last competition for a new kiosk. But it was overtaken by events. The Commission expired, in 1999, at roughly the same time as the telephone box, the latter by now redundant except as a photo opportunity and a glorified advertisement hoarding.

V | Climate change

Besides the physical impact of wars and the internal combustion engine, the Commission had to navigate a world of attitudinal and structural changes. Occasionally these made things easier. Mostly they made them harder. Either way, they needed to be skilfully managed in order for the Commission to remain influential and effective.

Concentrating power

One area of flux was state intervention, which ebbed and flowed over the course of the twentieth century. There was growth in state architectural patronage even before the Second World War – fifty-six employment exchanges and three hundred post offices and telephone exchanges were under construction in 1929 – but it expanded massively through nationalisation and indeed Keynesianism, which acted as a prompt to public investment in transport infrastructure. Since the Commission was set up for the purpose of advising public bodies on capital programmes, it was ideally positioned to deal with the explosion of state patronage that began out of necessity in wartime and was carried on very deliberately by Attlee after 1945. This was not foreign territory but fertile ground. Here were identifiable clients who wielded centralised and nationwide power; and being in the public sector they spoke the same language as the Commission, making them in theory more amenable.

The scaling potential of state control carried risks and opportunities. Almost overnight it created Leviathans which had the capacity to design things well or badly. The effects for good or ill were magnified, and at the same time any organisation able to exercise influence had before it the prospect of making a real difference. Knowing this, the Commission tried to find an inside track, pushing where possible for design teams within nationalised industries. Much of its success in bettering the design of power stations and gas works stemmed from successful pressure to use architects, which a simple diktat from the controlling board was able to embed as industry-wide practice. Discussions between the Commission and the Gas Council in 1951 brought particular dividends: instead of local gas boards obtaining their own tenders for plant based solely on technical requirements, leaving construction and design to the manufacturers, they now had integrated delivery teams that included designers. Alex Gordon, one of the Commissioners who took part in those discussions, was impressed with the results: the new gas works, he said, 'not only look better but do their job better at less cost. They no longer look so ashamed of their appearance that they have to be concealed behind a belt of trees'.

In its report for 1948–49, the first since large-scale nationalisation and still very much at the bedding-in stage of state control, the Commission also praised the Central Electricity Authority for giving a lead in the design of large buildings and standard equipment. In Sir Cyril Hurcomb the industry had an enlightened director, someone who saw the aesthetic but also practical value of good design; if, as he rightly suspected, the Government was likely to feel obliged to back the Commission in any row, he knew that it made strategic sense to encourage the Commission's involvement and get it onside. As a result, he was always keen to push for the Commission to be consulted on design matters. And in turn the Commission had a powerful figure to cultivate. This it did to good effect with both Hurcomb and his successors at the Central Electricity Generating Board, where it had additional inside influence through William Holford's status as the Board's architectural consultant in the late 1950s and early 1960s. The Commission was adept at pressing home its advantage, using access to senior industry figures to push, say, for 'super-grid' transmission lines as a way of concentrating the agony in sensitive areas; its hand was also apparent in the redesign of transmission towers to reduce their height and cut the number of cross-arms.

Largely by ensuring that architects were employed from the outset, it helped improve the standard of power station design to the point where it could afford to turn its attention to the separate issue of siting, especially of the coal-fired power stations needed to cater for the huge increase in electricity consumption in the 1950s. From the Government perspective this was a far trickier matter, as siting bore far more than design on questions of national industrial strategy, and it was hardly surprising that the idea of allowing the Commission a say met stiff resistance within Whitehall. But there were pragmatic arguments for a flexible approach, as a Ministry of Fuel and Power memorandum of May 1956 made clear:

'If we adopt a purely negative attitude towards the Royal Fine Art Commission they have a prescriptive right to criticise us in public and plenty of opportunity to do so...The Commission are certainly not qualified to comment on the strategic, economic or scientific reasons for the choice of site but it must be accepted that the Commission represents the most distinguished body of

critical opinion that the Government can bring together on a subject of great public interest ... It is a choice of evils. Either the Central Electricity Authority embark on a large-scale, long-term guerrilla warfare with the Commission, in which case all its decisions with regard to sites will be subjected to hostile criticism which is given the widest possible circulation in the informed Press, or it does its best to earn the Commission's sympathetic cooperation.'

Those advocating the latter approach won,[52] giving the Commission a voice – not an influential one, but a voice nonetheless – on some key strategic decisions. Soon John Piper, qualified presumably by his skills as a landscape artist, was despatched across the country to investigate the suitability of sites from the visual perspective, his views relayed back to Holford for onward transmission to the electricity industry.

Nationalised industries were not, of course, universally enlightened, and those that were did not always remain so. In its report for 1962–65, the Commission sweepingly condemned them for causing damage to areas of natural beauty, complaining that most of its recommendations aimed at preventing such damage had been overruled. This, then, was the downside; in the absence of due care and attention, or where aesthetics were pushed down the hierarchy of values, the visual results in the form, say, of ugly pylons and street lights could be painful, and painfully widespread. Nationalised industries that deviated from the path of enlightenment could be destructive juggernauts. But even then there was at least the theoretical possibility of correcting errors and educating the decision-makers. When a state-owned body erred, as the General Post Office was widely thought to have done in building Faraday House 'higher than the London County Council limit, without any warning', there was still a basic supposition that any repetition could be prevented: a sense, as *The Manchester Guardian* put it in 1935, that the Commission could 'exercise its good offices to prevent the State from again setting a regrettable example before the public'.

It was far harder for the Commission to maintain productive relationships and exert influence, still less control, in the *laissez-faire* world of the later twentieth century; not only had clients multiplied but they were answerable to shareholders rather than Ministers. Even those public sector bodies that had survived and were still commissioning buildings were less biddable, partly because they had to operate in a more aggressively commercial climate and partly because that sense of obligation to better the built environment, so powerful between the wars, had by degrees diminished. Most generations deplore what they see as a decline in standards, but the architecture critic Charles McKean had a point when he wrote in *The Times* in 1980 that

> *'patronage in Britain is on the retreat. The Post Office's buildings are designed by the Property Services Agency and are only rarely exciting. British Steel is not really in a position to commission exciting new buildings. For the most part, commercial developers are content that Britain's reputation for architectural patronage is the lowest in Europe. The faint glimmer of hope that London Transport would build Norman Foster's exciting scheme for Hammersmith Broadway has been killed, apparently, at the behest of Dutch developers who prefer a 'safer' architect. If so, it is sad to see the fledgling steps of an important British public authority towards enlightened patronage cravenly abandoned at the command of a foreign developer.'*

In these awkward, often confusing, conditions, when the decision-making process could be opaque, the Commission could either retreat or redouble its efforts. On the whole it chose the latter course, and it sometimes paid dividends. In 1991, it achieved a significant success by forcing the Inland Revenue to hold an open architectural competition for its new headquarters in Nottingham, instead of taking a design and build procurement route that would have given far less control over project management. The result was a fine building by Michael Hopkins: proof that where public sector clients took their civic responsibilities seriously, the end product could still be an adornment.

Deference and confidence

The Commission also had to cope with a marked shift in attitudes to authority as the century progressed. Initially there was an almost reflexive reverence. The bureaucrat, the man from the Ministry and the officially-sanctioned expert were assumed to be right and their judgements unassailable.

By the 1960s, the temper of the times had become far less amenable, far more inclined to question pronouncements from a committee of experts, far less tolerant of an Olympian body. And where the Commission's involvement might once have been welcomed almost with gratitude in the provinces, it was now just as likely to be seen as interference in local affairs. An early sign of this was the resistance shown by Cheshire Police Authority, in 1964, to pressure from the Commission to reconsider the design of its proposed headquarters building; eventually the Authority came up with the novel, not to say bizarre, idea that 'only if the building is erected can the public and posterity judge whether the designers were right or wrong'. And in 1965, when Sir Hugh Casson and Arthur Floyd visited Birmingham to discuss the proposed treatment of the new inner ring road, they faced in Alderman Thomas, Chairman of the Public Works Committee, someone who was in no mood to brook opposition from day-tripping aesthetes from London. Birmingham, he said by way of introduction, 'was quite well able to look after its own roadworks', and he himself

'only listened to the Royal Fine Art Commission because I have been told by my officers that otherwise the Ministry of Transport could refuse to sanction the works'.

The rise of strident pressure groups, so full of certainty and dismissive of doubt, also led to impatience with the Commission's measured and contemplative approach. When the Commission raised no objection to a proposed 100ft hotel overlooking the Avon Gorge — admittedly a piece of parasitic architecture that sought to exploit a view without beautifying its context in return — it found itself criticised for appearing supine, especially when the project was scuppered by other protestors. Once this sort of criticism started it became impossible to stop, and indeed became harsher and louder, shading at times into ridicule. By 1980, the Chairman of the Greater London Council's Covent Garden Committee felt able to dismiss the Commission's views (in favour of preserving the Jubilee Hall) as a 'rambling diatribe'. Perhaps the English were simply rediscovering their native tendency to prick pretensions in arbiters of taste who seemed to speak *de haut en bas*, as if a version of *L'Academie Française*. That was never a fair description of the Commission, but it could easily be caricatured as such by those wanting to stifle criticism of their projects.

The shift was mirrored in the press. Newspapers had been indulgent at the outset, *The Times* especially so. The Commission was seen, hopefully, as a harbinger of a new enlightenment, 'a purer standard of public art'. It was cast without hesitation or cynicism as a guardian of public amenities, a protector of the public interest. The Commission's annual reports up to the early 1960s were not only summarised by *The Times*, still then a diligent newspaper of record, but were usually the subject of editorials. If these were often laudatory, there was a very good reason for that, at least in the 1950s: *The Times* employed an architecture correspondent, J.M. Richards, who happened also to be a serving Commissioner, and it is reasonable to assume that at least some of the

(unsigned) leaders that backed the Commission were written by him. To a degree, then, *The Times* in the 1950s was a surreptitious mouthpiece for the Commission, the recipient of inside information and in return its public defender. When Brighton councillors criticised the Commission's suggestion of a comprehensive plan for the whole of central Brighton, saying it was 'planning gone mad', it was true to form for *The Times* to counter with an editorial entitled 'Planning gone Sensible'. In a curious twist, though, Richards was not beyond using *The Times* to exert reverse pressure on the Commission when he knew that the Commission was in two minds and might be pushed; in that sense, *The Times*' coverage can be taken as a kind of barometer of the Commission's own internal dynamics. Many readers will have been unaware of the subtext, but when *The Times* was, for the first time, really critical of the Commission — in late 1959 over the Monico scheme in Piccadilly Circus — it was in truth one of the Commission's own members trying to nudge his colleagues towards outright opposition to the scheme. It worked: within days the Commission had dropped its neutral stance and subjected the proposals to a very public mauling.

By 1970, any hope that the press would act as a complaisant messenger for the Commission had long since vanished. The new tone was one of irreverence at best. Sometimes the barbs were cloaked in humour, even fondness. Where Prince Albert had Mr. Punch, the twentieth century Commission had Osbert Lancaster *et al.* as quirky social commentators. One Lancaster cartoon from 1970 had a husband and wife puzzling over a new monstrosity: 'But, darling, it *must* have been approved by the Royal Fine Arts Commission — it's so hideous.' A few weeks later, a Louis Hellman cartoon in *The Architects' Journal* showed Basil Spence lying coquettishly in Hyde Park, his new Household Cavalry Barracks sprouting priapically behind his pelvis while the Royal Fine Art Commission, in the form of a policeman, tells him off for indecent exposure.

Sober coverage of the Commission's actual work tailed off even further after the mid-1980s. It was still discussed, but more often in reproving opinion pieces and catty commentary than in straightforward reporting.[53] So the Commission's words, once dutifully reproduced, were minced and repackaged. The media mediated, as it were, and there was little room for the careful development of an argument. At its worst, that led to the Commission's views being not just misrepresented but inverted. In commenting on a project it liked, it often suggested tweaks to make the finished product even better, but it was all too easy for these niggles to become the headline and for the favourable 'big picture' to be forgotten. The ready wit and vivid turn of phrase of its last Chairman, Lord St. John of Fawsley, created an added vulnerability in an age when the press was eager for soundbites rather than substance and preferred discord to consensus. Terry Farrell's 1991 scheme for Paternoster Square, next to St. Paul's, exemplified these problems. The Commission praised it as 'brave, bold and comprehensive', but as an aside suggested improvements to a couple of proposed pavilions – relatively minor elements in the context of a major project – and in passing drew a probably ill-advised comparison with Disneyland. *The Times* picked up on this: 'Disneyland jibe at St. Paul's plan', its headline screamed. 'It's that dreadful Marcus Binney of *The Times*', Lord St. John said to Peter Lennon of *The Observer*, who with some glee reported the conversation *verbatim*. 'He has distorted the whole thing … We did say some silly little temples would be like Disneyland. We are not saying the whole thing looks like Disneyland.'

This tonal shift among both press and public had its roots, in large part, in a loss of confidence in public authorities to deliver the kind of buildings and places that people wanted. Heavy-handed interventions had come one after another, in the shape of comprehensive redevelopment that obliterated the urban grain, housing estates that belittled the individual and urban motorways that severed communities. These

had arisen from noble intentions. But they had caused a collective trauma that meant, in Robert Browning's phrase, that it was 'never glad confident morning again'. Architects shared the blame, but no-one escaped it entirely. If dystopian estates and grim environments were the product of a world where specially-appointed public bodies safeguarded the public interest, what then was the point of such bodies? In these circumstances, when theory increasingly collided with observable fact and where unappealing buildings were literally a standing reproach, how was the public meant to keep faith? All this cast a long shadow: even in 1998, Alan Powers, writing in *The Spectator*, was able to say that 'on the basis of past experience, many people are suspicious that the aim of 'high art' architecture is to make them feel miserable or threatened'.

In the midst of all this, the Commission was in some ways in an especially awkward position. Unlike other bodies which could simply oppose demolition – in itself never a difficult thing to do – the Commission could not confine itself to wishing a building saved; it generally had to pronounce intelligently on the proposed replacement. And if it thought the replacement satisfactory, that could be construed, unfairly, as complicity in demolition. Even worse was a phenomenon which became something of an occupational hazard for the Commission: association with a bad design because it was determined to do its duty and try to improve it. In other words, by an unfair paradox its very diligence contributed to a loss of public confidence. Lord Crawford summed up the problem in a note to Arthur Knapp-Fisher, the Commission's Secretary, in 1946 – the subject was the relatively piddling one of postage stamp design, but as he knew such minor things could loom large in the public's mind: 'I imagine what will happen will be that two or three very poor designs are submitted and that we will be asked to plump for one of them; after which it will be said that this was a design selected by the Fine Art Commission, and we, instead of the Postmaster-General, will get all the blame'. This became such a problem that the Commission was moved to address it in its 1950 annual report, noting that when its advice was ignored it was 'then faced with the alternative of either withdrawing its interest entirely or of trying to improve in detail a scheme of which it fundamentally disapproves. In many cases the Commission feels that its duty to the public requires the second course, but by adopting it, it runs the risk of being made partly responsible in the eyes of the public for the final result'.

And even when the Commission offered no comment – sometimes a euphemism for distaste, sometimes stemming from a genuine wish not to get involved – it could be extrapolated by a process of Chinese whispers into something like a blessing. This was perhaps inevitable: subtlety will always be lost in a zero-sum game where a building is either built or not, and people want to know if bodies like the Commission are for it or against it. But the resulting confusion did require some disentangling. When in 1955 the Commission reviewed plans by the United Kingdom Atomic Energy Authority for a building in Lower Regent Street, it suggested a couple of small adjustments but otherwise said nothing. The Authority's Chairman, Sir Edwin Plowden, misinterpreted this as approval and passed it on to the Marquess of Salisbury, who as Lord President had ultimate power of refusal. In doing so, he added the entirely inaccurate point that the Commission wanted an ornamental scroll (instead of a bronze by Lynn Chadwick) to enliven the blank corner panel. Salisbury then wrote to Lord Crawford, a close personal friend, saying that he thought the building 'pretty ugly, but I am quite willing that it should go through as it has your approval'. Crawford replied that:

'the A.E.A. building seems to me a very poor affair – second rate, impersonal, dreary; the sort of thing that could have been built anywhere in the world during the last twenty years and which will become characteristic of London before long, unless anyone cares enough. The Commission first saw it with a very heavy cornice, which the architect disliked, as we did. The Commission preferred the second, lighter treatment: but nobody liked the building. All we said was that we 'had no further comment to make' – we never gave any indication of approval at all. Nor did we ever recommend the introduction of an ornamental scroll, or sculpture...From the drawing it looks as if the architect wanted something just to make his very dull wall a little less so. I don't myself think that a bad building can be improved by sculpture, though it may be made less dull by it...Anyhow it is clear that someone has said that the Commission approves the building and recommends sculpture. Neither is true – and this denial may clear the air for Sir Edwin to go ahead and eliminate the sculpture. We won't object.'[54]

There was ample room in all this not just for innocent misunderstandings but for deliberate mischievousness on the part of scheme promoters. The Commission generally avoided giving its 'approval' to projects – it smacked too much of lending its imprimatur – but developers were often a good deal less particular. The mere act of consulting the Commission was sometimes paraded as if it amounted to tacit approval. In 1954, *The Manchester Guardian* recognised the problem: 'The Royal Fine Art Commission commands the services of some of the most eminent men in architecture and its allied professions; their advice is to be had for nothing and need not be taken. One would have expected it to be sought eagerly, not applied for at the eleventh hour to cover the developer against possible critics, who can be silenced by the retort that the Commission was consulted'. But developers were indeed adept at using the simple fact of contact to imply that they had the Commission's blessing, or at any rate to suggest that any lingering deficiencies were not the fault of the client; how could they be when the plans had been examined by such eminent men?

As time went on, the public was also less inclined to put automatic trust in confidential discussions – sometimes a necessary part of the Commission's work, especially at pre-planning stage when the details of projects might be commercially sensitive, but one increasingly at odds with the trend towards transparency. On controversial schemes such as Basil Spence's Home Office building in 1972, the fact that the Commission was given access to designs which were otherwise kept secret engendered not so much a sense that the public interest was being looked after as one that collusion, amounting perhaps to a conspiracy against the public interest, was playing out behind closed doors. As *The Times* suggested, the idea that only the experts or those contractually involved need know the details of a scheme was less and less tenable:

'This is not an obscure corner of London for which an obscure building for an obscure government department is going up. By every standard this is a building whose plan and elevation are a matter of public interest. It may not be possible now to discover how this cloud of secrecy collected but one way of avoiding a repetition would be to give the Royal Fine Art Commission more power to publicize buildings submitted to it. The more information that is put before the public, the more articulate opinion will embody a real collective sensibility and not simply be tiresomely obstructive. It should be possible to amend this design in response to an informed public feeling.'

This is a fairly bald statement: not only should the Commission not necessarily have the last word, it should not have privileged information. In fact, as the Commission itself realised, greater openness would probably have helped; at a point when it no longer benefited from a default assumption that matters were safe in its hands, it would have gained a good deal from greater public knowledge of the quiet, and often quietly effective, work it did behind the scenes.

Tower of Babel

To believe fully in expert design assessment, such as that exercised daily by the Commission, requires a parallel belief that quality can be appraised objectively, in a world beyond subjective relativism. What is good in architecture is not simply what anyone might decide to like, or what the vicissitudes of fashion might push to the top of the pile. Moreover, what is good is more likely to be discerned by experts in possession both of knowledge and superior critical faculties.

Broadly, these beliefs were widely held between the wars, when the Commission's judgements were seen as definitive, but they became unfashionable not long after as patience wore thin with an 'official' idea of what constituted good architecture. Partly this resulted from a growing pluralism in architecture. This was evident immediately after the Second World War, in the arguments over how best to rebuild the blitzed Coventry Cathedral. As *The Times* said, the task of producing a satisfactory design was 'all the harder in an age which, in architecture as in other arts, has produced no style that meets with universal and unhesitating acceptance...It is a dilemma that is almost inescapable for those who plan public buildings in this age of experiment and uncertainty, especially those with the responsibility of building among precious historical relics'. The challenge was even greater than a century before, when Classicism contended with a resurgent Gothic; but now both of those were merely two voices in a Babel of pluralism that was increasingly hard to decipher.

In that context, the idea of objective truth, an objective assessment of quality, becomes if not unsustainable then at least harder to sustain. It is a short step before the views of

Everyman are worth the same as those of experts, especially if architecture is seen as a social construct where the obligation to make lives better trumps the need to please the cultured eye. And not long after that, the Commission becomes no more than one voice in a cacophony, and not necessarily the decisive one. Throughout its existence, the Commission clung to the idea that quality was discernible regardless of style, but that became harder to trumpet as a mantra to an audience stung by sometimes quite bitter experience.

By the late 1960s, the City of London was inviting the general public to act as a *de facto* Royal Fine Art Commission, asking its views on the proposed Mies van der Rohe tower at Mansion House Square. Tim Rock in *The Observer* was perplexed. 'Why are we suddenly consulted on what is architecturally an unusually distinguished building by one of the gods of twentieth century architecture, when the one thing most of us longed for was the power to stop the banalities of post-war City rebuilding?' Similarly, in 1970, the two options for Richard Seifert's NatWest Tower in the City of London were exhibited at the Royal Exchange, with the public invited to say which it preferred: a single 600ft tower with more public space around the base, or a 500ft tower with a 184ft tower next to it, which Seifert had reluctantly designed as a compromise. In this scenario, everyone was supposedly an expert and all views were equally valid. In fact, the Corporation was hoping that the public would agree with the Commission, which had controversially backed the first option, against protests in the House of Commons. Effectively, the Commission was being pitted against Parliament in the court of public opinion.[55]

That court was increasingly canvassed, in more or less unscientific ways, in the post-war decades, the clear assumption being that, ultimately, the public knew best – or rather, that public support could not easily be gainsaid, and was therefore the support most worth having. The Commission

was not above playing the game; as early as 1964, it appealed direct to the public to support its view that the Chester Police Authority's scheme for a headquarters building was unworthy of its setting. Nor were Government Ministers, when it suited them; which was usually when they thought the public could be trusted to give the right answer. When public participation was especially in vogue in the 1970s, Anthony Crosland (as Minister of Public Buildings and Works) invited the public to give its views on plans, exhibited in the Banqueting House, for a new Home Office on the east side of Whitehall. Clearly it was no longer enough to ask the Royal Fine Art Commission – less reliable and certainly less manipulable – to adjudicate on the public's behalf.

The trend gained pace in the 1980s. In 1983, it was the public, or that very small part of it which attended an exhibition of the rival schemes, who voted for the Ahrends Burton Koralek scheme to extend the National Gallery in Trafalgar Square.[56] In the same year, with the Commission locked in dispute with the Royal Borough of Kensington and Chelsea over alternative schemes for Kensington Town Hall, both sides ended up appealing to public opinion. The Commission accused the council of misrepresentation in claiming, without meaningful evidence, that the public would dislike a scheme by MacCormac Jamieson Prichard. 'We believe the opposite would be true if a public exhibition were held', it said. The matter was never put to the test, but it is revealing that, for presentational purposes at least, both parties treated the popular judgement as definitive.

On one level this was simple democratisation of decision-making, but again the root cause was a crisis of confidence. Speaking at the Royal Institute of British Architects in 1981, the Commission's Secretary, Sherban Cantacuzino, attributed much poor design to 'a collective loss of instinct about what is good and what is bad'. The practical result was very often confusion. Not only did developers tend to choose architects for their ability to manipulate a complicated planning system, but there was jostling for position among those seeking to influence which designs were built. In November 1990, by which point The Prince of Wales had long since added his voice as a kind of one-man Royal Fine Art Commission, a frustrated Denys Lasdun noted in *The Guardian* that 'you have the Prince, you have the Commission, you have Uncle Tom Cobley and all'. In this crowded environment, the official aesthetic censor had a harder job than ever.

Chasing efficiency

As the planning system grew in complexity in the 1930s, and again under Attlee with his 1947 Town and Country Planning Act, some came to think of the Commission as just one more obstacle to overcome before approval could be given. In the simpler 1920s it was easy enough to live with its interventions, as it operated in a world relatively free of planning restrictions, but as those restrictions grew it was more likely to be seen (and resented) as an additional drag on progress.

This was especially true in the twenty years after the Second War, when the need for speed in post-war rebuilding made it hard to argue for the primacy of aesthetic over economic considerations, or even their equivalence. The Central Electricity Board set the tone as early as May 1945 when it complained to the Electricity Commission, which had just invited the Commission's views on a proposed power station near Birkenhead, that it was 'becoming more and more concerned at the continual delays that have to be overcome before new stations can be built. Consulting the Commission consumes a lot of time and we do not welcome its intervention'. The Commission did indeed add a hurdle – there was no point pretending otherwise – but it was careful not to argue that aesthetics *per se* were paramount: it was sophisticated enough to present itself, with some justice, as a friend of

cost-effectiveness in times of austerity. In its report for 1948–49, it said that it was 'pleased to note an increasing realisation of the fact that, handled with imagination, a simple housing for the large-scale electrical equipment required for power stations can be much more impressive than a cathedral-like structure'. Superficially that remark was about aesthetics, but the Commission knew that the subtext would be picked up in Whitehall: that in advocating functional simplicity over grandeur, it was advertising its ability to help deliver efficiency in design.

It did so most notably over Bankside Power Station, proposed just after the fuel crisis in the winter of 1946 – a febrile time of industrial disruption, mounting unemployment and domestic hardship. Bankside was a rare and late example of an inner-city, oil-fired power station,[57] intended for the south bank of the Thames immediately opposite St. Paul's. The city-centre location meant that a taller chimney was needed, to carry away the pollution produced by the burning of fuel oil, and the result was a massive brick monolith with a domineering central chimney. Neither the urgent need for power nor the eminence of the architect, Sir Giles Gilbert Scott, could save it from a savaging. The London County Council, the City Corporation, Southwark Borough Council and the Dean of St. Paul's all protested. Sir Edward Keeling led objections in the House of Commons, saying the proposal 'to put up immediately opposite St. Paul's a power station as big as St. Paul's will do irreparable injury to London and will be resented all over the British Empire'. *The Times* called it 'a brutal impediment to the seemly development of the South Bank' and in a similar vein Lord Latham told the House of Lords that it would condemn the area to industrial use from which it could never hope to escape. Objectors asked the Prime Minister to seek the advice of the Royal Fine Art Commission; and the Government, while refusing to consider a less central site on the grounds that it would delay the project, relented on that point. But it was not quite the safeguard the objectors had hoped for. Although some Commissioners, such as Albert Richardson, had severe reservations, publicly the Commission backed the project, saying that the site was far enough from St. Paul's to avoid visual competition.[58] It recommended the setting back of the building from the riverfront to allow the potential for amenity space, and indeed argued that the architecture, already pared back, would have benefited from being even more utilitarian. With the Commission's qualified support, the Minister of Fuel, Lewis Silkin, was able to face down continuing demands from London County Council that the power station be moved to Rotherhithe.[59]

The cycle of growth and recession that marked the British economy in the second half of the twentieth century did, though, create difficulties for the Commission. If amenity concerns came a distant second under Attlee's austerity, they came second again in the 1950s when Britain returned to growth and there was a rush to develop. Buildings went up quickly, giving London the office accommodation it needed, but at such an expense of quality, even in the most sensitive areas of London, that questions were asked about whether enough use had been made of the Commission. By 1954, the Minister of Works, Sir David Eccles, was fretting that a better balance needed to be struck between quantity and quality. 'Many people', he said in a speech at Mansion House, 'have been disturbed by the clumsiness of design, the inappropriateness of style and the lack of concern for surroundings. Indeed it may be said that blocks of offices represent the one category of contemporary architecture[60] of which Britons have real reason to be ashamed.' He went so far as to refer to 'a process of brutalization', by which he meant an over-dependence on 'fat and familiar, mediocre and characterless neo-Georgian architecture'.

A decade later, the push for growth under Harold Wilson created further pressures. Buildings like the Imperial Institute in South Kensington were scorched in the White Heat

of Technology, when the need to produce scientists and technicians to fuel industrial progress took precedence and better road communications were seen as a key to economic growth. In its nineteenth report, covering 1962 to 1965, the Commission laid bare the difficulties it faced in protecting both urban and rural amenity: 'Where (as is always the case) the alternative to avoiding important damage to natural beauty involves some degree of extra cost, it requires a super-human effort to win the battle .... This is surely a most short-sighted policy, for, given the expansion of population which is foreseen, unless there is a change of heart, in a fairly short space of time the inhabitants of large parts of England will have to make long journeys before they see any real country. The loss in terms of human happiness will be incalculable.'

If growth generated problems, so too did recessions. Although a brake on development, they were usually accompanied by measures to kick-start economic activity; and this usually meant greater latitude in planning, as in London's Docklands in the recessions of the early 1980s and 1990s. As at Canary Wharf, the Commission was vulnerable to being blamed for delays and missed opportunities, including employment opportunities. In many ways, indeed, the Commission was a poor fit for a brash world of enterprise zones, *laissez-faire* economics and streamlined planning recast in the service, above all, of economic growth. Its interventions in the cause of discretionary things like superficial design were unlikely, on balance, to find a receptive audience.

But there were those who understood that the Commission was not just, or even mainly, about applied aesthetics. Good design, then as now, is about buildings that work well, a far more rounded concept than just external appearance. In straitened circumstances it offered a route to functional efficiency and indeed economies. This was true not just after the Second World War but after the Great War too, and in many ways throughout its existence. When created in 1924, it was seen by some as a means of reining in extravagant and costly designs. The ability to help clients towards more efficient buildings that minimise waste is a skill that perhaps resonates more now than in the twentieth century, for much of which consumption was nothing if not conspicuous, but it was a service the Commission always attempted to offer.

Mutating architecture

There was another tectonic shift that occurred in the twentieth century. Buildings were not the same things at the beginning of the century as at the end. Naturally they looked different, but the way they were created and what they represented also changed in ways that tended to take them outside the control of bodies like the Commission. The architect Reinier de Graaf, in *Four Walls and a Roof*,[61] notes that 'what we witnessed was not a succession of architectural styles...but a shift towards a fundamentally different role of buildings. If before the 1970s (roughly speaking) buildings were primarily regarded as (public) expenditures, after the 1970s buildings became mostly a means of revenue, a shift that caused further downward pressure on construction projects'. And methods of procurement too became less straightforward, with a growing tendency towards short-termism. Where buildings had been built, on the whole, for a defined client with longevity in mind, they came to be built by contractors and then leased to the client as a medium-term asset. At the end of the century this was the norm for public buildings, partly as a way of shifting capital expenditure off the balance sheet, and the effect on the standard of civic architecture was largely appalling. Ruskin's dictum that 'when we build, let us think that we build for ever' had been junked in favour of disposable architecture with a life expectancy of perhaps thirty years: we had gone, as it were, from Ruskin to the bin. Where did quality fit in that equation, and what room was there for meaningful discourse, close attention to detail,

sensitivity to context? Those were questions the Commission grappled with, for example in *Design Quality and the Private Finance Initiative*,[62] but in truth they were not questions to which a satisfactory answer was possible.

The Private Finance Initiative was the logical conclusion of trends that had gathered pace over the previous quarter-century. Public-private partnerships had been gaining in popularity from the end of the 1970s and could work well: half the cost of converting Manchester Central Station to an exhibition complex in 1983 was met by a Government grant, and the Commission praised the results for their intelligence and sensitivity. But the main precursor was 'design and build' procurement – generally a quicker and cheaper way of getting buildings delivered, but one which downgraded the architect. As Martin Pawley put it in *The Guardian* in 1990,

> 'In the old days it was the architect who delved deeply into what the client wanted; appointed engineers and other specialists; talked to local authority planners; consulted the fire officer and possibly the Royal Fine Art Commission; designed the building; obtained planning permission; sought bids from builders, and then kept an eye on the building while it was going up. The new way is that the builder signs a contract with the client, recruits an architect direct and promises to deliver a building for the client at a certain price on a certain date. One third of the construction industry is run this way.'

This was a problem for the Commission because, as a rule, its most fruitful relationships were with architects able to respond intuitively to what the client wanted; and its most satisfying successes came from working with such architects to tease out the best solution. Where the architect was employed by the builder, at one remove from the client, such relationships were more or less impossible. The Commission's attempts in the late 1980s to assist the B.B.C. with its expansion plans illustrated the difficulties. Initially, in 1986, the B.B.C. engaged Norman Foster to design a new radio centre on the site of the Langham Hotel in Portland Place, opposite Broadcasting House. Four painstaking years later, during which the Commission had sat alongside the architects, the B.B.C. changed chairman and its auditors questioned the need for such a pricey location; the Langham Hotel site was sold and the old greyhound track at White City bought instead. The B.B.C. then signed a design and building contract with Balfour Beatty for a 'simple building' on a site where there was 'no need for an architect of international stature'. Reactions were not long in coming. There was general dismay in architectural circles at the loss of the Foster building and the Commission said outright that the design and build route would produce bad architecture. Lord St. John of Fawsley intervened direct with Marmaduke Hussey, the new B.B.C. chairman, and won an undertaking that the Commission would be consulted as the designs evolved. The main practical effect was that Scott Brownrigg & Turner, the architects employed by Balfour Beatty, were forced to introduce a rotunda to reduce the monotony of the façade facing the elevated A40 Westway, which in effect served as a public viewing platform. But essentially an envelope as big as St. Paul's Cathedral was built and fully fitted out in just over two years – impressive in its own way, but not likely to produce impressive architecture.

The Commission often recommended competitions as a way of injecting intelligent discipline – and criteria other than cost-reduction – into the process of selecting architects. As we have seen, in 1991 it pressured the Inland Revenue into jettisoning the design and build approach and holding an architectural competition for its Nottingham Headquarters, an intervention generally hailed as one of its most productive and successful. But competitions were not failsafe; they too could be a messy and *ad hoc* mechanism, out of which good

architecture emerged, if it did, more by luck than judgement. Much depended on the conditions. What was their underlying purpose? Who judged them? Who implemented the results, and how carefully?

While approving the principle, the Commission tried to keep its distance from those practical questions. Only once did it actively manage an architectural competition, in the late 1990s when a Falkland Islands Memorial Chapel was sought for a site at Pangbourne College in Berkshire; but that was a relatively straightforward project, albeit one where the Commission was determined to deliver a worthy design.[63] Its more usual stance was established early on in response to Government requests to run competitions; as it explained in a 'strictly confidential' paper to the Royal Institute of British Architects in 1929, it always declined for fear of being placed in a conflicted position if it helped select an architect and was then asked to comment on the resulting design. Its preferred solution was to pass on the task to the R.I.B.A.

Generally, its later experience confirmed the wisdom of that approach. The Kensington Old Town Hall debacle in the early 1980s was a case in point. Much of the disused building was secretly bulldozed one night in June 1982 by the Royal Borough of Kensington and Chelsea in order to pre-empt, and thwart, an imminent Greater London Council preservation order. In retaliation, the G.L.C. issued a preservation order on what little remained, leading to a peculiar halfway house where the remnants could not be completely demolished, nor a new building built. The result was 'a gaping eyesore'. To try to resolve the impasse, Kensington and Chelsea agreed to a design competition for a new building and sought Royal Fine Art Commission advice. The Commission, slightly repelled by the whole messy business, stressed the importance of selecting an architect rather than a design: in its words, someone 'sensitive to the surroundings who could both design good architecture in its own right and respond to the existing buildings and spaces'. That advice was not taken. Five architects submitted plans for a mixed-use office and retail scheme and the council selected an entry from Frederick Gibberd and Partners. But the Commission dissented, saying that MacCormac Jamieson Prichard's entry stood 'head and shoulders above the others' and insisting that 'the best design be selected irrespective of whether it appeared to be also the best commercial deal'. Upping the ante still further, it accused the council of skewing the results by undervaluing the potential commercial return from the MacCormac scheme, adding that it 'deplored the short-sighted commercial approach to a site which is prominent and environmentally sensitive', and telling the council that it intended to ask the new Environment Secretary, Tom King, to intervene. Nicholas Freeman, the council leader who had ordered the illicit demolition, hit back: 'We have chosen the architect who would produce a scheme leading to planning consent...which will then enable the council to sell the site for the best possible price. I am sorry the Royal Fine Art Commission should have been so blinkered in its approach to this problem.' As it happened, neither scheme was built, but the Commission was right to argue that the MacCormac design, with a street-level escalator taking visitors into a glass-topped courtyard, was both innovative and a potentially exciting addition to Kensington High Street.

Even messier in its way was the open competition for the Sainsbury Wing of the National Gallery. In 1981, the Commission agreed to Michael Heseltine's request to assist with the brief, but for a nominally public building there were deep commercial overtones: developers were asked to submit plans for a commercial development which they would enjoy rent-free for 125 years on condition that the National Gallery was given at least 20,000 square feet of free gallery space. The gallery's trustees favoured an entry from Skidmore Owings and Merrill, but the Commission thought it unacceptable and Heseltine told Lord Annan, chairman of the trustees, that it

was futile to push for it in the face of that opposition. The competition was simply abandoned in 1982 and the trustees asked Ahrends Burton Koralek to produce a fresh scheme which then went through several mutations: a barrel-vaulted ambulatory came and went, as did a circular gallery, as did a 93ft tower topped by a crown of flagpoles intended to echo the adjacent St. Martin-in-the-Fields. The trustees lopped bits off at their monthly meetings and the Commission, largely in the person of its Secretary Sherban Cantacuzino, tried to put them back on, managing for example to reinstate an elegant exterior curve that had been ditched along with the circular gallery. Despite the Commission's best efforts, the process was derided as 'a saga of bungled good intentions', in the words of *The Observer*. Financing the project by commercial property development was widely seen as a mistake; and the point was made that although competitions could be a way of raising architectural standards, they stood little chance of doing so without orderly execution. In the end, after the Ahrends Burton Koralek scheme was in turned killed off, this time by criticism from the Prince of Wales, a closed competition was held and was won by Robert Venturi. Martin Pawley, interviewing him for *The Guardian*, described him as being 'saddled' with the extension and as having 'already paid his respects to the Secretary of the Royal Fine Art Commission' — a nod to the importance of winning over the Commission, and doing so early, if any sort of success was to be achieved.[64]

If the increasing intrusion of commercial realities complicated matters, so too did the changes to architecture brought about by technological advances. Towards the end of the twentieth century, buildings were evolving quickly, as were client requirements. The relationship between elevation and interior often diminished to the point where the prefabricated façade was a mere wrapping in whatever style was chosen. And the trend towards overcladding in the 1980s — even James Stirling's celebrated Engineering Faculty building at Leicester

University was not spared – suggested that buildings were not so much perfectly-realised *objets d'art* as tools to be shaped and reshaped to meet changing demands. Richard Rogers's 1981 Lloyd's building, for example, was designed with replaceable external service towers in an attempt to cope with likely advances in technology over the fifty years to 2030. And the pace of change in London after the Big Bang of 1986 was bewildering. Almost overnight, buildings needed to be able to contain and conceal hundreds of miles of coaxial cable. Space requirements were expanding so fast in the late 1980s that storey heights at the Broadgate development next to Liverpool Street Station went up from 11'8" in the first phase to 15'2" in phase two and then 19 feet in phase three. Buildings were becoming technical instruments like computers, cars and video screens. As Martin Pawley put it in 1985, when commenting on Canary Wharf,

'electronic technology and floorspace demands have completely supplanted the old perusal of elevations and tinkering with cornice heights. Even today, six months before building is due to begin, no-one knows how tall the first phase tower will actually be. It will depend on the technical requirement of electronic banking, with its state-of-the-art fibre-optics, massive heating and cooling loads and unprecedented floor to ceiling heights. Under these conditions no delicate exercises in massing or proportion can ever make sense or – more correctly – ever be allowed to take precedence...This galloping evolution in building technology utterly destroys the raison d'etre of traditional regulatory bodies like the Royal Fine Art Commission that endeavour to judge the impact of new developments by their effect on the skyline or on well-known classic views over the City.'

VI | Making itself heard

With all these challenges, was it mission impossible? There were people who thought so. Sometimes the Commission itself seemed to come close to thinking so, especially during the difficult 1950s when troubles came in battalions. Its annual reports (which ceased to be annual after the end of the 1950s, until the mid-1980s) could read like a litany of affronts inflicted on a rather hurt and disappointed convocation of dons, to the point where Dame Evelyn Sharp,[65] commenting on a draft of the 1959 report, felt moved to contradict the slightly depressive tone, telling Lord Bridges that 'a very heartening proportion of the cases you refer to are success stories, are they not?' *The Manchester Guardian* had picked up on the pessimism much earlier, in 1953, saying with more than a hint of sympathy that 'the Commission's job often consists in trying to reconcile the irreconcilable. No wonder its reports are a little downcast'.

So how did the Commission manage to make sense of its enormous task of improving the built environment across England and Wales? How did it get itself heard?

A virtual veto

As we know, it had almost no hard power, its warrants conferring the right to advise but little more. It would be wrong to say it had none at all, because occasionally legislation or covenants required its consent. When the Buxton Memorial Fountain, erected in Parliament Square in 1865 to commemorate the anti-slavery movement, was removed under the 1950 Parliament Square Improvements Act, the joint presidents of the Anti-Slavery Society (Viscount Simon and Lord Winster) managed to insert a clause in the legislation giving the Commission joint power – along with the Minister of Works – to decide where it should be re-erected.[66]

The Commission had been handed even more power when, in 1933, the Commons approved an amendment to the Adelphi Estate Bill moved by Sir Arthur Steel-Maitland (the conservation-minded Member for Tamworth) to give the Commission the final say on the appearance of the buildings put up to replace the Adam Brothers' Thames-side terraces. Similarly, in 1944, when George VI gave Crown land bordering The Regent's Park to the Central London Mosque Trust, the deeds of gift stipulated that the mosque design should be approved by the Royal Fine Art Commission – a highly unusual step but in the end a momentous one. The Commission took its obligation so seriously that it forced the abandonment of the Trust's first scheme when it was eventually presented for review in 1964; and the original architect, Ramzy Omar, was replaced by Sir Frederick Gibberd.

There were occasions, too, when private donors insisted on the Commission's prior approval as a condition of their gift, mainly because they were anxious to avoid being dragged into an unseemly row and having their generosity besmirched. In 1962, the Dean of Westminster asked Lord Bridges for a precautionary *nihil obstat* for some chandeliers given to the

Abbey by Viscount Boyd of Merton; external permission of any kind was not technically needed but the wish to steer clear of controversy gave the Commission a key role.

Similarly, the King George VI Foundation, scouting for a suitable site for William McMillan's statue of the late King in 1953, was so desperate to prevent a repeat of the embarrassing rows attending the King George V memorial that it insisted, via the Minister of Works Sir David Eccles, that the Commission be brought in early. This worked up to a point: there was still a row, but at least it was conducted in private. The Commission objected to the Foundation's first choice, in Carlton Gardens, on the grounds that it would require breaching Nash's arcade along the Mall. Numerous other sites were then dusted down for consideration. One of them, bizarrely, would have required the demolition of a building in Abingdon Street, the very scene of the George V controversy. Others were the forecourt of Buckingham Palace (with the railings set back), the fourth plinth in Trafalgar Square, atop a new archway at the northern end of Whitehall or in place of Queen Anne outside the west front of St. Paul's Cathedral. Models for some were even prepared by Geoffrey Jellicoe. At last the preferred alternative was opposite the Cabinet Office in Whitehall, but The Queen considered it unsuitable. The Foundation then met Crawford to explain the awkward position in which it had been placed by the Commission's opposition to the Carlton Gardens site. Crawford relented, but the press release announcing the scheme omitted any reference to the Commission. The Minister of Works would say, if necessary, that he had approved it 'after consultation with the Royal Fine Art Commission' – a deliberate ambiguity that left people to guess what the Commission thought.

But all this was at once random and specific: so specific as to have no wider application. In all normal circumstances the Commission had no veto, and for political reasons it was never going to get one. For its writ to run, it needed to be adept at exploiting what might be called soft power: influence and authority derived from respect for its expertise, the weight of its input, even deference while it lasted. At times this could amount almost to a *de facto* veto: usually informal, sometimes only implicit, sometimes vicarious, but in its practical effect real power nonetheless.

Deference gave it that power in the 1920s and 1930s, when it was seen in some quarters as a final arbiter; but its frame of reference, limited by its warrants, was small. Its breadth of influence was far greater in the early post-war period. Although deference had largely gone by then, blown away in part by the war and by the need for action afterwards, Ministers were never more willing to direct new public bodies towards the Commission for advice, or to make their own consent for a project dependent upon the Commission's prior approval.

The sheer extent of state control under nationalisation made such conditions relatively easy to impose and enforce. In February 1951, Hugh Dalton, Local Government Minister, and Philip Noel-Baker, Fuel and Power Minister, told the Eastern Gas Board to involve the Commission in designs for extending the huge St. Albans Gas Works with a carbonizing plant and an array of tower purifiers. On the Commission's advice, the Ministers approved only a reduced extension, not the full-scale one sought by the Gas Board. The Ministry of Transport was also supportive. Attlee's first Transport Minister, Alfred Barnes, addressing a conference of the Association of Public Lighting Engineers in 1946, urged delegates who represented lighting authorities to insist on street-light designs that had been commended by the Commission. Two years later, funding for trunk road lighting was made conditional on the Commission's approval of its design. And in 1959 the Ministry decreed that all proposed buildings at the Toddington service area on the M1 should have their designs passed by the Commission, a precondition that led to some curiously intense involvement with tiny details: in May 1960, the Commission was demanding that a police post be redesigned, that the word 'police' be removed from an outside wall and that a natural finish rather than varnish should be used for the salt bins. By 1972, as the tentacles of bureaucracy spread, submission of designs to the Commission had become one of an exhausting twenty-five steps in the preparation procedure for the lighting of trunk roads.

By these means, the Commission exercised real power over a disparate range of projects. One of its most effective interventions, measured purely by impact, was to scupper the original scheme for rebuilding Coventry Cathedral after the mediaeval building was largely destroyed in the 1940 blitz. Sir Giles Gilbert Scott had initially proposed a traditional Gothic design in the spirit of the old cathedral and in harmony with the surviving Perpendicular remains, which amounted to the spire and the scorched outer walls. Unhappy with this, the Bishop sought a more modern treatment and as a compromise Scott introduced contemporary elements to the interior – sloping, high-vaulted walls of reinforced concrete and a central high altar – while keeping the traditional shell. It was this awkward marriage of opposites to which the Commission objected; and indeed it pushed its objection to the point of writing to the Bishop, in December 1946, advising abandonment of the whole Scott scheme in favour of looking at the problem afresh. That entailed, in effect, writing off four years' work, as Scott had been given the job in 1942. But the Bishop complied, announcing in January 1947 that the Scott scheme had been scrapped because the Commission was 'dissatisfied with the present plan'.

Scott walked away, understandably, and Lord Harlech was appointed to chair a committee to restart the project. He recommended an open architectural competition, initially with the caveat that the new cathedral should be built in red sandstone in the English Gothic tradition; but this brought objections that it would handicap architects and cramp their

imagination; at the same time, there was a growing feeling locally that the new building should be a statement of faith in the future and a powerful symbol of urban renewal, rather than a harking back to past glories. By 1950, ten years after the war damage, the mood had moved decisively against a new exercise in Gothic; a revised competition was announced that required the new work to be 'in continuity' with the spire and walls but otherwise imposed no stylistic restriction. The winning design by Basil Spence, who had vowed to build a new cathedral while witnessing the shelling of an old church during the Normandy campaign, was less overtly modernist than the entries from Colin St. John Wilson or Peter and Alison Smithson, who designed a hyperbolic paraboloid in concrete that the judges wrongly thought to be unbuildable; but it was still a dramatic departure from traditional notions of an English cathedral. Far too much of one for some tastes: Spence received so many abusive letters that his wife had to intercept and burn them. But his design was warmly welcomed by the Commission. Holford said that 'if you want scale and colour, soaring vaults, cut-glass and stained-glass, tapestry, bronze sculptures, and the full yet detailed perspective of a large internal space, you will discover it by the time that Coventry Cathedral is consecrated in May, 1962'.

The Commission had a pivotal role in many other projects, from the restoration of the Norman Chapel at Durham Cathedral – 'nothing will be done without the approval of the Royal Fine Art Commission', reported The Times in 1950 – to a proposal in 1956 for a memorial at London Airport to commemorate the first aerial crossing of the Atlantic in both directions, by the R34 airship in 1919. The Commission's rejection of the original plan, for a marble representation of an airship seen against clouds, was especially awkward as donors and in-kind offers from manufacturers were already in place. But the scheme promoter, the Air League of the British Empire, had no option but to scrap it and start afresh. The new design

Opposite: Basil Spence's now-celebrated design for a new Coventry Cathedral, to replace the mediaeval cathedral that had been blitzed in 1940, emerged after a long and tortuous process. The original architect, Sir Giles Gilbert Scott, walked away after his revised hybrid scheme, a modern interior within a traditional envelope, was so heavily criticised by the Royal Fine Art Commission that it was abandoned. The Spence design emerged from a fresh architectural competition held in 1950. Illustrated here is his sketch of the nave, not exactly as built: the details, especially of the ceiling, evolved as the design progressed. *(Historic Environment Scotland Sir Basil Spence Archive)*

was no less controversial: Lord Brabazon of Tara opposed it, Lord Winster called it a 'monstrosity'. But the Commission liked it, leaving Lord Gosford, a Foreign Office Minister, to tell the House of Lords that 'in accord with normal Government practice, I feel that I must be guided by the advice of the Royal Fine Art Commission and do not see how I can veto the Air League's proposal'. And so the Commission, having killed one controversial design, breathed life into another.

This abiding sense that it was awkward and even embarrassing to contradict the Commission enabled it to intervene decisively elsewhere. One instance, the saga of the Jacob Epstein figures in the Strand, is nowadays hard to contemplate without amusement at the prudery on show, but it was a matter of deadly seriousness in the mid-1930s. Epstein had sculpted eighteen nudes for the façade of Agar House, designed by Charles Holden in 1907 as the headquarters of the British Medical Association. They caused a row from the start, major enough for Scotland Yard to visit the B.M.A. to caution against a possible outrage against public decency.[67] The National Vigilance Society huffed and puffed. 'I felt like a criminal in the dock', said Epstein. When the building was sold in the 1930s to the Southern Rhodesian Government, it too considered the nudes offensive and in May 1935 announced its intention to remove them. Another public row ensued, played out at length in the press, which revelled in the salaciousness. A direct appeal to the Rhodesians signed by the heads of art museums and societies had no effect.[68] The Commission – influenced by Holden, who had joined in 1933 – then intervened, calling the building 'one of London's finest unions of architecture and sculpture' and echoing Holden's professional view that the Epsteins could not be removed without destroying them. The Commission negotiated with the Rhodesians and extracted an assurance that the statues would stay. That agreement was honoured by the Rhodesians in letter but not, sadly, in spirit; they left the figures in place but in 1938

mutilated them on the pretext that body parts might fall and endanger pedestrians. Oddly, they butchered the torsos rather than the offending genitalia, which can still be admired today.

Another major row, again perhaps difficult to comprehend from the distance of another century, attended a 1958 plan to replace Grinling Gibbons' statue of James II outside the National Gallery with a statue of Sir Walter Raleigh. Cast to commemorate the 350th anniversary of the foundation of the Commonwealth of Virginia, the Raleigh was intended to form a pair with Jean-Antoine Houdon's statue of Washington on the other side of the portico. James II would be moved back to a site in Whitehall, outside the Ministry of Defence. The Commission strongly opposed the plan, even though James II had until the War stood outside the Banqueting House; it considered the Gibbons to be a work of such quality that it should stay on the superior site, surveying Trafalgar Square and the sweep down to Parliament. The Raleigh, which it thought a trifle by comparison, could occupy the lesser Whitehall site. And that is what happened, with Hugh Molson, Minister of Works, telling the House of Commons that he felt bound to follow the Commission's advice.

As time went on, the unwritten policy of deferring to the views of the Commission was just as likely to be honoured in the breach than the observance, but it still occasionally held sway in the later twentieth century, especially under Conservative administrations. In 1964, Sir Keith Joseph made Royal Fine Art Commission design approval a condition of his granting outline consent for a new covered way outside London Guildhall. And as late as 1990, when Chris Patten, as Environment Secretary, gave approval for John Simpson's huge office scheme (including a 240ft version of the San Marco campanile) for a site opposite the Tower of London, he added the very definite qualification that the Commission should be brought in to advise on the details.[69]

High-level support

Ultimately the Commission depended for its influence on the support of decision-makers, on a basically receptive attitude from major clients, public or private. Ideally, Government departments and others would genuinely want and seek its advice, recognising that it could help produce better designs. That benefit was felt more fully if advice was sought before a scheme had become solidified; once that point had been reached, the expense and inconvenience of unpicking a scheme, as well as the risk of bruised egos and hurt pride, could lead supplicants to approach the Commission with a degree of defensiveness that made constructive discussion more difficult.

Where Government was concerned, the tone came from the top, and at times the Commission had backing at the highest level. Ramsay MacDonald, accidental creator of the Commission, was instinctively supportive. In 1931, Sir Lionel Earle said that he was 'far more deeply sympathetic than any other Prime Minister I have ever known' – and he had known several in his long career at the highest levels of British administration. A year later, Max Beerbohm, who knew about such things, said that MacDonald was 'with the exception of Sir Robert Peel, the only Prime Minister who has cared about the visual arts. And he cares very much about them'. MacDonald had few challengers on that front among his twentieth century successors. Indeed, the Commission figured low in the consciousness of most post-war Prime Ministers until Margaret Thatcher, whose consistent support for the Commission was partly a mark of loyalty to its chairman Lord St. John of Fawsley, who had served as her Arts Minister. She was notably helpful in the establishment of the Royal Fine Art Commission Trust in 1987 and two years later both launched and contributed a foreword to the Commission's publication *A New Look for London*.[70] Even at the end of her third ministry in 1990, she offered strong support for a proposal by

Peter Palumbo, backed by Lord St. John, to create a special fund for the repair and maintenance of both Anglican and Catholic cathedrals.[71]

Everyday activity was conducted at a less rarefied level, of course, especially after the War. And the degree of influence enjoyed by the Commission often came down to some quite unsentimental calculations. A desire to involve the Commission could often be taken at face value – as a genuine wish for assurance that a matter would be dealt with properly and that considerations of visual design would be properly addressed.[72] But it might also appeal as a way of temporising on an awkward question, or avoiding it altogether. Hiding behind the Commission was an attractively easy way of ducking responsibility; it was much easier to avoid local flak for refusing a scheme if the blame could be pinned on expert advice from an independent body. Conversely any public body would be encouraged in facing down opposition if it could point to support from a body as august as the Royal Fine Art Commission. And the Commission might even be used by public bodies, notably by local authorities, in their skirmishes with each other; its backing for Sir Hugh Casson's Youth Hostel in Holland Park in 1955 was a strategic victory for the London County Council, which then felt emboldened to give it consent against the wishes of Kensington Borough Council.

Sometimes, then, there were ulterior motives for beckoning the Commission to intervene. For the Commission itself it hardly mattered: influence was influence. And for the supplicant it carried some risk, as the Commission could never be entirely relied upon to give the answer that was wanted. Councils expecting a perfunctory once-over, followed by a nod of approval, could be surprised to find their cherished schemes upturned. Nottinghamshire County Council baulked at the cost implications of a Commission recommendation to rework its plans for a new County Hall in 1954. And as we have seen Brighton Council, having innocently asked the Commission in 1960 for its views on three alternative schemes to redevelop a sea-front site, was alarmed to find the Commission rejecting all three in favour of a comprehensive plan for the wider area. Far from settling the matter, the exercise had simply galvanised local objectors, leading to a petition of 11,500 signatures supporting the Commission's stance. Convince the Commission and you might neuter opposition; fail to do so and you might inflame it.

Others who went to the Commission for comfort or vindication, or simply for an impartial judgement on a difficult matter, were on safer ground. In the 1940s, the Electricity Commission was generally keen to encourage its input on sensitive sites because it knew that a proposal that had been robustly examined, and perhaps improved, was likely to encounter a smoother path; put simply, better proposals stood more chance of being acceptable to more people. On one especially contentious scheme in 1944, for 230ft cooling towers that intruded in the view of Lincoln Cathedral painted by Peter De Wint, the Electricity Commission made consultation with the Royal Fine Art Commission a key plank of its defence at the public inquiry. *The Manchester Guardian* reported the upshot as a 'notable success for a good cause: the advice of the Royal Fine Art Commission will be sought and the height and site of the towers and chimneys must be regulated by the need for preserving unspoilt the view of Lincoln Cathedral'.

Similarly, Government Ministers knew that involving the Commission could strengthen their hand. Sir Keith Joseph was especially aware of this, although he was far too civilised for it to be merely a ploy; on the whole he genuinely believed in the social and environmental value of good design. In 1973, when Health Minister, he met Sir Colin Anderson and Sir Hugh Wilson to discuss what the Commission regarded as the 'vast and inhuman scale' of new hospitals and the negative impact of car parking requirements on hospital design and massing.

Joseph agreed; his own preference was for more and smaller hospitals, and the Commission's backing gave him leverage with his civil servants – leverage that was doubtless needed as he had just arrived at a spending department with entrenched capital programmes. As a first step, the Chief Architect at the Ministry of Health was instructed to liaise with the Commission to ensure that discussions were held before any irreversible design decisions were taken.

Across the years the Commission took care to cultivate relations of this kind with Ministers, although the return on the investment was limited by what is commonly called the ministerial merry-go-round; the Commission might reach a point of easy intimacy with a Minister only to find him shunted to another portfolio, whereupon it had to start the process all over again with his successor. So it was with Duncan Sandys, Minister of Works towards the end of Churchill's wartime Government, who in April 1945 invited the Commission's input on a range of projects, from developing standardised designs for prefabricated housing to redecorating 10 and 11 Downing Street. On the latter Crawford replied gently that 'we are not interior decorators',[73] but he leapt at the opportunity to influence mass housing design. There was, though, time for only one exploratory meeting with the Ministry of Works before Sandys was out of office, Churchill having been defeated by Attlee. The Commission had a similar experience with Anthony Crosland, Secretary of State for Local Government and Planning in Harold Wilson's second ministry. In February 1970, a few months after taking office, he asked to see Sir Colin Anderson and told him that he 'looked forward to a system of closer contact with the Commission than had been possible with any previous minister'. But again the promise was unfulfilled. Within four months, Wilson had lost a general election to Edward Heath and Crosland was back in opposition. The Commission ploughed on, holding private briefings in the 1980s for the Conservative Environment Secretaries Michael

Heseltine and Patrick Jenkin. Heseltine indeed was hosted twice for lengthy sessions, but of all Environment Secretaries he probably had the least intellectual sympathy with the Commission, in that his instincts were opposed to the kind of design control on which the Commission depended.

Even if these contacts were often fruitless for the Commission, many of the Ministers involved – however transient they turned out to be – saw something in it for them. Some used the Commission to defuse tension. In 1950, when Hugh Dalton controversially announced the demolition of houses on the north side of Mecklenburgh Square in Holborn to make way for an extension to Herbert Baker's London House, he added a rider that 'to fortify the faith I have decided that the Royal Fine Art Commission should approve the design when it is made'. And Ministers soon came to realise that an undertaking to involve the Commission was useful as a sop to public opinion and as a means of pacifying Members of Parliament – and often quite a painless one at that, as there was a fair chance that the Minister would be in a different job by the time things became truly awkward.[74] Even Manny Shinwell, whom no-one would accuse of having a highly-developed aesthetic sense,[75] promised, when taking his 1947 Electricity Bill through the Commons, that the Ministry of Power would 'take all reasonable measures to ensure that the Royal Fine Art Commission, wherever practicable, will be acquainted with proposals for new generating stations'.

Many Members of Parliament exploited these possibilities. Seeing the Commission as a way of advancing their own particular enthusiasms, they pressured Ministers accordingly. Sir John Mellor demanded that it be asked to review a 1938 scheme, widely-criticised, to install memorials to Earls Beatty and Jellicoe inside the fountain basins in Trafalgar Square.[76] Also in the 1930s, Alfred Bossom often used Commons debates to press for the Commission to be used to help 'check destruction of beauty in town and country'. He and

other members like Sir Alfred Beit and Geoffrey Mander saw the Commission as a bulwark at a time when powers to preserve fine buildings covered only those built before 1714, and then only if they were unoccupied. Mander thought the Commission should be made the final judge of all controversial proposals to demolish buildings – a veto too far for any government, and it is not clear with what resources the task would have been performed, but it is notable that the Commission was once again presented in the Commons as the route to salvation.

Being assertive

Others, then, projected their own hopes and fears onto the Commission. Had it yielded to those expectations, and begun to see itself as all things to all men, it might easily have collapsed under the weight, but generally it was secure and confident in its role. Perhaps too much so: on the whole it took few pains to explain itself, beyond its formal *communiqués*, and went to little trouble to manage public relations.

This was especially true in the early years, when the Commission had to wait to be consulted. By 1931, wearying of this, it produced a pamphlet summarising its duties and its work thus far, mainly in an attempt to get itself more widely known and thus more often consulted. This was an unusual and (by its standards) radical step, but one that was proved necessary by its own data. In its first seven years, it had been consulted formally by public bodies on sixty-eight schemes, an average of about ten a year. Nineteen of those had concerned memorials (including the statue to its own Lord Curzon in Carlton Gardens); thirteen were for historic buildings; ten were town planning schemes; eleven public buildings; nine bridges and another six were schemes of interior decoration. Only ten per cent of schemes reviewed were outside London and the South-East. Given the reactive nature of the Commission at this time, before the loosening of the warrant restrictions gave it the power of initiative, this suggests both a failure of engagement on the part of provincial authorities and a failure of the Commission to advertise its services outside London. Whatever the reasons, it was certainly at this time a nationwide body only in a nominal sense.

The Commission's overtures brought an immediate response from the Royal Institute of British Architects, which in October 1931 told Sir Lionel Earle that it would recommend to its Fellows and Associates the practice of referring difficult questions to the Commission. But otherwise the exercise was fairly desultory, Earle taking the view that 'as the Commission is partly intended for the guidance of those who have made mistakes in the past from lack of knowledge or taste, no harm will be done by sending the pamphlet to all universities, to individual colleges at Oxford and Cambridge, where there is still a risk of unfortunate things being done, and to Deans of Cathedral Churches'. It was, again, all quite endearingly donnish.

Even after the Second World War, when a small workload was the least of its problems, the Commission tended to operate behind the scenes, shunning a public persona. There was a certain logic to this. Sound and fury were fine for those (such as newspaper critics and pressure groups) without responsibility, without the obligation to make hard choices; the Commission often had to be more measured, more understanding of the dilemmas facing those charged with making decisions in the national interest. Sometimes problems were brought to it in confidence; if it was given a privileged preview, it was not always at liberty to cause a public fuss, or not without jeopardising future involvement and the trust on which early discussions are based. Moreover, persuading architects to modify their designs was at the best of times a challenging business, one not made easier by being conducted in the public spotlight; one architect even tried to take legal

action against the Commission on the grounds that its criticism of his drawings undermined his standing with his client. And although the Commission operated in the public interest, it was not in any direct sense dependent on the interest of the public; it knew that chasing headlines and courting popularity had a way, sooner or later, of rebounding. Stridency usually, in the end, creates an equal and opposite backlash. It knew also that going public with its frustrations could simply have the effect of advertising not its importance but its impotence – certainly the fact that any private pressure on Ministers had been fruitless. Why would a Royal Commission with direct access to Ministers not be able to rely on more private channels to achieve its goals?

This reticence worked for a while, but it could easily be mistaken for soporific quietism at a time when demands were growing for a noisier public advocate. Discretion looked like diffidence. There was impatience with its 'Sphinx-like utterances', beautifully-honed but lacking force. 'When it comes to producing an annual report', said *The Manchester Guardian* in May 1955, 'Commissioners can stand shoulder to shoulder with the uprightness of politicians faced by a general election', before adding that 'fine art should not be a euphemism for endless sleep'. To some extent the impatience was shared internally: Sir Colin Anderson, in a private note to Lord Bridges in 1962, wondered whether the Commission's letters were not 'too cautious in their utterances, with their flights of escape clauses', but he reasoned that perhaps these 'oblique tiptoe methods' were 'the best way of dealing with our wary quarry when we have no control but through guile'.

Ultimately, though, the back channels were not quite enough; and public opinion, from being relatively unimportant, became too important to ignore. The balance tipped decisively at the end of the 1950s. The Commission had tried to deal direct with the Minister of Housing on the 1959 Monico development in Piccadilly Circus, much as it would have done thirty years before: a quiet word behind the scenes, an assumption that a private nudge would be sufficient. On that basis it declined to appear at the public inquiry, and indeed the Minister told Parliament that he would hear the Commission's views privately before coming to a final decision. But that would no longer do. The Commission was being second-guessed in the press to the point where it felt forced to go public with its views; on the day of the inquiry, it issued a statement damning the scheme. A major row ensued, with the scheme's proponents accusing the Commission of sharp practice, even of cowardice and a dereliction of duty. With, it has to be said, a certain tendentious relish, they argued that the inquiry had been fatally prejudiced. Poor Sir William Holford, who was appearing for himself, was cross-examined on the matter by Sir Milner Holland, counsel for the developer, who complained that the Commission had sprung from nowhere to pronounce a sentence of death on the scheme.

'Can you tell me why the Commission thought it necessary when giving the Minister their views to issue a Press handout?', asked Holland. 'Don't you think it was a little unfortunate that the Commission should make public their views on the day on which the inquiry opened, at the same time not giving evidence?'

'That was the only way in which the Commission could make their views known,' Holford replied. 'I think it is impossible usefully to examine or cross-examine a committee on taste at a public inquiry.'

It was an awkward moment, and it marked the point at which the Commission understood that it had to muddy itself in the public arena, rather than relying on *ex cathedra* judgements that were disclosed to the public months or even years afterwards in its published reports. Lord Bridges was hesitant, as might have

been expected of a career civil servant; he worried aloud to his colleagues that the Commission would be embarrassed if it appeared 'to lead a crusade against Government departments which it is our duty to advise and assist'. Reassurance came, unsurprisingly, from J.M. Richards. Part of his argument was that greater publicity would stop people jumping to the wrong conclusions about what the Commission thought: silence was always filled with gossip, to a greater or lesser extent ill-informed, and the only antidote was information. But he also considered public opinion to be the Commission's main, and sometimes only, weapon: 'We command much public respect, and the mere knowledge on the part of the public that some project under discussion was being pressed forward in defiance of our views would have an effect. Has not the Commission a duty, in its capacity as a watchdog on behalf of public amenities, to see that such knowledge is made available in time?' Advice of this kind was predictable from a journalist, as Richards himself realised, but it was more in tune with the times than Bridges' very proper discretion.

The Monico press statement was soon, then, followed by others, some of them directly critical of Government departments: one regretted that 'the special committee appointed to advise the Minister of Transport on the landscape treatment of trunk roads has been inadequately consulted. It was not assembled in time to advise, from the beginning, on the first section of the London to Yorkshire roadway and, since then, it has been brought in only after major decisions on alignment have been taken'. In its report for 1962–65, the Commission announced that it would rely more on such statements; a more populist stance certainly, but one in part forced by a recognition that its voice was less readily heard in the corridors of power. In 1968, it took what *The Guardian* reported as 'the remarkable step of issuing a public statement condemning the 435ft tower proposed for the Criterion site in Piccadilly Circus'.

This promise, or threat, to go public was a recurrent one, but the fact that *The Guardian* thought the step remarkable indicates that the Commission never quite embraced the concept. Indeed, when Sherban Cantacuzino became Secretary in 1979, he made clear that he wanted the Commission to hold regular press conferences to publicise its decisions; even then, in other words, public engagement was seen as an innovation. To some extent his new policy fed through into practice. In September 1980, the Commission appeared in public for the first time when it was represented by Cantacuzino at a public inquiry into the proposed John Lewis development in Kingston-upon-Thames; and here the Commission came not to oppose but to praise, defending the scheme on architectural grounds against a consortium of rival stores for whom the new development represented unwelcome competition. And it continued to appear very selectively thereafter, usually in support of projects: in 1995, its then Secretary Francis Golding gave evidence in favour of Richard MacCormac's proposed Tesco supermarket on the cattle market site in Ludlow.[77]

The Commission had to choose its words carefully in the quasi-legal context of a public inquiry; less so outside, and it tended to be much more publicly assertive from the mid-1980s under the chairmanship of Lord St. John of Fawsley. At times it came so far down Mount Olympus that it turned into a streetfighter. There was a price to be paid: exercising skilled critical judgement is a nuanced job and nuances are easily lost in a less rarefied atmosphere. The spikier tone also invited criticism in return, which it got in abundance. Indeed it was involved in some fairly impressive rows, one provoked by a Lord St. John speech in 1990 lamenting the quality of new buildings by American architects, who, he said, had failed to understand Britain's town planning tradition. Swanke Hayden Connell's designs for Spitalfields and Pelli Clarke Pelli's tower at Canary Wharf were singled out for criticism. This was characterised in the press, and not just the popular press, as the 'Yanks Go Home' row. If there was not a great deal of subtlety involved, the intervention had at least got the Commission noticed: perhaps subtlety, a tendency to be too gentlemanly by half, had been one of its defects. By 1990, when public discourse was coarser, that approach no longer got attention in a cacophonous world.

VII | People power

Above all, though, what made the Commission influential and compelled others to pay attention was the quality of its advice. Ultimately, all advisory bodies, even Royal Commissions, operate in a free market and live or die by saying things of value to others. For the Royal Fine Art Commission, that value was generated by its Commissioners.[78]

Throughout its existence, even as its focus narrowed from the widest matters of amenity to detailed questions of building design, it retained a breadth of expertise among its members. Architects predominated, as was reasonable, but were always balanced by other relevant professions and indeed generalists: men of culture and polymaths. It was a broad enough church to include, say, Sir Thomas Merton, Professor of Spectroscopy at Oxford, who in 1916 had 'reproduced in the laboratory features of spectra of hydrogen and helium, previously seen only in light from the stars'; he was, besides, a connoisseur of Italian Renaissance pictures and an expert in the scientific side of conservation.

A balance was also struck, as a matter of policy, between professional and lay members. The chairmen were always laymen, though their backgrounds were varied. The founding chairman, the 27th Earl of Crawford, had been First Commissioner of Works in the second Lloyd George Coalition and for a time had had Ministerial responsibility for policy on the formation of the Royal Fine Art Commission; in the pantheon of those to whom the Commission owed its existence, he shares the highest pedestal with his confidant Sir Lionel Earle, who served as his Permanent Secretary at the Office of Works.[79] Though dutiful and committed – he missed only two of two hundred Commission meetings – Crawford was not necessarily a natural chairman, and his obituaries are masterly attempts to be generous without sacrificing accuracy. Lord Lee's appreciation in the *RIBA Journal* recalls 'the strange antitheses of a complex character: abstemious yet instinctively epicurean; sensitive and meticulous yet robustly appreciative of the Rabelaisian; the proud Chief of an ancient House, yet humble worker amongst London's poor; on occasion dictatorial yet enjoying the complete loyalty of colleagues'. Chalton Bradshaw added a nice rider that 'while some of his opponents might have winced at his trenchant manner and forthright views, on other occasions a disarming gentleness concealed his stubborn determination. Despite a certain brusqueness, he was really most approachable'.

His death in the spring of 1940 happened when the Commission was in any event entering a period of enforced dormancy – ironically at the point of greatest assault on physical culture in England since the Reformation. There followed a curious interregnum. Churchill had the Battle of Britain to contend with and, as Downing Street pointed out in November, he 'could not be troubled with the chairmanship during the summer crisis and it is rather doubtful whether he would want to be troubled with it now'. He had, however, appointed Lord Reith as First Commissioner of Works, which indicated, said The Treasury, 'that he considers that the Government should pay attention to reconstruction problems, and that he might regard the appointment of a new chairman of the Royal Fine Art Commission as an incidental if somewhat tiresome part of reconstruction'.

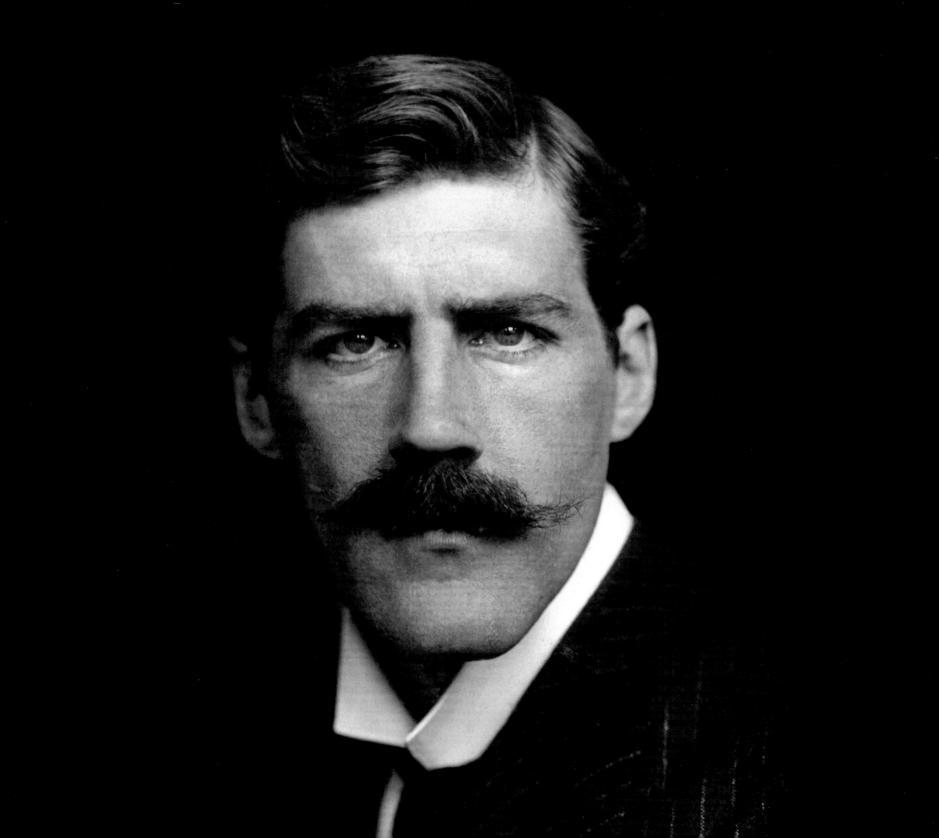

Opposite: The 27th Earl of Crawford, photographed in his prime at the beginning of the twentieth century. As First Commissioner of Works in the 1921–22 Lloyd George Coalition he was instrumental in laying the groundwork for the creation of the Royal Fine Art Commission, before serving as its first Chairman from 1924 until his death in 1940. Some of the characteristics noted by his obituarists, notable brusqueness, tenacity and Scots fierceness, come across in this arresting shot. (National Portrait Gallery)

Most qualified candidates, though, were otherwise engaged, or simply unsuitable: Lord Harlech, a particular favourite of the Government's, was in the north-east as Civil Defence Commissioner, and shortly after left for South Africa as High Commissioner. Lord Baldwin, the former Prime Minister whose Government had fallen on the very eve of the Commission's creation, was 'too old and tired'. Even Lord Reith was quietly canvassed, in the Lords by Lord Esher, Lionel Brett's father. That appointment would have been odd indeed, as Reith would have operated, in effect, as his own watchdog; happily he declined on the grounds that 'his long experience was that the State was not to be trusted and that an expert eye must be kept on its activities'. He did, though, take a serious interest in the Commission's potential for helping with reconstruction, and indeed was a prime mover in keeping the Commission alive, at some level, during the War; without him, it might have drifted into terminal decline, its functions taken over by a new Central Planning Authority to which, in 1941, the wartime government was committed. Realising that the Commission needed direction if it was to be sustained, Reith gave some thought to chairmanship candidates, ultimately suggesting Lord Crawford's son, by now the 28th earl. This too was a peculiar choice in some ways; although the younger Crawford was not wholly inexperienced, having been a trustee of the Tate and the National Gallery in the 1930s, his experience was decidedly limited. Perhaps Reith saw that as a plus, giving him a malleable junior partner. At any rate, at this stage, in the autumn of 1941, the Government considered Crawford to have the opposite defect to Baldwin: too young and too green.[80]

By this point the Government was left with candidates who, for one reason or another, it considered dubious: an unsigned Treasury minute says that 'one or two people are afraid that Kenneth Clark may be suggested... His appointment would produce violent reactions. The Commission is not a place for an autocratic chairman but one who can produce a common mind out of discordant elements'. In the end, the 'expert eye' sought by Reith was that of Lord Lee of Fareham, who cannily waited until the field of battle was littered with corpses and then suggested himself. Even more cannily, he put himself forward only as a stopgap. He was in many ways supremely qualified, having been a Commissioner since 1926 and an informal policy adviser to the Office of Works on Commission matters since the 1920s. And he had become something of a professional chairman, serially leading investigations into the public services in India, police pay and pensions, cross-river traffic, police powers and even radium.

The Government considered Lee too belligerent, and he must have been well aware of such doubts about his temperament. Why else, after all, had he not been approached? But he gambled that of all deficiencies, belligerence at least might be allowable in wartime. In July 1942, he sent a cleverly-crafted letter to Churchill, effectively a job application that anticipated and dealt with all the objections. 'One temporary solution that I have already ventured to suggest', he concluded, 'is that I should be officially appointed to occupy the chair for the duration of the War on the understanding that I would retire at any moment in favour of a younger man if and when he can be found'. The next sentence suggests that Reith had already had a quiet word with Churchill: 'I understand that it has been your desire to appoint the present Crawford to follow his father in the chair and that he has not yet felt able to accept, partly on the ground of inexperience of the duties involved'.

Churchill consented to this arrangement, calling it 'generous and prudent'; doubtless he was grateful to be handed a ready-made solution. Crawford fils thus became chairman-designate under Lee, and took over from him not much more than a year later, in 1943. Like his father he was punctilious, and partly on account of that found the job taxing. A Sunday Times profile in the 1950s notes that 'when he might be enjoying himself in the

Bargello or at the Capodimonte, Lord Crawford is more likely to be found at his desk with an ancient piece of hand luggage at his side; from this he draws the vast correspondence to which he replies in long-hand, in a fist which even his grandfather might be hard pushed to decipher'.[81] He resigned in 1957, ending a family connection with the Commission stretching back to its foundation. He had wanted to go in 1955, exhausted by the pressure of work, the sapping criticism and the endless round trips from Scotland, but felt obliged to stay until a suitable successor was found; and once the Commission was dragged into the public row over the future of the Imperial Institute in 1956, he felt constrained to hang on in case his departure was misinterpreted in the press as a petulant resignation.

Finding a replacement turned out to be a tortuous process. John Betjeman and Sir Arthur Richmond, Crawford's *de facto* deputy, were ruled out as lacking authority. Sir Kenneth Clark was considered again (and was Crawford's first choice) but by this point was committed elsewhere, in particular to the Arts Council which he chaired. Lord Radcliffe, who had partitioned British India and was now a Law Lord, was said by Crawford to have 'nibbled' but was ultimately too busy drawing up a new constitution for Cyprus. Crawford asked the Prime Minister (Anthony Eden, a personal friend) for other ideas; he in turn asked his Chancellor of the Exchequer, R.A. Butler, and suggested consulting Sir Edward Bridges, Head of the Home Civil Service and Permanent Secretary at the Treasury. From then on, Bridges managed and refereed the process, informally interviewing and appraising candidates. But hope after hope was dashed. Sir Alan Lascelles, Private Secretary to George VI and Elizabeth II, was approached but, Bridges told Sir Russell Johnston at the Treasury,

'refused with a degree of determination and fervour which was quite startling. His reasons were: (i) that he was nearly 70; (ii) that he knows nothing about architecture. Until two years ago he had never heard of Gibbs and he had had to look Gibbs and Kent up in the encyclopaedia to learn something about them. He also disclaimed any knowledge of any of the arts except music. When I said I couldn't believe this and that he managed extremely well on the Historic Houses Commission his answer was that the only way in which he managed on that body at all was because he did happen to know something about country houses. But his determination to have nothing to do with the idea at all is so fierce that I had to drop it like a hot brick.'

In an effort to be helpful, Lascelles offered his own suggestions, each more improbable than the last: Lord David Cecil, Peter Fleming, the Duke of Devonshire ('by a Cavendish out of a Cecil, so he ought to have the qualities of a chairman') and the Marquess of Lansdowne, who had only just demolished the greater part of his Robert Adam seat in Wiltshire. 'He is able', said Bridges, 'but if he was appointed the *Evening Standard* might say his chief contribution to architecture was the pulling down of Bowood'. Brendan Bracken was also fleetingly considered, but Bridges scotched that with the withering put-down that 'if I was to judge him from his performance in the war I should regard him as a rather terrifying prospect'. As in the 1940s, then, the battlefield was littered with bodies, this time round with Bridges as sniper-in-chief. And by a curious unrecorded process which only a truly seasoned mandarin could contrive, the person who emerged victorious from all this was Sir Edward Bridges himself. Freshly raised to the peerage as Lord Bridges, and having been reassured by Crawford that Duncan Sandys' planned new Civic Trust would not invade the territory occupied by the Commission, he was appointed by The Queen to succeed Crawford in September 1957.[82]

Bridges took over just as the Royal Fine Art Commission was entering the most torrid period in its history, for which he needed all his formidable political, intellectual and administrative skills. Churchill, whom he had served at close quarters as Cabinet Secretary, was a definite admirer, attributing to Bridges the 'complete harmony' between the civil and military staffs of the wartime Treasury. The irony of his Treasury background did not escape the press – *The Daily Telegraph* noted that 'he must have spent a great part of his life in refusing public money for the arts' – but as an ex-gamekeeper he knew how the system worked and his brilliance as an administrator made him ideal at a time when an organisational overhaul was long overdue. Better preparation and more effective delegation were his watchwords; on the face of it simple, but in reality a ponderous and distracting business, not least because of endless awkward questioning by John Betjeman, who feared that sub-committees were an underhand way of bypassing the laymen and reducing the full Commission to a rubber stamp. His suspicions were deepened by the fact that the so-called technical committee, which predated Bridges, had only architects and engineers as members and produced no record of its meetings; its job was to reach a provisional view on schemes for presentation to the full Commission, having discussed schemes with their architects, but Betjeman argued that 'architecture as assessed by the Commission is never just or wholly a technical matter, and things such as relationship to historic buildings and landscapes would not necessarily occur to architects'. That was a fair point, and Bridges' reply that 'it is easier for architect members of the Commission to talk to other architects if laymen are not present' was not wholly convincing. Bridges did manage to add a preparatory committee with the job of sifting incoming schemes, but Betjeman gave that too a cool reception, worrying that schemes worth reviewing were being winnowed out. Bridges reacted as a headmaster might to an errant pupil, largely holding his ground and saying wearily in a riposte circulated to all Commissioners that

'*Betjeman seems rather suspicious of delegation. If he means that really important issues should be considered by the Commission as a whole I am with him. If he means that nothing except the utmost trivialities can be decided without submission to the full Commission then I say that one has to choose between the situation in which nothing of any significance is settled without the whole Commission seeing it and, on the other hand, the Commission having time to do the big things well.*'

All this was of course trying, however much it played to Bridges's strengths as a shrewd operator. 'My efforts to secure delegation of the unimportant business of the Commission I find very hard work', he said to Sir Colin Anderson in 1962. A hint of his impatience is given in his *Times* obituary in 1969, which remarked that of all his numerous high-powered appointments – one of his last was being asked by Harold Macmillan to inquire into the theft in 1961 of Goya's *Duke of Wellington* from the National Gallery[83] – 'the Royal Fine Art Commission was closest to his heart: his interest in architecture was deep and he found this difficult and sometimes frustrating assignment consistently absorbing'.

It was Anderson who succeeded Bridges. Having served an apprenticeship, and to some extent acted as Bridges's confidant, he was well-briefed on the various internal machinations and personal foibles. To his annoyance the tendency towards navel-gazing, inherited from the Bridges era, spilled over into his tenure, again often stoked by Betjeman. It reached its nadir in the convoluted 'Playfair-Davies Memorandum' of 1962 on the subject of sub-committees and other aspects of internal organisation. Anderson was left to echo Bridges's lament: 'many of us live with this problem of delegation in our daily lives and delegate like mad, because our jobs would seize up if we didn't. The Betj has never experienced this of course'. When he died in 1980, *The Times* noted that Anderson might have seemed a wealthy *dilettante* but for his practical contributions to architecture, for example as client for the P&O Building in Leadenhall Street.[84] It added that 'in the 1930s, when 'modern' art was still deeply controversial and widely despised, he played a role not much less significant than that of Kenneth Clark in championing and patronizing such emerging artists as Bacon, Moore and Sutherland'. But as with Bridges, it presented the chairmanship of the Royal Fine Art Commission as something of a penance: 'he was unfailingly on top of his dossiers', it said, 'but the Commission's inadequate powers must have been a source of frustration to so devoted a patron of good design'.

Much quieter were the tenures of Lord James of Rusholme, a distinguished educationalist who strove for consensus in the war of attrition between conservationists and developers, and the engineering scientist Sir Derman Christopherson, who had an early bruising exposure to the Commission in 1962 when it severely criticised his project for an arts building at Durham University, where he was a college warden.[85] These long years of low-key diligence strongly influenced the next, and final, appointment. As the Commission had largely disappeared from public view, with only one report issued between 1971 and 1984, the Government wanted a populariser to raise its profile; and from that perspective it chose well in the charismatic Norman St. John-Stevas, always ready with a pithy and acerbic quote. 'A kind of Lord Queensberry of taste at the prow of the Royal Fine Art Commission', said *The Observer* in 1991 in a fairly off-beam comparison. But perhaps a degree of pugilism was needed after too long lurking in the shadows with gnomic, *sotto voce* utterances. To a degree he came to personify the Commission, partly because press releases were usually rendered as direct quotations from the chairman rather than as impersonal missives from a collegiate body. That made for quotability but exposed a vulnerable flank to persistent snipers like Deyan Sudjic, who in 1995 complained that the Commission

had become a reflection of its chairman's personal prejudices. But if, as Sudjic said, the Commission's previous chairmen had come to 'enjoy a profile as visible as that of the Egg Marketing Board', that was incontestably no longer so under Lord St. John (as he became in 1987). He had done as asked and raised the Commission's profile, as well as greatly expanding its educational work; and if there was a whiff of the unexpected about some of the Commission's pronouncements, they were at least eagerly awaited.

These then were the leading laymen, all of them notably able; their main attribute, a critical one for the role, was a capacity to coax a common view from alpha practitioners, many of them egotistical, some of them belligerently defensive of their own work. It was impossible, across three-quarters of a century, to avoid eruptions altogether, and Blomfield was not the only Commissioner to resign in high dudgeon, or the first: Sir Giles Gilbert Scott preceded him to the exit by six months when the Commission initially objected to his designs for a new Waterloo Bridge. Kenneth Clark followed them in December 1951, unable to stomach the Commission's support for Basil Spence's Coventry Cathedral.[86]

But the rarity of these exceptions illustrates, more than anything, the success of chairmen in maintaining harmony and a collegiate spirit. When the Marquess of Anglesey resigned in 1971 – owing to the pressure of literary deadlines and the toll of repeated return journeys between Anglesey and London – he congratulated Sir Colin Anderson on 'so skilfully steering us through invariably difficult, often stormy and sometimes unfriendly waters': an acknowledgement of difficulties faced, but also the capacity to meet them.

A subsidiary laity was found in the ordinary membership. This lay dimension was usually seen as a strength; here were people who were not *parti pris*, offered a different visual perspective – almost literally, as Betjeman said, they saw things differently from architects – and were perhaps closer in perception to the man on the Clapham omnibus, who after all was and is the ultimate (and often involuntary) consumer of the architectural product. Sir Hugh Casson was among those who saw public relations value in that last point. Writing to Sir Colin Anderson in April 1971, he said

'I am often attacked at lectures all over the country on the subject of the Royal Fine Art Commission, the most difficult charge to answer being the very high proportion of practising architects who form its membership. Like you, I know the defensive noises that can be made, but I am bound to say that I think we are perhaps less enterprising than we could be in this respect. My own view is that the architects should be a majority, but only just.'

John Piper and David Piper – unrelated, the one an artist, the other an art historian – were fairly typical of the lay membership, in that they formed a kind of unofficial bulwark against architects. It was almost as if the architectural profession was seen, in a Shavian sense, as a conspiracy against the laity. In an eightieth birthday *festschrift* to John Piper in 1983, David Piper recalled the two of them sitting together on the Commission, 'consolidating satisfactorily a little block of Pipers that from time to time said no to architects'.[87]

A few laymen, such as the scientist Sir Thomas Merton, felt themselves unqualified to contribute to specialised discussions on architectural design. But not many. Most were fairly forthright, notably Curzon, who had been appointed to the Commission, right at the start, as a counterbalance to the architects and their supposedly cliquish tendencies. Only a month before his death in March 1925, prevented by ill-health from attending a meeting with the London County Council over the proposed demolition of Waterloo Bridge, he was using the columns of *The Times* to make a public plea for its retention: an extraordinary move given that the Commission

had been set up on the clear basis that it would speak only when invited, with the implication that discussions would take place *in camera* between public bodies rather than in the newspapers. But Curzon was already impatient with those limitations and frustrated by its obligation to stand by while currents of controversy swirled around. When the Commission offered no resistance to the proposed Artillery Memorial at Hyde Park Corner, Lord Curzon launched an independent howitzer of his own, saying that 'a thing of ugliness should not be allotted a place on one of the finest sites in London'.[88]

It was of course tempting for others to denigrate the lay membership, especially when it let loose like Curzon. That was so from the start but as time went on it became easier to caricature them as *belletrists* pontificating on increasingly technical matters, and in a less deferential world where the financial stakes were high there was far less compunction about doing so. They were particularly easy prey at public inquiries, owing to their lack of relevant professional expertise. A cameo from the Monico inquiry in 1960 illustrates the problem. The developers' Q.C., Sir Milner Holland, was cross-examining J.M. Richards, a qualified but not practising architect and at the time a Commissioner, though appearing for himself as a self-styled 'critic and writer':

Sir Milner Holland: 'You have not yourself designed a building of any kind?'
Mr. Richards said that he had not.
Sir Milner Holland: 'And you came here to give us a little lecture on your views about this building?'
'Yes.'
'Well, thank you very much for coming.' (Laughter).

As a theatrical debating point it had fleeting comic value, but most observers – and certainly the inquiry chairman, Sir Colin Buchanan – will have recognised in Richards a sensitive critic with a deep understanding of architecture.[89] Godfrey Samuel, who saw Richards perform monthly on Commission business, told Downing Street in 1958, in the course of a discussion on reappointments, that he was 'really good at giving worthwhile and sensible criticism on the architectural problems that come before us'. Other lay Commissioners had equally impressive credentials, the architectural historians Sir Nikolaus Pevsner and Sir John Summerson among them. There was, however, a clear need for sufficient professional expertise to cover the technical terrain, which grew and altered over time.

The earliest specialist requirement was in engineering. From the outset, when the Commission considered St. Paul's Bridge in 1924, the question arose of whether the Commission could sensibly assess the problem without expert engineering advice. And when Curzon challenged the conclusion of the London County Council engineers that Rennie's Waterloo Bridge could not be repaired or rebuilt, he had no colleagues on the Commission with the professional competence to back him up. The omission was eventually repaired when roads and bridges became such a staple of the Commission's work that it would have been absurd, and reputationally damaging, to have persisted without engineers. Not only did technical issues require technical expertise, but by the mid-twentieth century form was increasingly seen as following function; in that context, aesthetic questions could not be entirely separated from structural and functional ones. And, frankly, engineers by that time were having as much visual impact on Britain as architects. As the Commission itself put it in a 1959 statement on the relationship of motorways to landscapes, 'the outlook and achievements of Britain in this generation will be judged in no small measure by her major engineering works'. It added that 'it will be a grave indictment of the way the present opportunity is being handled if the new motorways fall short in any respect of the highest standards of which we are capable'. And to help on that front it recruited the finest structural

and later civil engineers. Admittedly it had to do without the stellar Ove Arup, blackballed by Downing Street on the grounds (pushed by the Institution of Civil Engineers) that the appointment of a foreign engineer would reflect ill on the ability of native English engineers – spurious grounds indeed as Arup was born in Newcastle, albeit to Scandinavian parents. But it did manage to recruit Sir Ralph Freeman, designer and engineer for Sydney Harbour Bridge;[90] Sir Alexander Gibb, consulting engineer for Rosyth Dockyard and the High Dam at Aswan; Sir William Halcrow, another Scots engineer with extensive global experience of major projects, from the Johore Causeway to Glen Affric hydroelectric project and the Bakerloo Line extension in London; and Sir Allan Quartermaine, Director-General of Aircraft Production in the Second World War and Chief Engineer to the Great Western Railway.

The Second War, indeed, was the decisive point at which the 'fine art' element was displaced by an almost exclusive focus on architecture and town planning; with the pressing concerns of rebuilding and the huge infrastructure demands, it could hardly have been otherwise. Sculptors retained a foothold[91] and there were periodic attempts to increase the number of painters – a series of distinguished correspondents including Augustus John, Bernard Shaw and Ralph Vaughan Williams advocated exactly that in *The Times* in 1945.[92] But those calls sounded more and more old-fashioned, as if lacking comprehension of the challenges ahead. The Commission, as we have seen, embraced those challenges even during the War via the appointment of planning experts such as Abercrombie, Holford and Hubert Worthington, in readiness for its new role supporting the Ministry of Town and Country Planning on post-war reconstruction. In a similar way, two property developers – Stuart Lipton and Trevor Osborne – were appointed in the 1980s to help the Commission cope at a time when it was presented with enormous private developments such as those at Canary Wharf and London Bridge City.

These specialists brought new and valuable perspectives, but the main business after 1945 was new architecture, and unsurprisingly architects took centre-stage. Some of them were very much accustomed to that position and almost matched Blomfield for combustibility, giving the Commission's successive chairmen a delicate task in managing internal dynamics. Basil Spence and Frederick Gibberd were opinionated and outspoken, and in the middle decades of the twentieth century were often at the forefront of public controversy on their own account, Gibberd for example writing to *The Times* in 1968 objecting to a proposed Tate Gallery extension which the Commission had already accepted. Inevitably, the convention of collective responsibility was sometimes stretched. The Commission depended on that convention to a degree but it could not enforce it absolutely; while it preferred architects to be team players, it had to accept that practitioners at the top of their game would not always be the most pliable of personalities.[93]

Nor were some of the non-architects, notably John Betjeman, a contrarian who was appallingly undiplomatic in his treatment of some fellow Commissioners, not least Nikolaus Pevsner, whom he lampooned as the 'Professor Doktor'. Betjeman required delicate handling, a task that fell mainly to Lord Bridges, who almost exhausted himself in the process. The two were horribly bad bedfellows: Bridges the brisk and solitary Treasury man who usually lunched alone at The Athenaeum and, as *The Times* said, 'gave the impression that much of the ordinary run of human converse came to him more by study than by instinct'; Betjeman the gregarious gadfly who took perverse pleasure in goading Bridges, accusing him of prolonging meetings to make him miss his train home and claiming he was too dismissive of Victorian architecture[94] – to which Bridges responded by reminding Betjeman that he was the grandson of one of the greatest of Victorian architects, Sir Alfred Waterhouse.[95] At times the relationship was strained to

breaking point: Bridges was especially riled by Betjeman's habit of leaking confidential information in his newspaper articles. 'I had a frank little talk with Mr. Betjeman', he records in a file note in 1959, 'and told him that on a number of occasions I had been left with the impression that he did not always pay very much attention to what was confidential. I think I shook him a bit'. In turn, Betjeman wrote to Bridges in March 1966 complaining of Bridges' 'rudeness' to him and his habit of 'brusquely dismissing' his suggestions.[96]

Ultimately the Commission wanted and needed these people. Men like Spence and Gibberd could be guaranteed to enrich the Commission's discussions and greatly increase the respect in which its conclusions were held. And Betjeman, however difficult, was tolerated for his brilliance. Tellingly, Bridges kept recommending him for reappointment, saying to Downing Street in 1967 that 'Betjeman is of course an individualist, but that has never worried me. His great service to the Commission is that he brings to our notice many instances where there is danger of damage being done to old buildings or small country towns up and down the country'. And indeed the Commission's files have plenty of more or less desperate pleas, passed on by Betjeman, from people seeking his support: from Spike Milligan wanting to save Brent Lodge in Finchley; from Lady Rathcreedan on behalf of Lady Agnes Syston of Mapledurham Park, which needed urgent repairs; from Robert Vernon Harcourt wanting help in stopping a women's prison from being built in the grounds of Hill Hall, near Epping.[97] At a time when it might easily have ceded the field to others, Betjeman did more than anyone to ensure that the cause of preserving historic buildings and places remained within the ambit of the Royal Fine Art Commission.

VIII | Thinking for itself

People needed to know that the Commission's conclusions represented the best impartial advice from open-minded experts. And so operational freedom, neutrality and a robust mechanism for dealing with the inevitable conflicts of interest were all needed to give the Commission its most essential attributes: independence of mind and independence of action.

Independence of mind

Avoidance of stylistic bias was a key factor in getting and keeping respect: the Commission would hardly have survived as an authoritative body had it been partisan. Its mantra, that design quality mattered far more than architectural style, sustained it well over the years. And quality was most likely to be achieved when all the elements in a building – height, bulk, alignment, scale, proportion, rhythm, texture and colour – were both internally coherent and responsive to their surroundings; in other words, quality had to do with intelligent layout, planning and contextual analysis as well as a pleasing external appearance. As the Commission itself said, 'this is not support for anodyne contextualism; rather it implies criticism of the architect who designs from the outside inwards, deciding on the style of a building before considering function and purpose, structure and materials and the appropriate use of technology'.

Such principles can seem glib and mechanical when set down in cold print, and indeed it is impossible to create or judge good architecture by following a checklist. Ideally,

though, application of those principles, allied to a good brief and a good architect, should make quality possible regardless of style, and Commissioners were chosen for their ability to discern it in whatever guise it came: an ability derived largely from an informed eye backed by judgement, skill, intuition and experience.

But of course individual Commissioners had their preferences; so too did the Commission's successive Secretaries, and as they were permanent fixtures wielding executive authority, and normally the ones who discussed schemes with outside clients and architects before the Commission itself reviewed them, their views were important. These preferences were often deducible from extra-curricular lectures, articles and other pronouncements, but they were not always as clear-cut or consistent as might have been supposed. As intellectually curious people, Commissioners were generally empiricists who followed evidence rather than dogma. For the engineers that was no less than a professional necessity, but it applied to architects and laymen too. Gibberd evolved over his career from functional modernism to a freer and more fluid language. Summerson could be a bag of apparent contradictions: an architectural historian who opposed conservation areas, a traditionalist who strongly supported the Mies tower proposed for Mansion House Square. Albert Richardson, though an anachronism who read eighteenth-century newspapers by candlelight, produced nuanced works, such as Bracken House in the City of London for *The Financial Times*, that were very far from copies of

Georgian prototypes. Frank Fielden, Secretary from 1968 to 1979, was intellectually sympathetic to functionalism but knew very well that it could lead to monotony; he was staunch, too, in resisting the vogue for tower blocks. And while his successor, Sherban Cantacuzino, leant towards modernism, that was hardly an exclusive world-view; he was also an early proponent of the sensitive reuse of old buildings, publishing on the subject long before it became fashionable, and he criticised the kind of architectural solipsism that disregarded context. 'Appropriate architecture', he told an R.I.B.A. conference in 1981, 'is mostly that which responds to what is already there'.

If individuals were rarely wedded to a single stance, it was even more likely that any two Commissioners would hold different opinions. Where Betjeman was an early champion of Victorian architecture, J.M. Richards took the more conventional mid-century view that it was 'intrinsically atrocious'. And for every occasion when an architect like Giles Gilbert Scott was dismissive of a modern approach – say for the new House of Commons, after it was bombed in the War – it would be possible to quote another architect saying more or less the opposite, such as Lord Llewelyn-Davies arguing in the House of Lords in 1964 against a proposed new extension to the Palace of Westminster in the Gothic style. 'Will Ministers bear in mind', he said, 'that the architecture of the new building should reflect the century in which we live?'

The Commission, then, was not just one body across time: it had changing priorities, attitudes and of course personnel. Insofar as it had a collective personality, that was not immutable; it stood outside neither time nor its own historical context. The founding Commissioners of the 1920s, schooled in traditional methods, tended to be reflexively conservative, none more so than Blomfield whose *Modernismus*, published in 1934, was a counterblast against what he saw as the visual horrors of much new architecture.[98] A later generation, prominent for about twenty-five years from the mid-1950s,

had their attitudes shaped by the Modern Movement; Sir Anthony Cox, a founder of the Architects' Co-Partnership and Commissioner from 1970, was one of its scions.[99] But it is also fair to say that the preferences of its individual members did not generally equate to institutional bias. It is possible for people to sublimate preferences and fairly judge the quality of others' work, even if they would never have produced it themselves. That is a mark of a refined critical faculty, and it was something of a job requirement for an effective Commissioner.

Whether it always came across like that on the outside is another matter. It often did not, although sometimes that stemmed from frustration that the Commission did not always say what people wanted to hear: conservationists might think it too pro-development one week, developers might think it too pro-conservation the next. In many ways those frustrations were evidence not of bias but rather the lack of it: a determination to treat each case on its merits.

If there was a stylistic refrain that ran through the Commission's pronouncements over the years, it was probably a marked preference for simplicity over complication and ostentation. Despite its supposed conservatism, which in architectural terms might have translated into a desire for ornament, this was evident early on, notably in its advice on bridges. The Commission sought as a rule to embrace lightness of structure and avoid the ponderous: 'greyhounds rather than elephants', as one commentator put it. It had a radical effect on the design of Chelsea Bridge in 1934, in an intervention that was widely seen as a success and exemplar:

'We recommended that it should be drastically simplified, as we felt that the structure should be notable for lightness; in fact we considered that its success would depend on the direct and unembarrassed expression of its purpose. We accordingly asked that certain architectural features not required for structural reasons should be

Opposite: Chelsea Bridge, designed by London County Council architects and opened in 1937 – a design radically simplified by the Commission, through whose influence the steel pylons were left unfaced with masonry. It was also a marked simplification on its Victorian predecessor, which was beginning to fail structurally by the 1920s but in the view of Sir Reginald Blomfield and others had always failed artistically: Blomfield said in 1921 that 'its travesty of Gothic architecture in cast iron, its bad construction and its text of *Gloria Deo in Excelsis* above the arch between the piers, are redolent of 1851, the year of the Great Exhibition, the *locus classicus* of bad art, false enthusiasms and shams.' *(Architectural Press Archive/RIBA Collections)*

avoided. We urged that it was unnecessary to cloak the steel pylons with masonry. In our opinion the result has fully justified our representation.'[100]

The Times, reporting approvingly, said that 'most people who have really looked at one of the best bridges in London will cordially agree with the Commission; and, allowing for differences of purpose, 'the direct and unembarrassed expression of its purpose' might well be adopted as a slogan when any proposed structure comes up for consideration'. Similarly, the Commission forced a drastic reworking of the bridge at Richmond-upon-Thames in 1929, after the Ministry of Transport had approved it. The architect, Maxwell Ayrton, had designed a vaguely fortified structure with four 70ft towers, which some thought 'snarled like sentinels at the peaceful scene below'. Under pressure from the Commission, Ayrton first omitted the towers on the Surrey side, then cut their height on the Middlesex side; finally he omitted all the towers, having sensibly concluded that leaving two stunted towers as a kind of afterthought had little to commend it in logic, looks or utility. *The Manchester Guardian* thought it 'one of the first important signs that the Royal Fine Art Commission is actually influencing the country', a rather backhanded compliment that suggested impatience at the slow headway being made, but a compliment nonetheless. By the mid-1930s, indeed, designers and decision-makers had definitely got the message, partly because Crawford had driven it home with the Transport Minister, Leslie Hore-Belisha, telling him in January 1935 that

'there is a popular misconception (which flourishes to this day) that having designed the bridge, there is 'plenty of scope for architectural treatment'. We read that the bridge at Datchet was enriched with squared rubble towers 'to avoid conflict with the Norman architectural surroundings'.[101] *These illustrate difficulties encountered*

by the Royal Commission, based on the fundamental error of thinking that a bridge should be embellished by superimposing architectural features...When the engineer tries to make 'something worthy', the result is generally bad'.

Hore-Belisha was persuaded to reissue a design circular first published in 1925, but to strengthen it by specifying that works financed through the Government's Road Fund would need, as a condition of funding, to exhibit 'well-proportioned simplicity' rather than 'undue elaboration'. Wandsworth Bridge, designed later in 1935, was one of the first bridges to emerge under the new dispensation. The local authority congratulated itself that the Commission had 'expressed approval in warmer terms than was customary' for a bridge that was, indeed, notably devoid of curlicues.

The Commission also consistently argued for simplicity in the design of power stations, where it deplored the tendency to aggrandise them into *ersatz* cathedrals – its main negative comment on Bankside was that it represented 'a departure in some respects from the principles put forward by the Commission, that the utilitarian functions of such a building should predominate'. When, in 1948, it produced guidance for architects employed by the Central Electricity Authority, it emphasised that 'designs should be based on clear functional expression... The temptation to give the larger elements of a power station a heavy monumental character more suited to places of public assembly should be avoided'.

Nuclear power stations presented different design problems – for operational and safety reasons they were usually sited on remote (and scenic) coasts – but here again the Commission advised plain and simple treatments, arguing that as these buildings, unlike cathedrals, had no emotional significance, to monumentalise them was to debase the currency of architectural values and to run the risk of making them ridiculous. Architecture should not, it thought, be applied to a structure in order to titivate the work of engineers. It had allies in this. In *The Observer* in March 1957, Robert Furneaux Jordan noted of the proposed nuclear power station at Trawsfynydd that 'there are ominous signs that in order to harmonise with the landscape, a little architecture – vaguely Egyptian – is already being prepared to drape around the reactors'. The Ministry of Fuel and Power pounced on what it saw as an opportunity for economy: whereas to the Commission monumentality might have equated to bombast, to the Government it meant extravagance. The Ministry set up a committee under Sir Hugh Beaver to articulate its vision of a pared-down civil engineering and building programme. The Commission was roped in as an expert witness, its plea to avoid monumentality quoted in support of the new policy of economising – which in practice, according to the Ministry, meant more functional designs, the avoidance of brick except where necessary and the use of asbestos as a cladding material: its light grey tones, it thought, would harmonise best with British landscapes.

Part of the point about simplicity was that it made people think harder about design. There was nothing wrong with ornament in itself (although some of the more doctrinaire functionalists might have thought so) but it could be used as camouflage for muddled thinking, a means of distracting attention from weak design. And simplicity, in the Commission's view, could be applied across architectural styles.[102] It did not, therefore, prevent the Commission from taking a latitudinarian approach to style, of the kind shown early on when, in 1926, it recommended that the architects extending Ewan Christian's National Portrait Gallery and Waterhouse's Natural History Museum should 'feel free to make additions according to their own ideas'.

Nonetheless, the Commission could hardly avoid being caught in the style wars of the latter half of the twentieth century, when skirmishes were fought between what might crudely be called progressives and reactionaries. In the 1950s, it was accused in some quarters of being at the centre of a modernist nexus, but accusations are easy to fling around. The wider world tended to obsess about bias, but for each occasion the Commission pushed for modernity (not necessarily the same thing as modernism) there are counterbalancing instances. In 1955 it persuaded the Minister of Works, Nigel Birch, to have the British Embassy in Washington extended in a contemporary idiom, rather than in the Queen Anne style used by Lutyens for the main embassy building;[103] but at the same time it was perfectly capable of welcoming historicist designs from classical architects, such as Albert Richardson's extension to Samuel Wyatt's Trinity House at Tower Hill. And Richardson himself was the polar opposite of a modernist: his distaste for its products (some of them, to be fair, debased products) was never far from the surface: its offices were 'expressionless concrete containers' and its schools 'mere incubators', to quote two of his milder descriptions. His retirement in 1956, to be replaced with Basil Spence, shifted the balance slightly, but that was soon redressed by the appointment of Raymond Erith, one of the most able classicists of the twentieth century.

Indeed, until the late 1950s, the Commission was just as likely to be regarded as a force for conservatism. Hugh Dalton, when Attlee's Planning Minister, certainly took this view (and as we shall see he tried hard to do something about it by manipulating the composition of the Commission). So too, up to a point, did Dame Evelyn Sharp, the civil servant responsible for planning from the mid-1950s, who said in 1957 that 'I am so afraid that with this control, even by the highest in the land – I refer to the Royal Fine Art Commission – we are repressing all experiment and excitement in architecture'. A year later, *The Manchester Guardian* was remarking that the Commission 'may be overweighted on the side of the traditional and the familiar'. As if to make the point, the Commission then reviewed plans for Southwark Roman Catholic Cathedral, bombed in 1941, and recommended scholarly reconstruction after the 1840s designs by A.W.N. Pugin.

The power struggle in the wider world between modernists and traditionalists intensified in the 1960s, and again the Commission could hardly be insulated. 'I am conscious of more than one rift in our midst', said Sir Colin Anderson to Bridges in 1962, remarking on 'a resentment burning in Erith's breast against the doctrinaire assumptions of the *Architectural Review* set, Richards in particular'. Donald McMorran, a friend of Erith's and almost his equal as a classical architect, was worried enough to intercede on his behalf, telling Bridges in August 1962 that Erith had been distressed by an attack on his work in *The Architectural Review:* 'the Richards group fear Erith's integrity and would go to some lengths to suppress him: their methods seem questionable and in Erith's case I find them intolerable because he is one of the best architects we shall ever have'. By this time, Spence had been joined on the Commission by Hugh Casson and Leslie Martin: Godfrey Samuel called them 'the moderns', although that was evident more in a shared outlook than in concerted action. There was, nonetheless, a serious risk of divisions deepening into schism. Bridges was understandably keen to avoid that: 'it would be a very sad thing for all of us', he said, if 'the silly and damaging gaps' that were evident elsewhere infected the Commission.

The Guardian[104] half-jokingly implied that the two camps had achieved a kind of equilibrium to the point where they neutralised each other, noting 'the splendid impartiality that comes from the fact that Professor Holford and Mr. Betjeman are members'. And indeed the Commissioners with the best attendance records in the 1960s formed a remarkably balanced group: perhaps they felt impelled to attend in order to keep an eye on each other. Between May 1964 and November 1968, Anderson, *de facto* deputy to Bridges, attended forty-six

of fifty-one full Commission meetings, as well as thirty-five of forty-nine meetings of the technical committee, by now rechristened the examination committee and admitting laymen. He was followed closely by Esher, Erith, Holford, Gibberd, John Piper and Casson.[105]

In general, though, the Commission remained as ecumenical as its membership, scrupulously working to improve projects regardless of designer. In 1963 it amended and then commended a design by Denys Lasdun for a monumental new building in Parliament Square for the Royal Institution of Chartered Surveyors, to replace its old headquarters building by Alfred Waterhouse.[106] But equally, and in spite of Richards, it supported Erith's design for Jack Straw's Castle, a proposed public house on Hampstead Heath that provoked noisy opposition from Hampstead Borough Council, which objected to what it called the 'old-fashioned, pseudo-historic front elevation, and particularly to the wooden battlements'. Erith replied that he thought any public house with the word 'castle' in its name should embody a feature instantly recognizable as belonging to a castle, hence the crenellations. From a distance of almost sixty years the Commission's positive attitude looks far-sighted; although sadly no longer a public house, the building has grown into its role as an appealing *jeu d'esprit*.

As the centre of gravity shifted towards conservation in the 1970s, and the world around it moved, the Commission could seem less traditionalist in its sympathies even though its essential objectivity was unchanged. And with a growing tendency towards partisan lobbying, the Commission could find itself pilloried for taking a dispassionate view based on an informed assessment of merits. By the 1980s, it was more and more difficult to chart a steady course amid a stylistic pluralism that at times seemed to border on anarchy; there was nothing so simple any more as a binary choice.

The word 'pastiche', pejoratively used, crept into discourse until it became almost meaningless, a catch-all denunciation

Opposite: Denys Lasdun's (unbuilt) scheme from 1962 for the Royal Institution of Chartered Surveyors in Parliament Square, a notably bold architectural approach for a building sitting alongside Westminster Abbey, the Palace of Westminster and St. Margaret's Church. The Royal Fine Art Commission supported the scheme, as it did Lasdun's equally uncompromising design (now Grade I listed) for the Royal College of Physicians in The Regent's Park. *(Lasdun Archive/RIBA Collections)*

of anything that appeared historicist; to the point where the Commission, finding its use tiresome, defined it as the illiterate misapplication of precedent (as opposed to scholarly reproduction or interpretation). In this confusing cacophony, arguments about style became a kind of substitute for considered debate on merits. And abusive soundbites increasingly passed for architectural criticism.

Nonetheless, it was still possible even in the 1990s to hear respected commentators say, or imply, that the Commission was a modernist cabal, albeit an increasingly decrepit one. 'Most of them have their roots in modernism', Terry Farrell was quoted by *The Observer* as saying in June 1991 after criticism of his Paternoster Square scheme. And Deyan Sudjic, also in *The Observer* in 1994, suggested that the Commission was still dominated at that point by modernist architects touting ideas from the 1960s. This was stretching a point by the mid-1990s, becoming almost a parody of an argument that might once have been half-valid, but in 1994 the Major Government seemed implicitly to acknowledge the problem, even if it was only a presentational one, by appointing two noted traditionalists in Quinlan Terry and Giles Worsley. The preferred solution seemed to be not to excise stylistic preferences – rightly, as it would have been futile – but as before to neuter them with equal and opposite ones.

Operational Independence

A key (and unique) ingredient of the Commission's work was disinterested appraisal untainted by economic or other ulterior motives, its legitimacy derived from Royal Warrants and not from the Government of the day.

Did it actually work like this? How independent of a paymaster is it possible to be? Evidence of freedom of action lies to some extent in a willingness to disagree, privately and publicly, with the Government; and as the Government was a major architectural patron in the post-war years of extensive state control, opportunities for disagreement were plentiful.

The Commission was prepared to be hard-hitting with Government departments where necessary, well beyond the point of making things awkward. In 1955, the Ministry of Works was deeply irritated when the Commission continued to press in public for revisions to a block of seafront flats in Dover, even after the Government had intervened to do the Commission's bidding and cut the height from fourteen to nine storeys. Internally, civil servants described the Commission's behaviour as 'a backhander and rather discourteous in view of the fact that every practical step has been taken to meet their wishes'. But there was little that they could do. In 1957, Dame Evelyn Sharp protested to Lord Bridges, just installed as chairman, that her Ministry of Housing and Local Government 'deserved the full support of the Commission' and that it was 'disheartening when we march breast forward into battle for amenities to find ourselves stabbed by our friends'. The occasion for this outburst was a proposed Government amendment to the Advertisement Regulations to introduce areas of special control. Sharp saw this as a positive tightening of controls in sensitive areas but the Commission chose to interpret it as a relative loosening of controls elsewhere, creating a two-tier system with some prettified ghettos and everywhere else left prey to advertising blight. Sharp considered this bizarre in its ramifications: 'of course strict controls might be applied in Bath but not in shopping or industrial areas', she said. Bridges, who a few weeks earlier, as Head of the Home Civil Service, had been Sharp's superior, calmed things down, but the point was made that the Commission was there to think its own thoughts, not to await instruction.

Its determination on that front was just as evident in the 1960s, exemplified say by its robust opposition to a 300ft telephone exchange proposed in 1969 for a site between two historic quarters in the middle of Bristol. The Government had resisted a decentralised location on cost grounds, but the Commission reminded it of the unquantified but significant cost of 'sterilising valuable central space with a pile of machinery'. It went further and challenged the advice of the city engineer, on which the Bristol Corporation had relied in giving the scheme permission. Having established that all the switch gear could in fact be put in a low building, it told the Minister of Public Buildings and Works (at the time, John Silkin) that there was 'no need at all for a distinguished area of Bristol to become dominated by an architectural monument devoted to telephone equipment'.

On several other occasions, the Commission took a radically different position from both Conservative and Labour Governments: on the Euston Arch, New Zealand House, the Imperial Institute, Bucklersbury House, Knightsbridge Barracks, the Park Lane Hilton and the Cutler Street Warehouses near Petticoat Lane, to give a flavour of what could be a very long list. As that list also shows, the Commission was far from guaranteed to get its way. Governments naturally found it easier to back the Commission when it supported a development scheme; Sir Keith Joseph did so several times, twice in quick succession in 1964 over Holford's Paternoster Square and a scheme to reconfigure the Guildhall forecourt. But where aesthetic and amenity considerations clashed with economic ones, the latter usually won, leading a frustrated Woodrow Wyatt, in 1960, to ask the Prime Minister to appoint a Minister with responsibility for implementing the recommendations of the Royal Fine Art Commission.[107] As a yardstick of independence, though, the end result was less telling than the argument that preceded it.

Governments could, however, try to rein in the Commission when they felt it was straying beyond its remit. Some civil servants took the untenable view that the Commission should confine itself to comments on the external appearance of buildings, steering clear of matters such as siting, massing,

height and plot ratio; the first was a question of amenity but the latter were planning matters. Entire Whitehall files are filled with agonising on the matter, but sensibly the Commission ignored such distinctions. Impossible to ignore, though, was the fact that Governments controlled appointments to the Commission. They exerted that control with varying degrees of intensity across the years, ranging from a nominal interest at times to a very close one at others. This was not necessarily the arrangement envisaged at the outset, when *The Times* reported that 'the Commission itself will submit to the King the names of those whom it suggests for election or re-election'. That would indeed have been a genuine mark of independence, cutting out an intermediate stage of consultation with the Government. But in practice the convention was soon followed that appointments were made formally by the Sovereign on the advice of his Prime Minister, and usually those recommendations came after discussions between the Commission and Downing Street staff.

In turn, although the practice fell off after about 1970, Downing Street consulted the spending departments – a curious practice, as it was exactly those departments that could expect to have their capital projects appraised by the Commission and might, therefore, be conflicted in commenting on candidates for membership. Departments were not usually so brazen that they openly exploited this opportunity, and indeed if they jockeyed for position they quite often cancelled each other out, as Downing Street noted with wry amusement: 'the problem with these Royal Fine Art Commission appointments', said Churchill's Private Secretary Sir Anthony Bevir in 1955, 'is that people whom the Ministry of Works like, the Ministry of Housing are apt to mistrust and vice-versa and there is generally a triangular argument'. And of course Downing Street itself had an interest in stopping departmental aggrandisement; it is notable that Bevir had been keen on Sir Alan Lascelles succeeding Crawford as the

Commission's chairman for the simple reason that, as he put it, 'he could be relied upon to take a firm line against pressure from departments and other interests'.

Departments did not just react to names put forward by the Commission or Downing Street. Very often they suggested their own. Dame Evelyn Sharp was especially prone to this, and indeed vocal on any names that came before her.[108] Ironically, she did her utmost to veto her namesake Thomas Sharp, the distinguished town planner, telling Downing Street that 'the Commission would find him a very difficult colleague. It is a pity because he is a person of great knowledge, taste and discrimination but he has never been able to endure a difference of opinion'. And in 1965 the Ministry of Works suggested that Sir Edward Muir, who had just retired as its Permanent Secretary, be appointed to the Commission to succeed Sir Edward Playfair, who had been Permanent Secretary at the Ministry of Defence. It might have seemed a straight swap, but Bridges vetoed it on the grounds that 'much of the work of the Commission consists in examining and often criticising the designs of buildings put forward by the Ministry of Works'. Muir, he thought, would not be sufficiently disinterested.

At times the annual appointments round led to squabbles as the Commission resisted attempts by the Government to saddle it with people it saw as unsuitable. More often than not the process lacked any discernible logic, with names coming and going seemingly at random, but occasionally Ministers had an underlying strategy. Labour ones in particular wanted to push the Commission towards a less traditionalist stance. Its emasculation of Maxwell Ayrton's designs for Richmond Bridge rankled with Herbert Morrison, who told Ramsay MacDonald that the Commission 'may sometimes be inclined to play for safety and discourage innovations without which architectural design petrifies into formalism. A too conservative outlook of this sort would be a mistake on the part of a progressive government'. Attlee's Government was even keener to try to

steer the Commission. In 1948 the Treasury vetoed Crawford's suggestion of Sir Lancelot Keay, Liverpool City Architect and former President of the Royal Institute of British Architects, on the grounds that he had 'gone out of his way to set himself up as the leader of the reactionaries in the architectural profession'. When Frederick Gibberd was nominated in 1950, his candidacy was bizarrely referred to the Chancellor of the Exchequer, Sir Stafford Cripps, for approval.

But it was Cripps' predecessor as Chancellor, Hugh Dalton, who was most interventionist, taking an active interest for example in who succeeded Maxwell Fry when he stepped down in 1951 to join Corbusier in designing Chandigarh in India. Like Morrison before him, he characterised the choice as one between traditionalists and modernists, and totted up who on the Commission belonged where: Fry, Gibberd and Holford he counted as modernists; Louis de Soissons, Edward Maufe, Albert Richardson and John Summerson he put in the traditionalist camp. In his view, then, the balance needed to be redressed with another modernist, and on that account he vetoed both Crawford's first choice of Harry Goodhart Rendel and the Ministry of Works' preferred candidate, Sir Howard Robertson, whom he dismissed as 'a very uninteresting traditionalist'. Instead he pushed the claims of the young architect Lionel Brett, fresh from designing housing in Harlow New Town and, Dalton thought, 'much interested in new ideas and techniques of construction'. Crawford resisted, thinking Brett 'unripe and too fashionable'. At this point Downing Street stepped in and asked the Prime Minister to settle the matter, believing he would back Crawford. But Dalton got in first. As Sir Edward Playfair described it, 'Dalton went to see Attlee and talked him round to appointing Brett. The Prime Minister then saw Lord Crawford who failed to talk him back again'. Brett it was.

Alongside these heavyweight wrestling bouts where the balance of the Commission was at stake, there were lesser skirmishes which sometimes shaded into comic absurdity.

'I suspect No. 10 do not fully appreciate the difference between an interest in painting and sculpture and an interest in architecture and planning', said Godfrey Samuel to Bridges in 1965 after Downing Street had suggested Evelyn de Rothschild on the grounds that he was 'said to have a sensitive appreciation of the Arts'. Three years later, the Treasury – which exercised a shadowy influence throughout the Commission's life, by no means only on financial matters – thought it would chip in with suggestions for engineer Commissioners. It already had form in the area of wayward judgements, having in 1954 written off the eminent engineer Sir Allan Quartermaine as a 'railway-bridge man' – to which Crawford replied with a scribbled 'cf. Brunel'. But now it excelled itself by putting forward two people called A.J. Harris and P.J. Barker, recommending the latter as someone 'interested in music'. Anderson of course was exasperated. 'I do not want to dampen their ardour', he wrote to Samuel, 'but I must somehow indicate to them how we come by an engineer member, which is certainly not by appointing unknown gentlemen who are passionate about music'. Anderson also blackballed the sculptor Oscar Nemon as a replacement for Henry Moore when he was finally allowed to retire in 1971. Nemon's name had emerged from discussions between Downing Street and what were always referred to, in slightly Orwellian terms, as 'The Departments'. Anderson was having none of it. 'Can you beat it?', he said to Moore. 'Over my dead body, I need hardly say'. He told Downing Street that Nemon's work was 'poor stuff, sadly lacking in either distinction or originality'. The appointment would 'arouse derision'. No more was heard of it.

He was even more bullish over Duncan Sandys, the subject of a fierce row in 1971 when Sandys, then Member of Parliament for Streatham, was pushed hard as a candidate by Julian Amery, Minister of Housing and Construction under Edward Heath. To Anderson, this smacked of a direct attempt to politicise the Commission. He believed Amery wanted a

Conservative; and Downing Street officials confirmed this in private conversations, telling Anderson that 'no-one, no matter how brilliant, will be acceptable to the present Government unless he is a declared Tory supporter'. Their under-the-counter advice was to try to trump Sandys with a superior Conservative; and thus the Duke of Grafton, wholly unwittingly, became the stop-Sandys candidate. But Amery refused to back down. The *dénouement* was a meeting between Anderson and Amery at the Department of the Environment on 8 October 1971, which degenerated on Amery's side into a rant against the Commission. Anderson reported it in a file note:

> *'Amery claimed, incorrectly, that it was his function to advise the Prime Minister on appointments to the Commission. He pressed the claims of Sandys and asked why I objected. I said if a Conservative was appointed why not nominees from other parties? Amery said Sandys had fought almost alone for St. Paul's after the War to try to save it from office developments which Amery considered should never have been allowed. 'Why had the Commission been so supine? Why had it not stopped these developments?' I said it had no powers. 'Why had we not resigned?' I said I didn't think that was a recipe that would have cut much ice – but that we had done our job by protesting against the quality of the buildings. Amery also defended Nemon. He said we did not seem to have a balanced representation of opinions on such matters in the Commission. I said it was not the aim to have a Commission representing untrained as well as trained taste. After more of this sort of thing he said he would have to put the matter to the Prime Minister, who might well reject the Commission's views.'*

Anderson relayed this conversation to Downing Street on the same day and asked officials to explain his point of view to the

Prime Minister, if possible before Amery saw him. Later that day, Anderson was telephoned by Robert Armstrong, the Prime Minister's Private Secretary, who had spoken to the Prime Minister and found him opposed to appointing a Member of Parliament. However relieved Anderson was by this immediate outcome, he still pressed the wider point, saying that the attempt to pack the Commission had been an ill omen. Armstrong replied that Amery 'would have to learn his place and that this rebuff ought to be a very salutary one'. After all this, the Duke of Grafton was appointed.

A milder spat occurred in 1985 when the Commission was told by Downing Street that Margaret Thatcher had offered the chairmanship of the Commission to Lady Soames, ironically Duncan Sandys's sister-in-law.[109] This was presented as a *fait accompli*, but Sherban Cantacuzino telephoned Downing Street to say that the Commission 'strongly objected to someone being approached without our being consulted or even alerted beforehand'. In the event Soames fell out of the picture, to be replaced as favourite by Sir John Boynton, former Chief Executive of Cheshire County Council. Since he had also overseen the Rhodesian elections of 1980, under the Governorship of Lord Soames, it is conceivable that the suggestion came from Lady Soames. At any rate that too came to nothing; and in June 1985 Downing Street wrote again to say that 'the Prime Minister has decided to offer membership, and subsequently the chairmanship, to Norman St. John-Stevas'. This again was seen by the Commission as a quasi-political appointment, but the outgoing chairman, Sir Derman Christopherson, was not inclined to resist. 'N.S.J. has had a long experience of artistic matters', he told Cantacuzino, 'and obviously cares a lot about them. He is a public figure whose statements attract public attention and respect. The only ground on which we could oppose the appointment is that we do not want anyone who would be seen as a 'political' appointment. To oppose it on that ground alone

would, it seems to me, probably produce a confrontation with Downing Street. The end result might be that N.S.J. would refuse the offer, and we might be landed with a much less qualified politician.'

The Commission of course had its own thoughts across the years on who might be suitable for membership, and far more suggestions came from the inside than from without. The archives have plenty of longlists annotated in manuscript, names struck through and others added, marks of enthusiasm and the occasional gruff veto, other names that are pushed forward hopefully year after year but never quite pass muster. Into that last category comes Anthony Blunt, an alarming prospect in retrospect but an obvious candidate at the time. 'Too busy', scribbled Bridges, with unwitting irony. The Commission's chairmen were adept at identifying a certain something, not quite definable, that made them hesitate. Temperament was key: could they be collegiate and rise above their personal preferences? Some outlandish suggestions were ruled out on that account, notably Tom Driberg[110] and Ian Nairn, who was accused by Anderson of having 'the hairy romantic approach'. Others who flickered on the radar were Osbert Sitwell, Lord Snowdon, Clough Williams-Ellis and Donald McMorran. In hindsight it is often hard to discern a unifying logic, although Frank Fielden told Deyan Sudjic in 1979 that 'we have had some difficulty in the past with people who were too committed to one side or another. These days people who are considered too young or likely to rock the boat tend not to get appointed'.[111]

Rarely, it was the candidate himself who refused. In 1965, Robert Sainsbury turned down Harold Wilson's invitation to join, explaining that 'with my particular knowledge and experience I would not be able to make a worthwhile contribution'. Wilson was then left to appoint the Marquess of Anglesey, whom Bridges had placed above Sainsbury in his list of preferred candidates. Denys Lasdun, having been privately blackballed by Bridges as a likely dissident ('it would be quite fatal to appoint him', he told Downing Street), was then rehabilitated by Anderson and offered a place in 1969, but declined because he thought he could best make a contribution to the built environment by designing it himself: no false modesty there. It was another way of saying, perhaps, that he was a creator rather than a critic, and it was for that same reason that the architect Edward Cullinan also declined – at first, though he later relented. Writing to Sherban Cantacuzino in 1985, rather impressively from 'Kennedy Airport', Cullinan said that

> 'I am rather a poor judge of buildings that are inspired by different criteria to my own. I am afraid that I would either say 'yes' to them all or try to turn them all into my own: two most undesirable extremes. I now realise I am repeating the old argument that says that a 'doer' should not also be a 'critic', but I do sincerely hold to that view... The Commission does first-class work and I have reason to be very grateful for its insight, but I do look forward to the day when intelligent laymen with an interest in the Art of Architecture become both our critics and supporters, rather than the practitioners also being the critics.'

As those last words imply, it was a fairly closed world, and not just where the architects were concerned. Some detected in the Commission's composition, and thus its mindset, a kind of unconscious establishment bias. And of course it was part of the establishment, especially early on when strong bonds of friendship and even kinship linked the Commission with Parliament and the Civil Service, offering a closeness to and affinity with decision-makers that unquestionably oiled wheels. It meant that its voice was heard, and heard respectfully; and it allowed the kind of candour that is sometimes possible only between friends. The fact that Crawford could dash off a note

to his relative 'Bobbety' Salisbury, and that Bridges was on terms of easy intimacy with Evelyn Sharp, added to the Commission's influence. And the fact that serving Commissioners often recommended other candidates – Llewelyn-Davies was suggested by Leslie Martin, for example – helped the Commission recruit critics who were respected by their peers.

But even so it was always a cudgel that others could take up, particularly from the 1970s when such apparent incestuousness was frowned upon. A 1981 *Spectator* review of *A Broken Wave* by Lord Esher caught that mood when it noted 'the powerful intellectual establishment which has dominated and controlled the appearance of Britain since 1945; modern architects and planners who have exploited the nexus of patronage and influence created by such bodies as the Royal Fine Art Commission'. It identified Esher, a former Commissioner, as 'a central figure in this world. The names of the members of this establishment, all so committed, so charming, all apparently friends of the author, recur like a litany throughout his book'. Three of those it picked out – Sir Leslie Martin, Lord Holford and Sir Hugh Casson – had served on the Commission alongside Esher.

It was easy then for critics to paint the Commission as a mutual appreciation society, its members preening each other in pursuit of the next big job. And it is clear that some interventions by the Commission did indeed lead directly to work for Commissioners, especially when it advised, as it often did, that a consultant architect should be engaged. For anyone receiving that advice, the obvious person to go to was a serving Commissioner; aside from his eminence, he was already familiar with the scheme and had thought about it in detail. And, whether justified or not, an outsider might well gamble that the Commission would be indulgent towards the work of one of its own, so giving the project a smoother ride. Thus when the Commission advised Brighton to engage a consultant architect to draw up a comprehensive plan for central redevelopment, the council offered the job to Sir Hugh Casson. At the Monico site, where the Commission objected to the developers' piecemeal approach, a final comprehensive plan was produced by Sir William Holford. After it forced the abandonment of the first scheme for the Regent's Park Mosque in 1964, the (Muslim) architect was replaced with Sir Frederick Gibberd, who was also the beneficiary when the Commission objected to Howard Lobb and Partners' designs for the British Council building near Trafalgar Square in 1969; the Commission welcomed Gibberd's replacement scheme. In 1992, after the Commission had pressured the Inland Revenue into holding an architectural competition for its Nottingham Headquarters, Sir Michael Hopkins got the job.

The Guardian was among those who saw all this as a back-scratching exercise, saying in 1972 in the context of the Spence's Home Office building, which the Commission had finally come round to accepting, that 'the Royal Fine Art Commission was hardly likely to criticise the architectural quality, in any circumstances. At least half of its members are practising architects and, at the time the building was considered, Sir Basil was himself a member'. It quoted an anonymous architect as complaining that 'people were hardly likely to criticise him, when their own designs might be coming up for discussion the following week'.

Lord Esher himself addressed these perceptions in 1970, in his article in The Times shortly after he had left the Commission.[112]

'Inevitably, I suppose, suggestions are made that the work of the Commission's architect members goes through with sinister ease. It is, of course, looked at in their absence and criticized with relish. But it is true that it generally gets built one way or another, and for two obvious reasons. One is that it is not easy to divert the leading members of any profession from what they believe to be right and are determined to do. Another is that their designs are sometimes quite good. Even so, one has heard it suggested that to ensure absolute justice no architects, or perhaps no architects whose designs are likely to need to be considered, should serve.[113] The short answer to this is that it would be very difficult to find enough acceptable persons willing and able to give as many man-hours,[114] and that even if one could, neither the planning authorities nor the architects who submit projects, nor perhaps the public, would regard such a body as authoritative.'

And those were fair points. If Commissioners were indeed prone to mutual admiration, it may be said in response that there was a great deal to admire. And if Commissioners were the best architects, as the public had a right to expect them to be, it is fair to assume that they would produce if not always the best work then certainly work of a consistently high standard. Spence's Home Office and Hopkins' Inland Revenue building are, on any objective assessment, powerful and rigorous buildings that become more impressive with time. The praise that went back and forth was more a logical outcome than a deliberate strategy; it might even be said that the Commission showed a commendable fearlessness and dedication to the pursuit of merit in praising its own members regardless of how it might seem to others.

In truth it was no particular respecter of reputations.[115] And there were some who subscribed to a counter-argument, probably also suspect, that Commissioners were set higher hurdles because the Commission overcompensated in an effort to appear impartial. Gillian Darley, writing a sympathetic profile of Stuart Lipton in The Guardian in 1992, notes that he had to 'step outside while his fellow Commissioners gave his Ludgate Place development a rough ride'. But here as elsewhere the interpretation that comes closest to the truth is probably the simplest one, that Commissioners criticised where criticism was due and offered praise where praise was due.

IX | Drawing to a close

Towards the end of the twentieth century, all those climatic changes which made the Commission's life harder were threatening to cause an existential crisis.

There was less willingness (not least among architects) to defer to a commission of great men. Frustration had always been there – an unnamed architect is quoted in *The Manchester Guardian* as far back as 1933 as saying the Commission was a 'great bugbear… The undercurrent of discontent seems to be flowing more swiftly than ever before'. But the anonymity is itself telling – this was not a charge to be made openly. By contrast, the brilliant, pugnacious egotists of the post-war period, like Spence and Lasdun, were never likely to appear before the Commission as supplicants. They tended to be assured of their own rightness – and often they were right. As *The Guardian* in 1990 said in an article entitled *La Poesie Concrète*, 'What people like Lasdun got from Le Corbusier was not only a concern with volumetrics, but the disease of conceit'. By the 1990s, other architects were also willing to fight back, and publicly. In 1994, Marks Barfield did so, successfully, when faced with the Commission's opposition to the Millennium Wheel, now known as the London Eye.

The later twentieth century also saw a philosophical shift to small government and a shrinking state; whereas in 1934 *The Manchester Guardian* could confidently proclaim that 'art as well as industry is a daily concern of the State', such an assertion would have seemed peculiarly old-fashioned under Margaret Thatcher. In that sense, the Commission was a relic of a corporatist world: in spite of itself, it was at home under *dirigisme*, nationalisation and the Butskellist settlement of the post-war years; and by contrast rather lost in the *laissez-faire*, socially-fractured world ushered in from the late 1970s. The Commission was easily written off as a captious, pernickety critic, fiddling with finials while London burned, as parts of it literally did in the Brixton riots of 1981. However deeply unfair – it was always aware of the social dimension of architecture and its role in improving quality of life – this was still a perceptual problem.

That suggests another difficulty, that of failing to get its message across. The Commission was a *naif* in the dark arts of propaganda, of building up a fund of goodwill as an insurance in lean times. An unwillingness to explain itself was noticed as far back as 1953, when *The Manchester Guardian* noted that the Commission's eleventh report

'occupies a mere three and a half pages. The appendix, giving a list of matters which have been before the Commission in 1952, is more impressive than the report. It leaps from the development plans of Anglesey to the state of Cannon Street Station, from plaques on historic buildings at Abingdon to a veterinary school at Cambridge, from Wadham College, Oxford, to Shed 102 at Southampton Docks. What is missing is any detailed description of what the Commission had to consider and what it concluded. The report itself is an example of the most uninformative Civil Service prose.'

On the whole its failure to communicate effectively came from a noble desire to remain above the fray, to be sober and measured come what may, but it meant that at critical times there were few people to step in to defend it, least of all perhaps those who had suffered its strictures.

Another criticism, made by Alan Powers in *The Spectator* in October 1998, was that it never colonised new territory. This is not wholly true. In fact visual education was a recurrent concern, though never formally part of its remit. It recognised that it would always be engaged in a Sisyphean labour if it tried to improve bad designs; far better that the public should demand good design, clients commission it, architects produce it and planners recognise it. As *The Times* put it in 1950, 'a community tends to get the lamp posts it deserves'. Lord St. John of Fawsley grasped this in 1987 when he set up The Royal Fine Art Commission Trust, an allied charity with the aim of improving visual literacy among the public.[116] The Commission was also willing to be inductive, to extrapolate lessons from its particular experience – and few bodies had as much collective experience of architecture and the built environment. Conference proceedings and advisory circulars were published throughout the later 1980s and 1990s, covering topics such as the design education of engineers and the design of university buildings and speculative housing. And in 1994 Sherban Cantacuzino distilled its thinking in a treatise entitled *What Makes a Good Building?*, which after a quarter of a century still has value as an authoritative statement of general design principles.

But the 1990s had been a sterile time for British architecture, generally speaking; there were relatively few good new buildings and the overall tone was one of insipid insularity. The Commission was seen to some degree as symbolic of late twentieth century torpor. On the eve of a new millennium, its very name was a source of bewilderment. References to it betray this confusion – it was called anything from the 'guardian of official taste' to 'the official arbiter of aesthetics' and 'architectural watchdog', sometimes in the space of one newspaper article. But more particularly, it seemed an anachronism. 'Fine Art' fitted Prince Albert's Commission well enough but was never a precise description of what its twentieth century namesake did; and it became less and less accurate a description as the century went on, as its focus narrowed to architecture. It implied a preoccupation with nice questions of what a pillar box looked like rather than a muscular grappling with hard questions of building design. Lord Esher suggested this in his *Times* article in 1970, perhaps a defining moment when the echoes of the 1920s, and the environment in which the Commission had been created, finally faded away.

'Any group of men so absurdly entitled must expect to have its leg pulled, and not only by Osbert Lancaster. 'Fine Art' after all, by common consent of artists, no longer has any meaning, and 'Royal Fine Art' sounds mediaeval or even Ruritanian. That such a body should be appointed by the Queen on the advice of the Prime Minister to make official pronouncements on matters of taste is not merely against the spirit of this age: it is against the creative spirit of every other age later than the eighteenth century.'

When such perceptions take root they develop a momentum that is hard to stall. In 1994, the Conservative government asked Sir Geoffrey Chipperfield, Chief Executive of the Property Services Agency, to review the Commission. He delivered a highly critical report in May 1996, still under a broadly sympathetic Conservative Government, but it provided ammunition for the reform-minded Labour government that took office in 1997. Post-Chipperfield, every perceived flaw was seen as proof of dysfunction and matters that would normally have been overlooked were seized on as evidence of self-referential thinking or profligacy. The Commission was not always notably sensitive to this. Controversy arose in June 1996 when its Building of the Year Award[117] was won by The Queen's Building at Emmanuel College, Cambridge – an excellent building and a worthy winner, but one commissioned by Lord St. John of Fawsley,[118] who was also chairman of the judges, and designed by a Commissioner, Sir Michael Hopkins, who was also on the judging panel. All the normal safeguards had been in place: both Lord St. John and Hopkins recused themselves (Sir William Whitfield took the chair) and the other judges were unanimous. But it all fed the negative perceptions that were building up. Tendentious or not, frothy or not, the criticism created a climate in which it was easy to argue that fundamental reform was overdue. Anyone looking for excuses to abolish the Commission did not have far to look.

And by this time there were such people. For much of the twentieth century, there had been a basic supposition that the public interest, and indeed government itself, was best served by independent expert bodies that were more of a challenge to government than its servant. *The Manchester Guardian*, in 1933, referred to the Commission as a 'public defender', almost a quasi-legal designation. 'Until now', it said in reference to the 1933 Warrant extending the Commission's powers, 'the public has had no defender against its own civil servants'. That independence allowed robust criticism that tested assumptions, made thinking more rigorous and made decisions better. But the Labour Government elected in 1997 wanted a different sort of body: one that delivered government policy, especially in the social sphere, and advanced architecture as a tool of social policy across the country, helping clients to create buildings that, as it hoped, improved the experience of users. The Commission's 'Royal' prefix was perhaps an unwelcome reminder of its independence, a titular assertion that although the Commission might have been funded through the public purse, it was not operationally beholden to the government of the day. But the time had come when the government of the day preferred a body that did its bidding.

In those conditions, the Commission would have been vulnerable whatever its record. Although tabloid tales of alleged extravagance were unreasonable,[119] it hardly mattered. It was indicative of a mood and a trajectory that could only end in fundamental change. In January 1999, press advertisements were placed for a chairman for the Commission's successor, at that point referred to only as a 'new public body for architecture'. Its role would be 'to continue the national design review function of the Royal Fine Art Commission and consider its extension to the regions', but also to promote good architecture and encourage 'community involvement' and public understanding of architecture – by implication all that was missing, in the Government's view, from what the Commission offered. A serving Commissioner, the developer Stuart Lipton, was chosen.[120] The new Commission for Architecture and the Built Environment started work on 1 September 1999, on an annual budget that within five years had grown to roughly fourteen times that of the Royal Fine Art Commission. Naturally it had many more personnel as well, but many fewer of them were recognisable to the public. It lasted not much more than ten years, before itself being abolished in 2010 when its Government grant was withdrawn.

X | Was it worth it?

The Royal Fine Art Commission might have been caricatured as an anachronism, but in truth the business of improving design is not a matter of chasing the latest fashion; those who try to do so will almost always be left behind as fashions move on.

On the whole, across the years, the Commission comprised good and disinterested men (and later women)[121] genuinely trying to improve the quality of the built environment. It was, as Sir Lionel Earle put it, on the side of the angels. Sometimes, of course, it failed, and just occasionally its intervention, though well-meaning, was counter-productive; its success in 1926 in forcing the relocation of the Mercantile Marine Memorial away from the Victoria Embankment, in order to preserve Sir Joseph Bazalgette's river wall, led to the abandonment of a design by Sir Edwin Lutyens which, had it been built, would today be revered for its power and virtuosity; the substitute memorial, built at Tower Hill, is anaemic by comparison. But those are isolated episodes, and it is fair to say that the effort was worthwhile even if the Commission did not wholly or always succeed.

The crucial question perhaps is whether it made a difference. And there are two ways of approaching that: first whether it made a concrete difference, in the sense of changing particular schemes, and secondly whether it made a cultural difference, in the sense of shifting attitudes and perceptions.

On the latter, the Commission was in itself a powerful statement of civilised values. Clough Williams-Ellis made the point in 1926: 'We have a Fine Arts Commission which, even if at best ineffective and at worst actually mischievous, is none the less an official gesture of recognition towards the graces of life, with the authority of a popularly elected Parliament behind it. If it does in fact do harm, it will be with the best possible intentions.' In other words, the mere fact of its existence, independent of its actions, had an elevating effect.

Its actions were nonetheless important; and it showed an extraordinary level of care over humdrum things that were held in common and available to all, regardless of means. In recognising that the best was possible for, and deserved by, everyone, it demonstrated a universality that was truly egalitarian. The fundamental seriousness it accorded to the form and function of utilitarian objects like telephone boxes and street lamps was impressive; its painstaking attention might seem almost quaint from a twenty-first century perspective, but in fact it showed a deep appreciation of what might be called the public good.

If the Commission's judgements were Olympian, its impulse was far from elitist; rather, it was the unashamed champion of the notional Everyman. Its willingness to labour over detailed design, and to see the investment of time, energy and care as a civic duty, made a statement that good design had the capacity to uplift and enrich. Nothing, it seemed to say, was too good for the man in the street; and nothing was too insignificant to be designed well, or to merit the close attention of the most eminent men. That message itself had a reinforcement effect – if such people paid attention to it, it must matter. And if they were going to be scrutinizing it, then the designers had better do a good job.

It was perhaps comforting to know that a body existed to take a detailed and diligent interest in pedestrian matters for no reason beyond the fact that the outcome affected, for good or ill, the quality of life of the ordinary man. But it was more than comforting: it was also a manifestation of the finest ideals. As *The Manchester Guardian* put it in 1944, just after those ideals had been mortally threatened:

'The fight against the sacrifice of beauty in the nineteenth century was a pretty desperate guerrilla warfare. A noble building or a fine landscape threatened by private or public greed had to rely for its defence on groups of sensitive people who had enough public spirit to make an agitation. Ruskin was the most famous of the resisters. Their successes were few. Gradually it came to be seen that beauty had a place and purpose in the common world and that a modern civilised society should follow the example of ancient civilised societies and recognise this truth. The creation of the Royal Fine Art Commission was an important event in the history of this enlightening process. The more we insist on our credentials as a democracy the more jealously should we guard the beauty that the poor can share with the rich and the possessions that help to educate imagination and feeling. For a democracy must hold that its business is to make that education common to all its citizens'.

Twenty years later, Colin Buchanan wrote in *The Observer* that 'ugliness should be tackled, our inheritance from the past cherished; we should have no inhibitions about new architecture, and quality should be sought in everything'. Though not written or intended as such, that could stand as

a kind of manifesto for the Royal Fine Art Commission. One of its attributes was the ability to seek after quality in a way that transcended sectional interests and the limited views of local authorities, looking holistically at schemes that, in their visual impact, were often no respecters of administrative boundaries. The point was not to redesign projects, which would often have been futile, but to make architects think harder and reflect on how they could do better once they had undergone the discipline of a critique from those at the top of their profession. The Commission made available a unique resource – free access to the best minds, a means by which average architects could benefit from the wisdom and personal attention of the finest in their field. The value of that is unquantifiable, and plenty of architects left chastened, but potentially at least it was a positive rather than a negative experience.

As for concrete differences, those are perhaps harder to judge. Sometimes it is difficult to isolate the critical factor. All campaigning bodies are adept at conflating sequence with causation: 'the Royal Fine Art Commission opposed a scheme, the scheme was amended, therefore the Royal Fine Art Commission changed it' is a beguiling syllogism but sometimes false logic. Revisions often have several causes and are promoted by several bodies, meaning that it may be impossible on the available evidence to know who, if anyone, had the decisive impact; equally, it might have been pushing on an open door, so that any apparent impact is illusory.[122] Attributing credit is often an impressionistic art, not a precise science. It may be, of course, that criticism that failed in its immediate object nonetheless influenced future projects. When a building such as a tower block is criticised, the critic might not be thinking exclusively or even mainly about that particular tall building: it might be thinking, consciously or not, about the next one and the one after that, about changing the climate and setting parameters for the future. There might, then, be a victory lag: ultimately unknowable, but not to be discounted.

It is still possible to pick out individual successes, always remembering that beyond each celebrated success stand a hundred unheralded things across England and Wales. Certainly the Commission performed a valuable service in promoting striking new work that it felt deserved an airing. In its report for 1962–1965, it said that it felt it had a duty, on occasion, to support an original design which might encounter public opposition on account of its originality. And Frank Fielden, on the eve of his retirement as Secretary in 1979, reckoned that he had spent as much time giving worthy schemes a helping hand as trying to stop eyesores. With a tightly controlled planning system often run by people with limited visual awareness, adventurous designs could easily run into trouble from arbitrary or timid planning decisions. In edging forward promising schemes that would otherwise have had no champion, and which might have fallen victim to an institutional inertia that favoured safe options, the Commission was making a forceful point about the importance of creating good work to sit alongside the best of the old.

In the early 1980s, it backed a highly controversial scheme by Arup Associates for a library for Clare College, Cambridge, sited astride the long ceremonial route created by Giles Gilbert Scott and terminating in his University library. Local opinion was outraged, but the Commission considered the new work not only to hold the promise of fine architecture but to be so sophisticated in its spatial awareness that it enhanced rather than detracted from Scott's legacy. In the same period, the Commission strongly supported a scheme by Edward Cullinan for the imaginative reconstruction of the gutted St. Mary's Church in Barnes, in the face of vociferous opposition from local groups who wanted it rebuilt in replica. And at Bayswater, on the northern perimeter of Hyde Park, it welcomed a daring housing scheme that placed apartments in an exposed concrete frame around the surviving tower of Christ Church Lancaster Gate; indeed, it pushed the architects to have the courage of their convictions and expose the concrete throughout rather than facing it with brick at penthouse level, where the frame took on the expressive form of flying buttresses.[123]

Without the Commission, too, the airy elegance of Nicholas Grimshaw's Waterloo International Terminal would probably have been lost amid an office development that was planned to sit above the station; huge structural supports would have crashed through its roof and natural light would have been largely excluded. It was the Commission, again in the 1990s, which pushed a sceptical Durham City Council into adapting the disused Newton Cap railway viaduct to carry the A689 across the River Wear near Bishop Auckland, giving the viaduct an assured future and averting probable decay.

We might look, too, at the St. Paul's Cathedral Choir School by the Architects' Co-Partnership, the subject of a perceptive appraisal by Ian Nairn in *The Observer* in 1967. The design arose from a limited competition organised after the original proposals had been turned down by the Commission, and Nairn notes that 'this mature procedure has produced an exceptionally mature building, taking the site seriously without being stampeded into false deference. There is no chance here of feeling, as you do in the new precinct on the north side, that the designs might just as well have been built somewhere else; the choir school is indivisible from this particular purpose on this particular site. The separate blocks are screwed into the ground with such force that you can almost feel the architect's brow corrugating with the effort'.

Or we might consider the Epping Forest District Council Offices, a lauded example of the 1980s vernacular idiom. Commenting on its genesis in 1990, the architectural historian Gillian Darley said that 'the search for an architect did not begin auspiciously. In the early 1980s the council turned to a large commercial practice for designs. The result so appalled the Royal Fine Art Commission that it persuaded the council

to hold an architectural competition'. The winning design, by Richard Reid Architects, was a brick composition accented with an octagonal clock tower. Darley thought the council chamber 'a room of considerable distinction'. There are plenty of other instances where forensic involvement brought hard-fought successes: in Ormskirk, say, where the Commission brought about a dramatic improvement in designs for a police divisional headquarters, averting the threat of a forbidding and oppressive building; or in Hove, where a banal, warehouse-style ice rink on a prominent seafront site was transformed into an elegant structure with a tubular steel space-frame, and reconfigured so that car parking was placed at basement level rather than covering surface areas in unappealing asphalt. Those examples are from the end of the 1970s; for earlier references, we might pick out the general comment of Myles Wright, Professor of Civic Design at the University of Liverpool, on the post-war reconstruction of London: 'it is noticeable', he said in 1955, 'that the continued sharp comments of the Royal Fine Art Commission have resulted in an improvement in the architectural quality of recent buildings'.

Achieving these results required not just critical skill but an intuitive understanding of the art of the possible. The Commission knew the risks of being sucked into futile labour, that it was ultimately unnecessary to help an excellent scheme and impossible to redeem a dreadful one: it would have been gilding the lily at one end and putting lipstick on a gorilla at the other, both of which would have been a waste of resources. But there is plenty in between those extremes where judicious intervention can improve the bad and the indifferent. Raising the quality of the ordinary is a socially-useful calling, with a cumulative effect that over the years can be significant.

Making that difference is a good deal harder in practice than in theory, and occasionally the Commission tried to work out some general principles for internal use. An internal minute in 1946 to Lord Crawford from the Commission's Secretary,

Arthur Knapp-Fisher, set out a formula which broadly held good across the years when the Commission was faced with an inadequate scheme:

1   *Those buildings with no architect: recommend architect.*

2   *Those buildings badly designed by an architect of little renown:*
    a   *recommend trying again after tendering advice;*
    b   *recommend another architect;*
    c   *recommend consultant*

3   *Those buildings found wanting designed by an architect of renown: adopt principle of limiting criticism to fundamentals. The expression 'no comments' to be used as a last resort. Any comments to be on a broad basis and covering general principles only and not detail.*

4   *Generally, avoid getting into the position of having to redesign a building or getting into conflict over detail with an architect of renown.*

This desire to avoid redesigning buildings did, of course, invite the accusation that the Commission was merely obstructive, merely carping without offering solutions. That was the gravamen of several complaints. In 1954, Dover Council made plain its frustration that the Commission opposed a seafront apartment block 'but had no practical alternative to put forward'. It is difficult to see how sensibly it could have done so, in any meaningful way, without becoming an architect itself or getting sucked into titivation, which may not be the optimal use of eminent architects' time, although that is, to be frank, often what the Commission ended up doing: an adjustment here, and adjustment there, leading to some minor improvement that would have required some scrutiny of the finished product to notice. Its 1956 critique of the designs for Bowater House in Knightsbridge, where it recommended Swedish blue pearl mullions and grey aprons in place of a uniform travertine, was not wholly untypical. Such attention to detail had its uses, but as the Commission itself knew very well it was better employed at an early stage, influencing the formal and general principles of a scheme. That allowed it to be more obviously helpful, as it frequently reminded commissioning bodies. Meeting a group of Regional Health Authorities in 1980, Sir Philip Powell and Sir Alex Gordon argued that hospital designs should be commissioned from the best architects, rather than from architects who had come to be known as specialists in hospital design; and they made a plea, one of many, for the Commission to be brought in early on strategic matters, such as the choice of site and the suitability of the type of hospital for the site. Reporting back, they told Sherban Cantacuzino that the root cause of many of the deficiencies was 'an inherent Philistinism which in hard times was made into a virtue'. But that was another problem altogether.

How then do we read the life of the Royal Fine Art Commission? One way of appraising its performance is to ask whether it has been missed. Certainly its breadth of perspective is missing. In London especially, it offered a panoramic view – cross-river, cross-borough, cross-capital – that was not always present otherwise and which was sharpened by the fact that it was never *parti pris*. Planning battles have always been adversarial and have perhaps become increasingly so, more likely to be determined by who can shout loudest and afford the best lawyers. Important points are either never made or lost in trench warfare between supporters and objectors. What can suffer in that *mêlée* is sober contextual analysis, three-dimensional assessment, considered appraisal of both macro impact and micro detail. In particular, the wider picture is sometimes lost. Here we might

reflect on the tower in Stratford whose intrusion into the viewing corridor towards St. Paul's from King Henry's Mound in Richmond Park was simply missed at the planning stage and noticed only when its effect became apparent during construction in 2015. Or we might contrast the agonising over the planned Mies tower next to Mansion House with the lack of much more than a whimper to accompany the planning and building of the rash of towers, only some of them distinguished, that now form a backdrop to Mansion House looking east. Or we might consider the buildings that now appear behind Lambeth Palace as viewed from Victoria Tower Gardens in Westminster – a clear skyline for centuries but now crowded with a jumble of indifferent towers, all located some miles away. It is hard to believe that anyone reflected on that wider impact at planning stage, as the Royal Fine Art Commission specialised in doing; and if anyone did the effect was nil. It is in that failure to consider context both wide and immediate that the absence of the Commission has perhaps been most keenly felt.

What is missing too is that essential ingredient of the Royal Fine Art Commission, namely its independence. It was simply there to represent the public interest, embodying the civilised principle that the state and the government, and the people and the government, might have interests that are not always identical. Making the design adviser an adjunct of government, as happened in 1999, sacrifices that, turning it into a body that takes instruction rather than dispensing home truths. When Royal Commissions are recast as government quangos, set up and paid to deliver government objectives, they become in effect a branch of the home civil service. But objectives change as governments change; the result can be directionless drift as quangos try to keep pace with what is expected of them. Better, perhaps, a body that seems quieter, but where the focus runs deep. And the focus of the Royal Fine Art Commission was the public interest, not partisan whim.

And certainly nothing since has eclipsed or even come close to equalling it in eminence of membership. To take a random but fairly typical instance from the mid-1960s, for a routine meeting with Oxford University to discuss the future of the Emperors' Heads at the Sheldonian Theatre the Commission fielded Henry Moore, John Piper, Sir Basil Spence, Sir John Summerson and Lord Esher, as well as its Chairman Lord Bridges: astonishing intellectual firepower made available in the service of the nation and free at the point of delivery.

Today, there is as great a need as ever for independent expert advice of that kind. The Royal Fine Art Commission's transient successor turned out to be a poor substitute. Although design panels have multiplied, the space filled by the Commission is now largely empty. And the general standard of ordinary architecture, of the sort most people encounter daily, seems at least as deficient as ever in the qualities that enrich our lives.

Notes

Part I

1   The appointment of 'Her Majesty's Commissioners' was gazetted on 22 November 1841, establishing a body which, as a standing commission appointed by the Sovereign, is referred to throughout Part I as The Royal Fine Art Commission. While it existed, it was often informally called the Fine Arts Commission.

2   *Punch* lampooned the Cartoon Exhibitions at Westminster Hall so often that its humorous drawings became known as cartoons, a name that stuck.

Part II

CHAPTER 1 – FRESH IMPETUS

1   *House of Lords Debates*, 22 July 1901, Vol. 97 Col. 1082. Lord Stanmore, a younger son of the Prime Minister Lord Aberdeen, had been a colonial administrator, ending his career as Governor of New Zealand.

2   By this he meant the Victorian railway bridges at Charing Cross, Blackfriars and Cannon Street, especially the first, 'with its elephantine legs, straggling across the river, spoiling the view of one of the most beautiful structures in the world – Waterloo Bridge, which Canova said was well worth a journey from Italy to see'. Ironically, all three railway bridges are still standing and it is the one Canova admired, Rennie's Waterloo Bridge, that has gone, demolished in 1933.

CHAPTER II – AMERICAN PRECEDENT

3   Crawford held two earldoms, the other the Earldom of Balcarres, also the name of his ancestral seat in Fifeshire. He was commonly called the Earl of Crawford and Balcarres, and informally signed himself 'C&B'.

4   Curzon supposedly objected to the expanse of naked flesh on show; others objected to the artist on grounds that were fairly clearly anti-Semitic. At any rate, the Commission in embryo benefited from this general assumption – the more compelling for being wholly unfalsifiable – that had it existed it would have prevented this or that outrage. R.S. Meiklejohn, a senior Treasury civil servant, was one of those who projected his own preferences in this way: 'had such a body existed', he wrote in an internal minute in 1922, 'we might have been spared such a monstrosity in our streets as the Nurse Cavell monument'. (Not everyone had such a negative view of the memorial, which stands at the south end of Charing Cross Road and commemorates Cavell's courage in the face of persecution by the Germans that led to her execution in 1915; its sculptor, Sir George Frampton, was appointed a founding Commissioner in 1924 and in 2014 it was listed Grade I).

5   Mawson also had recent American experience, having lectured on urban landscaping at American universities from 1911 to 1916. That brought him into contact with the American Fine Arts Commission, which left a lasting and positive impression. He told the Prime Minister in January 1924 that 'I have always hoped that in this country we might have the help of a similar body of experts, and congratulate you on the progress which has been made towards the consummation of this progressive policy'.

6   This was a close-run thing: in February 1924, Crawford told Sir Russell Scott at the Treasury that 'we think Royal Fine Arts Commission would be a compendious name'. But a month later, in a scribbled postscript to another letter to Scott, he said that 'the name we propose is Royal Fine Art Commission'. Scott told Earle that 'The Commissioners prefer Fine Art to Fine Arts. I don't think it matters much'.

7   Very occasionally the Commission did assist overseas governments. In 1944 the Treasury, in recognition of Malta's courage and steadfastness during the War, gave the Commission special dispensation to advise on a case in Valletta – 'provided they do not ask to be sent out by bomber to inspect the site'. And in 1946, at the

request of Mountbatten, the Commission was asked to comment on proposals for new office buildings in Delhi as there were doubts about how well they fitted in with existing buildings by Lutyens and Herbert Baker.

8 A separate Royal Fine Art Commission for Scotland was set up in 1927. The Commission did receive a few requests for design advice from Ulster, for example in 1937 when the Ministry of Home Affairs asked for help with bridges on the Belfast-Holywood bypass. The Treasury refused on the spurious legalistic grounds that it would be *ultra vires*, although its real worry was about the cost involved. In 1946, when help was sought by the Ulster Transport Authority on bus stop designs, the Commission tried again, sensibly saying this time that it would cost no more than a shilling to give the advice. 'A shilling!', scribbled Treasury civil servants to one another, disbelievingly. But this time they contrived to say yes on the grounds that later Royal Warrants, unlike the 1924 one, made no reference to 'Our Realm of England'. Advice continued to be given very sporadically in the later twentieth century, on major projects such as the Foyle Bridge near Londonderry, completed in 1986, and the Lagan bridges in Belfast (1995).

CHAPTER III – IN ACTION

9 Eventually they were installed at Brangwyn Hall in Swansea, where they remain.
10 Crawford showed signs of tiring of the more piddling Parliamentary matters: in 1933 he minuted Lee to say: 'you will remember that tiresome and stupid question about the clock in the House of Commons. I think we ought to reply that if it is required for the convenience of members its erection will be justified. On the other hand it will certainly be unbecoming immediately under the canopy of Mr. Speaker's chair. This is one of the petty questions which the Office of Works put to us, while leaving out questions of fundamental importance'.
11 In *The Spectator* 1946, recalling the Great War in an effort to forestall a repeat after the Second.

12 Haig replaced Sir John French as Commander-in-Chief of the British Expeditionary Force in December 1915.
13 The statue was finally unveiled (by the Duke of Gloucester) in 1937.
14 As a tantalising postscript, Lutyens received a handwritten note from the architect Charles Voysey in May 1925, enclosing a sketch of a Gothic kiosk made of plywood and enamelled in bright vermilion, with aluminium cresting in a pattern of alternating crosses and fleurs-de-lis, all surmounted by a crown, with heraldic arms riveted to the sides. 'The whole could be easily cleaned by turning on a hose', wrote Voysey. Perhaps to the relief of the Commission, which cannot have relished rehashing, even in miniature, the Classical versus Gothic style wars of the 1840s, it was all far too late. Lutyens forwarded it to Crawford with the note 'I fear there is nothing further that can be done about it'.
15 Some kiosks were painted green in the North York Moors National Park, and near Sandringham at the request of George V (in honour of whose Silver Jubilee the kiosk was named). A large number in the Cotswolds were painted battleship grey. Many of these are still in use.
16 The building fairly soon achieved distinction on its own account, as the headquarters of De Gaulle's Free French government-in-exile during the War.
17 Oddly, the Crown Lands Commissioners came under the Ministry of Agriculture.
18 It still stands, as does Baker's South Africa House.
19 That still left room for Sir Reginald Blomfield, ever belligerent, to manufacture a row with Baker in the letters columns of *The Times*. Baker's design, he said, was 'irrelevant to Trafalgar-square as a whole' and placed it in peril. When another architect accused him of bad form in criticising another architect in the press, he fell back on splendid pomposity: the public interest demanded a public statement, he said, and circumstances may arise of '*amicus Plato magis amica veritas*'. ('Plato is a friend, but truth is a better friend' – Aristotle).

20 The original plan had been to allow the fish market to use the Custom House quay for waterborne deliveries, but staff at Custom House strenuously opposed the idea on the grounds that the smell of fish would be intolerable. The City then came back with the far more radical demolition proposal. The Commission's ambivalence towards Custom House was later shared by John Betjeman, who suggested in 1958 that it be sacrificed in order to save the Coal Exchange on the other side of Lower Thames Street, which was due to be widened. By that time, Custom House (having already been rebuilt in part in the nineteenth century after the central section collapsed) had been patched up in replica after significant war damage.
21 Herbert Morrison was by now Home Secretary, in Churchill's wartime Government.
22 There is no recorded instance of the power being used in earnest. Mostly, as Crawford predicted, the bluff was enough, as when the Power Minister Aubrey Jones agreed in 1956 to make plans for the siting of power stations available to the Commission at an early stage. 'We have never exercised this power', Crawford told him, 'and I am glad that your letter makes it unnecessary in this case'. When Norman St. John-Stevas (later Lord St. John of Fawsley) was appointed chairman in 1985, he asked Lord Hailsham, the Lord Chancellor, what it really meant. 'What happens if any person or body refuses us access or declines to come before us? With the House of Commons Select Committee one would go back to the floor of the House. Where do we go?' No reply is recorded from Lord Hailsham, but it is a fair assumption that his advice would have been much the same as Sir Granville Ram's in 1943.

CHAPTER IV – TWENTIETH CENTURY CHALLENGES

23 This had long been a favoured project of Lord Lee's, stretching back to his chairmanship of the Commission on Cross-River Traffic in 1926. Like Lord Wemyss before him, Lee regarded the railway bridges as 'notorious eyesores' and

pointed out that rerouting the railway lines underground would also avoid delays caused by fog – a practical argument that disappeared (along with the fog) after the 1956 Clean Air Act.

24 The City claimed that the sites of bombed churches and churchyards qualified as open space, but the Commission had in mind something less accidental.

25 Lutyens in fact drew up, in 1943, a scheme for comprehensive rebuilding around St. Paul's, the twentieth century equivalent of Wren's grand plan of the 1670s. It was Lutyens' last major project – he died in 1944, having remained a Royal Fine Art Commissioner up to his death.

26 Holford's Juxon House, the part of the Paternoster scheme abutting Ludgate Hill, was often criticised for intruding in views of St. Paul's, but actually it showed a nice appreciation of dramatic effect. It was replaced in the 1990s by a new (classical) Juxon House by Sir William Whitfield, also a Royal Fine Art Commissioner, who sensibly kept to Holford's building line so that St. Paul's revealed itself by degrees on the approach up Ludgate Hill.

27 Ironically set up at the suggestion of the Royal Fine Art Commission in 1956. Its first chairman was the rather more *simpatico* David Bowes-Lyon.

28 A similar argument is now put forward for leaving the A303 at Stonehenge as it is, rather than rerouting it or putting it in a tunnel.

29 *List of Historic Towns*, Council for British Archaeology, 1965. This was produced in response to Sir Colin Buchanan's *Traffic in Towns* Report, which had predicted that 'unless steps are taken, the motor vehicle will defeat its own utility and bring about a disastrous degradation of the surroundings for living... Either the utility of vehicles in towns will decline rapidly, or the pleasantness and safety of our surroundings will deteriorate catastrophically – in all probability both will happen'.

30 *Aesthetic censors without active power*, Viscount Esher, *The Times* 18 April 1970.

31 The campanile still stands, a bit forlorn and marooned amid 1960s buildings that look increasingly tired. But it still works well as an eyecatcher when viewed from Hyde Park and Kensington Gardens.

32 Some of the bomb-damaged terraces were rebuilt behind their Nash facades. The Commission accepted this as a necessary compromise, though its efforts in securing it were not appreciated by everyone. Kenneth Williams, in a letter to Gordon Jackson of 23 October 1969, describes sitting in his 'drawer in the sky, watching the reconstruction of the Nash Terraces and reflecting on the utter stupidity of the Fine Arts Commission... which has forced the wretched builders to scoop out the backs and not touch the fronts'.

33 Jellicoe was not alone in his assessment, even among conservationists. When the screen was finally removed in March 1967, Alec Clifton-Taylor wrote to *The Times* to say that he had visited Hereford Cathedral to view the effect and had 'sat rejoicing. The improvement is almost unbelievable'. The Cathedral Dean's original plan was to have it re-erected in the Herbert Art Gallery in Coventry, but in the event it remained packed away for decades until reassembled at the V&A, where it can now be seen, fully restored, looking down over the entrance hall.

34 Its judgement in both instances has been vindicated; the Rogers and Lasdun buildings are both now listed Grade I. The muscular stone façade of Cooper's Lloyd's building was kept as a freestanding object and now serves, not very satisfactorily, as a screen wall.

35 Churches were exempted from the height restriction, as were towers and turrets on other buildings in order to reduce monotony. But the limit was as much about practicalities as about aesthetics; in the 1930s the London Fire Brigade consistently opposed an increase as its most powerful water jets could only reach 100 feet and its longest ladders were 92 feet.

36 Because of the success of the St. Paul's Heights limits in keeping buildings low to the west of

St. Paul's, Faraday House has much the same negative impact today as it did in the 1930s, and from the south bank of the Thames at Blackfriars it is still easily possible to see what alarmed the Commission.

37 Now demolished to make way for the One Hyde Park apartments by Rogers Stirk Harbour.

38 This was especially true of hotel schemes, as the Government was concerned at the time about the lack of hotel rooms in central London and the effect of that on the tourist industry. This encouraged developers to chance their arm with some fairly outrageous schemes, such as the Lowndes Square one, in order to meet deadlines for Government grants designed to promote the building of new hotels. Developers naturally favoured towers on the edge of parks as a way of maximising the number of expensive rooms with premium views. This mad rush was not conducive to design quality. The Commission said in its Report for 1968–1971 that the standard was 'depressingly low', making hotels 'the dreariest of all modern building types'.

39 Ironically, Spence recommended Lancaster for appointment to the Commission, in a private letter to Sir Colin Anderson in April 1968. 'He would be most useful as he has a real passion for good architecture'.

40 Knightsbridge Barracks and The Home Office.

41 Bucklersbury House was demolished in 2015 and replaced by the Bloomberg Headquarters by Foster and Partners.

42 The compositional balance between the Shell Centre tower and adjacent buildings has been a casualty of the current redevelopment works, which have ended the carefully-contrived dominance of the tower by introducing a cluster of quite tall buildings around its base.

43 Lord Esher in *The Times* in 1970 said how perplexed he was that the Commission was thought to be conducting a vendetta against tall buildings. The accusation was not, he said, borne out by his own long experience as a Commissioner. But it was a common perception.

In 1969 Stephen Gardiner wrote in *The Observer* that the Commission was opposed to tall buildings, and as late as 1998 Jonathan Glancey said in *The Guardian* that in the Commission's view 'high buildings equal bad buildings'. But in truth the Commission's stance was always far more nuanced, and indeed more sophisticated, than that. Its insistence on high design standards and careful siting for buildings that were so visible, coupled with its challenging of assumptions that tall buildings necessarily offer higher densities (generally they do not), were sometimes misconstrued as principled opposition.

44 The few police call boxes that survive, all long since redundant, are protected by law as structures of historic interest.

45 A startling reference to the French revolutionary mob's habit of hanging opponents from lamp-posts, and a powerful indication of how large concrete lamp standards loomed in the demonology of those protesting against the disfigurement of Britain by the accumulation of ill-assorted paraphernalia. Sir Hugh Casson, Associate Editor of *The Architectural Review*, sent a complimentary copy of *Outrage* to the Commission covered by a letter which called it 'a tourist guide in reverse, picking out the bad... Immediate action on a broad front is essential if the whole country is not to become a jungle of by-pass squalor'.

46 This need was identified by Herbert Morrison, by now Lord President of the Council; the Commission danced an uneasy *pas de deux* with him across a quarter of a century, coming across him in one way or another in almost all of the portfolios he occupied.

47 One of those residents, the architect Sir Albert Richardson, happened to be a Commissioner. His gift for polemic matched that of Betjeman and he was more than willing to use it in defence of Ampthill in Bedfordshire, where twenty-five concrete posts were erected in 1957 – one of them right outside his Georgian house. Richardson was an extreme reactionary who lived as a

Georgian, to the point of using candlelight at home, and the sudden appearance of this concrete post with its sodium light caused him real anguish. He put up a sign denouncing the intrusion: 'These incongruous lamp-posts that detract from the beauty of this historic town were erected by the urban district council against the advice of the Royal Fine Art Commission', it said. He told the newspapers that 'the greatest vandals in many cases are the district councils. Men without taste should consult men with knowledge of aesthetics. This is not a personal thing at all – I am fighting for the taste of the country. Our beautiful little streets are to be ruined by these uncouth concrete standards'.

48 And plenty more besides. As Michael Middleton put it in *The Times* in October 1961, 'our urban open spaces are furnished with lighting columns short and tall, bus shelters, seats, litter bins, illuminated bollards, guard rails, flower tubs, sand bins, pillar boxes, transformer boxes, vent pipes, parking meters, telephone and police kiosks, notice boards, traffic lights and beacons, and road signs in staggering profusion; they may further include lavatories, rockeries, bandstands, statues and memorials, petrol pumps, poster hoardings, and a thick crochet of overhead wires'.

49 This paradox mirrored the Commission's lessening involvement in building preservation at a time when apprehension of the problem became more acute. The reasons for that are the same in both instances: its success in raising awareness of problems brought other players onto the field, at which point the Commission could pull back in the knowledge that good minds were still being applied to finding solutions.

50 Cunard wisely preferred to deal with the C.O.I.D., but did have to accept Anderson's argument that it should take expert advice on a project of national prestige to which the taxpayer was contributing. In the end it appointed ten designers, including David Hicks for the nightclub and casino.

51 There was a tendency for items of street furniture to follow a trajectory of being despised when introduced, then tolerated, then loved when threatened, and then at last considered inviolate.

CHAPTER V – CLIMATE CHANGE

52 Even if it was technically still an 'evil', albeit a lesser one. Advocates included Eric Bedford, Chief Architect at the Ministry of Works and one of the best public sector architects of the mid twentieth century. He told Evelyn Sharp at the Ministry of Housing and Local Government that the Ministry of Works had determined on a course of cooperation and had benefited. The Commission, he thought, was 'pretty reasonable'.

53 When, in 1969, the Commission gave a positive review of Frederick Gibberd's design for the Intercontinental Hotel at Hyde Park Corner, *The Observer* observed that such praise was 'notoriously, not necessarily a seal of distinction'.

54 The building went ahead, a perfectly polite affair by Trehearne and Norman with the repetitive grid, coloured spandrels and Portland stone panels that were typical of the mid-1950s. It still stands, an increasingly rare example of its kind. The Chadwick bronze was omitted, rather regrettably in retrospect and to the disappointment at the time of Henry Moore, who wanted to encourage Chadwick.

55 The Commission won, with the 600ft tower being built, although the promised open space at the base was partly built on in the 1990s.

56 Later abandoned in favour of a postmodern scheme by Robert Venturi, after the intervention of The Prince of Wales, who told the R.I.B.A. in 1984 that the A.B.K. design was 'a carbuncle on the face of a much-loved old friend' – probably the most-quoted piece of architectural criticism in Britain in the twentieth century.

57 The decision to use oil was partly an aesthetic consideration, as it avoided the need for apparatus to unload coal on the river front, of the sort that disfigured Battersea upriver – although a jetty was still needed for the berthing of oil tankers.

58 Sir Cyril Hurcomb of the Electricity Commission told the Ministry of Fuel and Power in April 1945 that 'I saw the Royal Commission on Fine Art yesterday. Professor Richardson referred in terms of alarm and despondency to the proposal which he understood to be afoot for erecting a large station opposite St. Paul's which Giles Scott is being asked to 'camouflage'. Richardson said that the proportions of the station would dwarf St. Paul's'. In fact Scott's chimney was eighty feet shorter than the top of the dome of St. Paul's, and 100 feet shorter as built because St. Paul's was on higher ground.

59 Lord Latham's worries were reasonable at the time, but the Commission's support for the project, and its amendment to the ground plan, turned out to be far-sighted. When decommissioned in the late twentieth century and reused as Tate Modern, with a pedestrian bridge by Foster and Partners, linking it to St. Paul's, Bankside Power Station was a prime contributor to the cultural renaissance of the extended South Bank.

60 In contrast to schools, housing and factories.

61 Harvard University Press (2017).

62 Royal Fine Art Commission (1997), arising from a conference with the same title.

63 The Commission conceived the competition after it was left underwhelmed by the original proposals: first to dismantle and re-erect a redundant Nonconformist chapel from Salisbury and, when that fell through, to build a buttressed and pedimented red-brick chapel. The Commission thought the winning design by Crispin Wride Architects, chosen from seventy-three entries, evoked the right sense of sorrow, sacrifice and quiet gratitude.

64 It was; the Venturi scheme was built and is now listed Grade I.

CHAPTER VI – MAKING ITSELF HEARD

65 Permanent Secretary at the Ministry of Housing and Local Government, 1955–1966.

66 The answer was Victoria Tower Gardens, next to the Palace of Westminster, although the fountain spent five years packed in crates while it was decided whether it or Rodin's *Burghers of Calais* would be given the focal site in the centre of the gardens. In the end the fountain was given that honour. It might have been better off left in crates or (like the Hereford Cathedral Choir Screen) unpacked at the V&A, since eight bronzes of British rulers that adorned it were stolen in the 1960s and 1970s, and the fountain soon stopped working.

67 Holden had feared that something of the sort might happen. Epstein records in his autobiography that when he received the commission in 1907 'I had been like a hound on the leash and now I was suddenly set free...At first I was somewhat held back by the admonitions of the architects, who, although they had given me a big commission, yet felt that I might do something rash. I already had a reputation for wildness; why, I don't know. It is quite possible my appearance at this time was that of a traditional anarchist'. (*Epstein: an Autobiography*, Hulton Press 1959, p.21)

68 The refusal of The Royal Academy to sign led Sickert to resign in protest.

69 The development saga of this central site, known as Potter's Fields, was another on which the Commission spent much time over the years. Its first involvement was in 1983 when it criticised a Kuwaiti-backed scheme, largely for offices but including a private hospital. Tom King, the Environment Secretary, decided against a public inquiry and the Commission worked to improve the designs but the scheme was abandoned, as was a later (1987) one by Philip Johnson for 1.2 million square feet of offices with two 17-storey towers. The Commission said it would make the Tower of London across the river 'look like a garden folly'. After the Simpson scheme also foundered, less commercial schemes came along in the 1990s – social housing by Alsop and Störmer and a temporary home for the Royal Opera House by Ian Ritchie – which the Commission welcomed. Ironically, having by then been abolished, it had no involvement in the scheme that was actually built on the site – an office development largely by Foster and Partners and including the Greater London Authority headquarters building.

70 The launch was notable, as *The Guardian* had it, for the Prime Minister threatening a purge of 'filthy' Britain; she recalled being appalled at the litter that had confronted her and President Mitterrand when they drove through London in 1987. For a solution, she pointed people towards the Liverpool Garden Festival, where litter and graffiti had been systematically removed until people got the message and felt pride.

71 The relationship between Margaret Thatcher and Lord St. John was not without occasional *froideur*. When security gates were installed at the Whitehall entrance to Downing Street in December 1989, Lord St. John was reported as not only criticising their design but reminding the Prime Minister that she was not Head of State and that trappings that suggested otherwise would bring resentment.

72 It was on this basis that *The Times*, in 1948, fell in behind a controversial project to remove a reredos in St. Paul's Cathedral. It took the Commission's willingness to accept the scheme as a convincing indication that the plans were properly conceived.

73 Crawford told Knapp-Fisher that the idea of involving the Commission in the redecoration of 10 and 11 Downing Street had come from Sir John Anderson, Chancellor of the Exchequer in Churchill's caretaker government immediately after the war, who 'feels that the wives of chancellors should not be allowed to alter the general scheme of decoration or of furniture to suit their own tastes, which may be, and indeed usually are, deplorable; but that the decoration of these two houses and their furnishings should be the very best and form a standard by which distinguished foreigners should be able to judge the taste of our country'.

74 *Ad hoc* Royal Commissions are often humorously accused of 'taking minutes and wasting years', but standing Royal Commissions like the Royal Fine Art Commission could also be a useful way of putting things on the backburner.

75 Notoriously, he drove open-cast coal-mining right up to the front door of Wentworth Woodhouse in Yorkshire, causing huge problems of subsidence that even today are the subject of legal claims for compensation.

76 There was some logic to placing them in the basins, as the centrepieces had been redesigned by Lutyens in tribute to Beatty and Jellicoe. In the end both Beatty and Jellicoe (later joined by the Second World War naval commander Viscount Cunningham) were commemorated in busts placed along the north retaining wall of Trafalgar Square, facing Nelson's Column.

77 Both the John Lewis and Ludlow schemes were built. The latter owed much to the Commission, which had resisted three earlier proposals, all in a weakly historicist idiom, and had nudged a nervous local authority into embracing MacCormac's elegant design. The result was considered a template for supermarket developments that could fit comfortably into historic settings and help to sustain the economies of market towns in the face of huge competition from out-of-town shopping centres.

CHAPTER VII – PEOPLE POWER

78 A full list of Commissioners from 1924 to 1999 is given at the end of this volume.

79 In 1939, Earle told Chalton Bradshaw, the Commission's first Secretary, that 'my having been able to persuade the Cabinet of the day to create the Fine Art Commission, in spite of the violent hostility of Lord Curzon, is the thing I am proudest of in the whole of my official career'.

80 If the appearance of an hereditary chairmanship was seen as an impediment, it was never mentioned as such; a peerage was in fact considered a practical advantage, as it gave the chairman a platform in Parliament to expound the Commission's views, if only in a personal capacity.

81 Fortunately from the archival perspective, and perhaps the business of the Commission at the time, his letters to the Commission's office from the family seats of Balcarres in Fife and Haigh Hall in Lancashire were transcribed on receipt. The Government refused to fund a personal secretary for Crawford and he lived, according to Sir Edward (later Lord) Bridges, 'in circumstances at Balcarres that forbid the use of a typewriter'. Presumably the clatter was too noisy.

82 Crawford, meanwhile, promptly took the chair of the committee that oversaw the reconstruction of 10–12 Downing Street while the Prime Minister moved to Admiralty House. He ensured that the plans – drawn up by Raymond Erith, a Royal Fine Art Commissioner – were reviewed by the Commission, which had no objections. *The Guardian* was less friendly: 'Perhaps the Royal Fine Art Commission ought to draw up a list not only of buildings not allowed to disappear but of estimates of how much it is worth spending on reproductions of them'.

83 The painting was stolen in an opportunistic theft only nineteen days after it was first hung in the gallery, having been bought for the nation with the help of a Treasury grant. It was eventually recovered from the left-luggage office at Birmingham New Street railway station after a tip-off to *The Daily Mirror*.

84 Designed by Gollins Melvin Ward as a pair to their adjacent Commercial Union Tower and completed in 1969. It has now been replaced by Rogers Stirk Harbour's Leadenhall Building.

85 It would be wrong to draw the inference that the Commission did less useful work under James and Christopherson. Efficacy and productivity cannot always or only be counted in headlines. Its daily work of improving schemes, especially outside London, made a significant difference to those affected.

86 Clark was succeeded by Betjeman, so the Commission gained nothing in overall equability.

87 *John Piper Myfanwy Piper*, Frances Spalding, Oxford University Press 2009, p.346.

88 It is difficult to imagine any other Commissioner getting away with this, but Lord Curzon had achieved such stratospheric eminence that he was untouchable. Lord Crawford and Sir Lionel Earle privately referred to him as the 'All Highest', which also hinted at Curzon's forbidding persona. It is interesting, if idle, to speculate what sort of body the Commission would have been had he accepted the offer of the chairmanship, and had he then lived longer. He might have reined himself in, but more probably the Commission would have been far more assertive and unpredictable.

89 He was editor of *The Architectural Review* from 1937–1971 and published widely on the functionalist tradition in European architecture. He was knighted in 1972.

90 His son, confusingly also Sir Ralph Freeman, was also an engineer Commissioner, though not at the same time. They were the second father and son pair to serve on the Commission, after the 27th and 28th Earls of Crawford. Two brothers also served, again at different times: Sir Hubert and Sir Percy Worthington, both architects. Hubert worked for a time with Lutyens, 'whose gay scholarly influence tinctured his designs', according to *The Times*. He served as principal architect for North Africa for the Imperial War Graves Commission and joined the Commission in the same year (1943) that he left to undertake a 3000-mile tour of North Africa inspecting sites for war cemeteries.

91 As they did to the very end, with some hugely eminent representatives including Henry Moore and Elisabeth Frink.

92 The lead signatory, the sculptor Sir Charles Wheeler, was (unknown to him) up for appointment to the Commission at the very time the letter was published. It almost wrecked his chances as it might have looked, wrongly, as if the Commission was caving in to pressure by appointing him. 'I was expecting this Bernard Shaw letter', said Crawford to Knapp-Fisher (Shaw wrote so many letters to *The Times*, mostly carping, that they formed a volume of their own in his collected correspondence). 'I naturally did not know that Wheeler would be so silly as to sign it'.

93 Some of these architects were indeed an acquired taste, both in person and in their work, which strongly divided opinion even within the Commission. Some Commissioners were so annoyed at the Commission's (eventual) acceptance of Spence's Home Office that they told the Secretary, Frank Fielden, that they were prepared to break ranks and brief the press on their continued objections. Fielden averted that, and indeed supported Spence throughout, saying of him when he died in 1976 that 'he had the misfortune to be bold in an age of small deeds ... In ten years, the odds are that the British will think Sir Basil a very good architect indeed'.

94 Some of his fellow architectural historians on the Commission were more guilty of this: Summerson referred to railway architecture as 'the junk of a century'.

95 His distinguished artistic lineage did not stop there – he was also the son of the Poet Laureate Robert Bridges.

96 At times it almost seemed as if Betjeman had a persecution complex. Interestingly, when his friend Anthony West (son of H.G. Wells and Rebecca West) applied unsuccessfully for the post of Royal Fine Art Commission Secretary in 1968, Betjeman said: 'Do you suffer from persecution mania? I can't remember. If you do, the job would drive one into a bin, because one is abused by the Press, the Ministries, the Commissioners, the local officials and private correspondents'.

97 Harcourt could not resist adding that recent burglars at his home had left behind two volumes by Betjeman.

CHAPTER VIII – THINKING FOR ITSELF

98 *The Times*'s (1928) obituary of another founding Commissioner, the sculptor Sir George Frampton, noted with nice euphemism that 'partly on account of his well-known lack of sympathy with modern endeavour in the arts, his appointment to the Fine Arts Commission on its formation in 1924 did not give universal satisfaction'.

99 Godfrey Samuel, the Commission's Secretary in the later 1940s and 1950s, was also steeped in it; in 1937 he helped organise the Modern Movement exhibition at the Royal Academy, attended by Corbusier, and later that year was one of the half-dozen young architects who formed the Tecton partnership under the leadership of Berthold Lubetkin.

100 Royal Fine Art Commission, *Sixth Report,* His Majesty's Stationery Office, 1935.

101 To be fair, so was Tower Bridge – and it has sometimes been criticised for the same reason.

102 Including classicism. Raymond Erith and Donald McMorran, whose Wood Street Police Station in the City of London was praised by the Commission and is one of the finest classical buildings of the second half of the twentieth century, developed a stripped classicism that remained rich without dependence on applied ornament.

103 The extension was designed by the Ministry's in-house architect, Eric Bedford. The Commission had no objection to this in principle: 'if you feel your people can produce something first-rate', Crawford said to Birch in March 1955, 'tell them to bring their project to us at a very early stage'.

104 *The Manchester Guardian* became simply *The Guardian* in 1959.

105 The least frequent attender in this period was Henry Moore, who attended fourteen of the fifty-one meetings, but he was nonetheless reappointed four times over the years, kept on for his eminence and the lustre he added rather than for any direct usefulness. At the other end of the spectrum, Holford was a genuine mainstay, even filling in as Secretary during the War after

Bradshaw died at his desk (with Holford in the room). Samuel said in 1958 that 'Holford has by far the best architectural brain on the Commission and indeed better than any other man in this country, and the Commission would lose enormously in its strength and prestige if he were to go'.

106 The scheme was abandoned and the Royal Institution still occupies its Waterhouse building.

107 Wyatt was a Labour M.P. at the time. Unsurprisingly, Harold Macmillan rejected the idea out of hand. And while superficially supportive of the Commission, the proposal would actually have been fatal to its independence, as the Government could not have allowed itself to be dictated to by a body over which it had no operational control.

108 Her name usually appears in conjunction with the adjective 'formidable'.

109 Soames was the daughter of Sir Winston Churchill; Sandys had married another of Churchill's daughters.

110 Driberg would have been a risky proposition as a Commissioner, being the archetypal loose cannon, but he was a candid friend to the Commission, occasionally agitating in Parliament for it to be given greater powers – not that it necessarily wanted them, and not that Ministers ever came close to granting them, but he meant well.

111 By which he meant combustible types of the sort who in the past had harassed the Commission from the inside: Blomfield and Spence in particular, and to a degree Betjeman. As for the informal ban on relative youth, this had relaxed enough by the mid-1990s for the architectural historian Giles Worsley to be appointed at the age of thirty-four.

112 Very shortly after, a matter of months, which led some at the Commission to regard it as bad form even though the article was broadly sympathetic and on the whole discreet. A correction was demanded to clarify that he was no longer a Commissioner.

113 John Smith, Conservative M.P. for Westminster and later founder of the Landmark Trust, was one of those suggesting this. He said after the British Council controversy in 1969 that 'it is high time that practising architects were removed from the Commission. On a committee of public taste of this kind, architects are bound to be inhibited in criticising their brother architects' work'. But such complaints usually came from those disappointed by a particular outcome, which led them, unwisely, to extrapolate their particular grievance into a general policy.

114 Commissioners themselves were often kept away by pressure of work, especially if they were overseeing projects abroad. Few had as grand an excuse for absence as Patrick Abercrombie in 1946, when his son reported that 'my father is at present in Ethiopia advising the Emperor on the rebuilding of Addis Ababa'.

115 It was highly critical, for example, of some aspects of James Stirling's postmodern designs for the Clore Gallery at the Tate in 1981, dismissing the north-east and south-east elevations as unworthy of the rest of the scheme and the roofscape as unresolved. And it was far from unknown for Commissioners to receive a mauling from their colleagues: Geoffrey Jellicoe was on the Commission when it ripped into his Oxford Roads Plan of 1963.

CHAPTER IX – DRAWING TO A CLOSE

116 The charity continues and is the co-publisher of this volume. It was privately endowed after a fundraising drive, actively supported by Margaret Thatcher, which attracted donations from numerous figures in the worlds of art, architecture and design, including Terence Conran.

117 The Building of the Year Award ran from 1989 to 2005, with winners including The Royal Courts of Justice in Truro by Evans & Shalev (1989), the River and Rowing Museum at Henley by David Chipperfield (1999) and the London Underground Jubilee Line Extension by various architects under the direction of Roland Paoletti (2000).

118 In his capacity as Master of Emmanuel.

119 In hindsight the annual cost of the Commission (£800,000 in 1998/99) looks remarkably low. And the Commission, always aware of the need for defensive briefing in a more or less hostile world, was adept at accounting for taste. In 1936, Bradshaw told Crawford that the annual cost of the Commission was £1,195, 'which is the pay of an Assistant Controller of Death Duties'. In August 1995, Francis Golding calculated the average financial value of a Commissioner's contribution at £37,795 a year excluding VAT; in other words, the country was getting free work to an annual value of nearly £700,000 from some of its finest architects and designers.

120 Lipton added significant value to the Royal Fine Art Commission, but his appointment as chairman of the new body departed from the Royal Fine Art Commission's established practice of reserving the chair for those not professionally involved in relevant fields. Failure to follow that practice led to difficulties over conflicts of interest that culminated in his resignation in 2004.

CHAPTER X – WAS IT WORTH IT?

121 The first woman appointed to the Commission was Elizabeth Chesterton in 1969 (as the Queen was overseas, the Warrant of Appointment was signed by Queen Elizabeth and The Prince of Wales), although only another three were appointed over the next twenty years: the Countess of Airlie in 1975, the sculptress Wendy Taylor in 1981 and Lady Nutting in 1986. In total there were seven female Commissioners from a total of one hundred and fourteen, a representation rate of 6%, or 15% after 1970.

122 The Ministry of Fuel and Power was mystified when the Commission used its report for 1953 to imply that its intervention had led the Government to drop plans for a power station at Machen in South Wales. An internal minute complained that the report was 'most misleading. The Commission's views had nothing whatever to do with the refusal to sanction Machen'.

123 The Commission also strongly supported the (abortive) Boilerhouse Extension by Daniel Libeskind for the Victoria & Albert Museum in 1997. Designed in the deconstructivist idiom in vogue in the later 1990s, the proposed building met resistance from those who thought it lacking in sympathy with the red-brick Victorian range that flanked the development site, but the Commission considered it daring and innovative; it was right, it said, that the building should be an expression of its own time.

Commissioners 1841–1863

Chairmen		Dates of chairmanship	Profession
HRH Prince Albert KG	1819–1861	1841–1861	Prince Consort
5th Earl Stanhope FRS (Acting) (member 1844–1861)	1805–1875	1861–1863	Antiquarian and politician

Commissioners		Dates on Commission	Profession
5th Duke of Newcastle KG	1811–1864	1841–1863	Politician
2nd Duke of Sutherland KG	1786–1861	1841–1861	Politician
3rd Marquess of Lansdowne KG FRS	1780–1863	1841–1863	Statesman
16th Earl of Shrewsbury	1791–1852	1841–1844	Politician
4th Earl of Aberdeen KG KT FRS	1784–1860	1841–1860	Statesman
1st Earl Russell KG GCMG FRS	1792–1878	1841–1863	Statesman
1st Earl of Ellesmere KG	1800–1857	1841–1844	Politician
3rd Viscount Palmerston KG GCB FRS	1784–1865	1841–1863	Statesman
2nd Viscount Melbourne	1779–1848	1841–1848	Statesman
1st Viscount Eversley GCB	1794–1888	1841–1863	Politician
1st Lord Ashburton	1774–1848	1841–1848	Politician and financier
1st Lord Colborne	1779–1854	1841–1850	Politician
1st Lord Lyndhurst	1772–1863	1841–1863	Lawyer and politician

Sir James Graham Bt GCB MP	1792–1861	1841–1861	Politician
Sir Benjamin Hawes MP	1797–1862	1841–1862	Politician
Sir Robert Inglis Bt FRS MP	1786–1855	1841–1854	Politician
Sir Robert Peel Bt FRS MP	1788–1850	1841–1850	Statesman
Sir Thomas Wyse MP	1791–1862	1841–1848	Politician and diplomat
Henry Hallam FRS	1777–1859	1841–1859	Historian
Henry Gally Knight FRS MP	1786–1846	1841–1846	Politician
Samuel Rogers	1763–1855	1841–1855	Poet
George Vivian	1798–1873	1841–1863	Artist
1st Lord Macaulay	1800–1859	1844–1859	Historian and politician
22nd Lord Willoughby de Eresby	1782–1865	1845–1863	Politician
7th Earl of Carlisle KG	1802–1864	1846–1863	Politician
1st Earl Canning KG GCB KSI	1812–1862	1846–1856	Statesman
1st Lord Llanover	1802–1867	1856–1863	Civil engineer and politician
1st Viscount Ossington	1800–1873	1858–1863	Politician
7th Duke of Rutland KG GCB	1818–1906	1859–1863	Politician
1st Lord Mount Temple	1811–1888	1860–1863	Politician

Secretary

Sir Charles Eastlake PRA	1793–1865	1841–1863	Artist and art historian

Commissioners 1924–1999

Chairmen		Dates of chairmanship	Profession
Rt. Hon. The Earl of Crawford KT FRS FSA HonFRIBA *(27th Earl)*	1871–1940	1924–1940	Politician and administrator
Rt. Hon. Viscount Lee of Fareham GCB GCSI GBE HonFRIBA *(member 1926–1947)*	1868–1947	1942–1943	Politician and administrator
Rt. Hon. The Earl of Crawford KT GBE FRSE *(28th Earl)*	1900–1975	1943–1957	Politician and administrator
Rt. Hon. Lord Bridges KG GCB GCVO MC FRS	1892–1969	1957–1968	Administrator
Sir Colin Anderson *(member 1959–1968)*	1904–1980	1968–1976	Shipowner and administrator
Lord James of Rusholme *(member 1974–1976)*	1909–1992	1976–1979	Educationalist
Sir Derman Christopherson FRS FEng *(member 1978–1980)*	1915–2000	1980–1985	Engineering scientist and academic
Rt. Hon. Lord St. John of Fawsley FRSL HonFRIBA	1929–2012	1985–1999	Lawyer and politician

Commissioners		Dates on Commission	Profession
The Marquess Curzon of Kedleston KG GCSI GCIE PC FBA	1859–1925	1924–1925	Statesman
Sir Aston Webb GCVO CB PRA FRIBA	1849–1930	1924–1925	Architect

Sir Reginald Blomfield RA FRIBA	1856–1942	1924–1933	Architect
Sir George Frampton RA FSA	1860–1928	1924–1928	Sculptor
Sir Edwin Lutyens OM KCIE PRA FRIBA	1869–1944	1924–1944	Architect
Sir David Young Cameron RA	1865–1945	1924–1929	Artist
John Alfred Gotch RA PRIBA	1852–1942	1924–1927	Architect
Thomas Mawson PTPI	1861–1933	1924–1925	Planner and landscape architect
Dugald Sutherland MacColl	1859–1948	1925–1929	Artist
Sir Percy Worthington FRIBA	1864–1939	1925–1927	Architect
Francis Derwent Wood RA	1871–1926	1925–1926	Sculptor
Sir Giles Gilbert Scott OM RA	1880–1960	1927–1932	Architect
Professor Stanley Adshead FRIBA	1868–1946	1927–1934	Architect
Sir William Reid Dick KCVO RA	1879–1961	1928–1942	Sculptor
Charles Ricketts RA	1866–1931	1929–1931	Artist
Sir Walter Peacock KCVO	1871–1956	1930–1934	Lawyer
Sir William Rothenstein	1872–1945	1931–1938	Artist
Arthur Davis RA FRIBA	1878–1951	1932–1936	Architect
Dr Charles Holden FRIBA MRTPI RDI	1875–1960	1933–1945	Architect
William Curtis Green RA FRIBA	1875–1960	1934–1943	Architect
Ronald Norman	1873–1963	1934–1949	Administrator and politician
Sir Alexander Gibb GBE CB FRS FRSE	1872–1958	1934–1939	Civil engineer
Professor Sir Patrick Abercrombie FRIBA	1879–1957	1936–1948	Planner
Sir Albert Richardson KCVO FSA PRA FRIBA	1880–1964	1937–1956	Architect
Sir Gerald Kelly PRA	1879–1972	1938–1942	Artist
Sir Ralph Freeman *(père)*	1880–1950	1939–1948	Structural engineer

1930s

1940s			
William, Lord Holford RA RIBA	1907–1975	1943–1969	Architect
Professor Geoffrey Webb	1898–1970	1943–1962	Art historian
Sir Hubert Worthington RA FRIBA	1886–1963	1943–1950	Architect
Kenneth, Lord Clark OM CH KCB FBA	1903–1983	1946–1951	Art historian
Maxwell Fry CBE RA FRIBA FRTPI	1899–1987	1946–1951	Architect
Sir Edward Maufe RA FRIBA	1883–1974	1946–1953	Architect
Raymond Mortimer CBE	1895–1980	1946–1951	Writer and critic
Professor John Wheatley ARA	1892–1955	1946–1952	Painter
Sir Charles Wheeler KCVO PRA	1892–1974	1946–1952	Sculptor
Henry Moore OM CH FBA	1898–1986	1947–1971	Sculptor
Sir John Summerson CH FSA	1904–1992	1947–1954	Architectural historian
Sir William Halcrow	1883–1958	1948–1954	Civil engineer
Louis de Soissons CVO RA FRIBA	1890–1962	1949–1961	Architect
Sir Arthur Richmond RA	1879–1968	1949–1961	Artist
1950s			
Sir Frederick Gibberd RA FRIBA	1908–1984	1950–1970	Architect
4th Viscount Esher CBE RIBA *(The Hon. Lionel Brett until 1963)*	1913–2004	1951–1969	Architect
Sir James Richards FRIBA	1907–1992	1951–1966	Architectural critic
Sir John Betjeman	1906–1984	1952–1970	Poet and conservationist
4th Lord Methuen RA	1886–1974	1952–1959	Artist
Sir Thomas Merton FRS	1888–1969	1952–1959	Physicist
Sir Howard Robertson MC RA RIBA	1888–1963	1953–1958	Architect
Sir Geoffrey Jellicoe RA FRIBA	1900–1996	1954–1968	Landscape architect
Sir Allan Quartermaine MC	1888–1978	1954–1960	Civil engineer

Sir Basil Spence OM RA PRIBA RDI	1907–1976	1956–1970	Architect
Sir Leslie Martin FRIBA	1908–1999	1958–1972	Architect
John Piper CH	1903–1992	1959–1978	Artist
Arthur Floyd CBE	1894–1978	1960–1968	Municipal engineer
Sir Hugh Casson CH KCVO PRA FRIBA RDI	1910–1999	1960–1983	Architect and artist
Raymond Erith RA FRIBA	1904–1973	1960–1973	Architect
Sir Edward Playfair	1909–1999	1961–1965	Administrator
Lord Llewelyn–Davies FRIBA	1912–1981	1962–1973	Architect
Sir Howard Colvin CVO FBA FSA	1919–2007	1962–1972	Architectural historian
The Marquess of Anglesey FSA FRSL	1922–2013	1965–1971	Historian
Sir Nikolaus Pevsner FBA	1902–1983	1966–1974	Architectural historian
Sir Peter Shepheard FRIBA	1913–2002	1968–1971	Architect and landscape architect
Sir Gilbert Inglefield	1909–1991	1968–1975	Architect
Sir Ralph Freeman (fils)	1911–1998	1968–1985	Civil engineer
Dame Elizabeth Chesterton FRTPI	1915–2002	1969–1994	Architect and town planner
Sir Philip Powell CH RA FRIBA	1921–2003	1969–1994	Architect
Sir Philip Dowson PRA FRIBA	1924–2014	1970–1997	Architect
Sir Anthony Cox FRIBA	1915–1993	1970–1985	Architect
Sir David Piper FSA FRSL	1918–1990	1970–1986	Art historian
11th Duke of Grafton KG FSA HonFRIBA	1919–2011	1971–1994	Conservationist
Professor Bernard Meadows	1915–2005	1971–1976	Sculptor
Sir Hugh Wilson PRIBA	1913–1985	1971–1986	Architect
Professor Sir Colin Buchanan	1907–2001	1972–1974	Town planner
Dr Mark Girouard FSA	1931–2022	1972–2022	Architectural historian

1960s

1970s

Sir William Whitfield RIBA	1920–2019	1973–1994	Architect
Sir Alex Gordon PRIBA	1917–1999	1974–1991	Architect
Edmund Ward RIBA	1913–1998	1974–1983	Architect
The Countess of Airlie DCVO	b1933	1975–1988	Courtier
Lord Reilly	1912–1990	1976–1981	Designer
Dame Elisabeth Frink CH RA	1930–1993	1976–1982	Sculptress
Sir Francis Sandilands	1913–1995	1980–1986	Insurer and administrator
Martin Moss CBE	1923–2007	1981–1986	Fashion retailer
Wendy Taylor CBE	b1945	1981–1999	Sculptress
Sir Richard MacCormac RA PRIBA	1938–2014	1983–1995	Architect
Patrick Nuttgens CBE RIBA	1930–2004	1983–1990	Architect
Lady Nutting OBE	b1941	1986–1999	Architectural historian
John Winter MBE RIBA	1930–2012	1986–1996	Architect
Professor David Carter CBE RDI	1927–2020	1986–1998	Industrial designer
James Sutherland FEng FICE FIStructE	1922–2013	1986–1996	Structural engineer
Donald Hamilton Fraser RA	1929–2009	1986–1999	Artist
Sir Michael Hopkins RA RIBA	1935–2023	1986–1999	Architect
Sir Stuart Lipton FRIBA	b1942	1988–1999	Developer
Hal Moggridge OBE PPLI RIBA	b1936	1988–1999	Landscape architect
Professor John Steer FSA	1928–2012	1992–1999	Art historian
Professor Margaret MacKeith CBE FRTPI	b1939	1993–1999	Planner
Trevor Osborne FRICS	b1943	1994–1999	Developer
Quinlan Terry CBE FRIBA	b1937	1994–1997	Architect
Dr Giles Worsley FSA	1961–2006	1994–1999	Architectural historian

1980s

1990s

Ian Ritchie CBE RA RIBA	b1947	1995–1999	Architect
Sophie Andreae	b1954	1996–1999	Architectural historian
Edward Cullinan CBE RA RIBA RDI	1931–2019	1996–1999	Architect
Edmund Hollinghurst FEng FICE FIStructE	b1944	1996–1999	Structural engineer
Graham Morrison OBE RIBA	b1951	1997–1999	Architect
Professor Sir Colin Stansfield Smith	1932–2013	1997–1999	Architect
Professor Nicholas Butler OBE RDI	1942–2012	1998–1999	Product designer

Secretaries

Chalton Bradshaw FRIBA	1893–1943	1924–1943	Architect
Professor Arthur Knapp-Fisher RIBA	1888–1965	1944–1948	Architect and academic
The Hon. Godfrey Samuel RIBA	1904–1982	1948–1969	Architect
Professor Frank Fielden RIBA	1915–2001	1969–1979	Architect and academic
Sherban Cantacuzino CBE RIBA	1928–2018	1979–1994	Architect and writer
Francis Golding HonFRIBA	1944–2013	1995–1999	Administrator

Honours listed represent lifetime achievements; some were conferred after the person concerned had left the Commission.

Short bibliography for Part I

Boase, T.S.R. 'The decoration of the New Palace of Westminster 1841–1863' in *The Journal of the Warburg and Courtauld Institutes*, vol. 17, 1954

Boeckmann, Daniel *Ludwig Gruner, Art Adviser to Prince Albert*, University of East Anglia, M.A. dissertation 1996

Eastlake, Charles Locke *A History of the Gothic Revival*, London 1872

Gruner, Ludwig *The Decorations of the Garden Pavilion in the Grounds of Buckingham Palace*, London 1846

Kurzer, Frederick 'Arthur Herbert Church FRS and the Palace of Westminster Frescoes' in *Notes and Records of the Royal Society of London*, vol. 60, 2006

Martin, Theodore *The Life of His Royal Highness the Prince Consort*, London 1875

McLean, Janet 'Prince Albert and the Fine Arts Commission' in *The Houses of Parliament: History, Art, Architecture*, eds. Christine Riding and Jacqueline Riding, London 2000

Rhodes James, Robert *Albert, Prince Consort* London 1983

Saumarez Smith, Charles 'The Institutionalisation of Art in Early Victorian England' in *Transactions of the Royal Historical Society*, vol. 20, 2010

Turner, Michael 'Prince Albert and Architectural Inspiration at Osborne', in *Künstlerische Beziehungen zwischen England und Deutschland in der viktorianischen Epoche*, eds. Franz Bosbach and Frank Bittner, Munich 1998

Vaughan, William *German Romanticism and English Art*, New Haven, Yale University Press 1979

Vaughan, William '"God Help the Minister who Meddles in Art": History Painting in the New Palace of Westminster', in *The Houses of Parliament: History, Art, Architecture*, eds. Christine Riding and Jacqueline Riding, London 2000

Willsdon, Clare *Mural Painting in Britain 1840–1940: Image and Meaning*, Oxford University Press 2000

Winter, Emma 'Prince Albert, Fresco Painting and the new Houses of Parliament 1841–51' in *Prinz Albert – Ein Wettiner in Großbritannien* ed. John R. Davis, Munich 2004.

Principal sources for Part II

The National Archives, Kew

BP2 Series (Royal Fine Art Commission: Correspondence and Papers) and BP4 Series (Royal Warrants)

CRES (The Crown Estate and predecessors) 36/76

HLG (Ministry of Housing and Local Government) 52/918, 71/1589

MT (Ministry of Transport) 39/300, 118/68

POWE (Ministry of Power) 14/148

PREM (Records of the Prime Minister's Office) 5/23, 5/85, 5/93, 5/110, 5/152 and 11/938

T (H.M. Treasury) 162/781, 218/101, 218/102

WORK (H.M. Office of Works and successors) 12/718, 12/724, 17/498, 22/308, 22/309, 22/350, 11088/2, RS3148

London Metropolitan Archives (LMA/4625)

Reports of The Royal Fine Art Commission, published as Command Papers by H.M.S.O.

Observations on the City of London's Report on Post-War Reconstruction, Royal Fine Art Commission, His Majesty's Stationery Office, 1945.

Parliamentary Debates (Hansard)

Newspaper and periodicals archives, principally those of *The Times, The Daily Telegraph, The Manchester Guardian (The Guardian* from 1959), *The Observer* and *The Spectator*.

Index